How To Become
a
Published Author

Idea to Publication

Includes

"Protecting Your Literary Legal Rights"

Mark Shaw
Author/Attorney

Publishing Partners

Publishing Partners
Port Townsend, WA 98368
info@Publishing-Partners.com
www.MarciaBreece.com

Publisher's Cataloging—In—Publication Data
Mark Shaw, 1945-
How to Become a Published Author: Idea to Publication by Mark Shaw
p. cm.

ISBN: 978-1-944887-06-3
eISBN: 978-1-944887-07-0

1. Shaw, Mark, 1945-
2. Authorship -- Marketing
3. Book Publishing
4. Authors and Poets
5. Writing Skills
6. I. Shaw, Mark, 1945- II. Title

Printed in the United States of America

Cover design: Marcia Breece
Interior design: Marcia Breece

Contents

Dedicated to

Wen-ying Lu,
My Shining Light

and

Writers Everywhere
Keep the Faith:
You Will Be Published

Mark Shaw Books

If there is a book that you want to read, and it hasn't been written yet, then you must write it.

TONI MORRISON
Nobel Prize-Winning Author

*Outside of a dog, a book is man's best friend.
Inside a dog, it's too dark to read.*

GROUCHO MARX

All good books have one thing in common—they are truer than if they had really happened, and after you have read one of them, you will feel all that happened, happened to you and then it belongs to you forever: the happiness and unhappiness, good and evil, ecstasy and sorrow, the food, wine, beds, people and the weather. If you can give that to the readers, then you're a writer.

ERNEST HEMINGWAY

Acknowledgments

How to Become a Published Author evolved from an idea to a book thanks to the assistance of many people. Without them, I could have never completed it.

Thanks are extended to Jodee Blanco, a valued friend, literary consultant, and competent author. She assisted me with the text and wrote the Foreword. Jodee continues to be a leading authority on book promotion and self-publishing.

Donna Cortese, Christina Williams, and Nancy Crenshaw contributed much-needed editing skills. Their assistance is most appreciated.

To all of the editors of my books, and various literary agents that have represented me over the years, I say thank you. To those readers that have offered comments and suggestions, I thank you as well.

Love and thanks to my wife Wen-ying Lu. Her support and caring ways are most valued.

Thanks are also offered to my loving canine pal, Black Sox. His companionship at five a.m. was most appreciated.

Above all, I thank the Good Lord for blessing me with the creativity and dedication necessary to become an author. Without His guidance, I am nothing.

Mark Shaw
Author

Foreword

If you have purchased this book, chances are you dream of being a published author one day, of having your name in bold letters written across the front of a book jacket. To that end, I have exciting news—your timing could not be better since the publishing industry is evolving at an unprecedented rate.

Fresh, new opportunities abound, especially for first-time authors. Traditional self-publishing flourishes. The Internet has been a blessing for authors and redefined the potential parameters for marketing books. The technology boom has also given birth to electronic books and digital printing. The bottom line—if your fantasy is to become a published author, there now exist many accessible avenues to transform that wish into reality.

Even though opportunities are there to be seized, an aspiring author, to take advantage, must understand the publishing industry. For example, what is the difference between mainstream advance-against-royalty publishing, as opposed to print-on-demand or traditional self-publishing? Does every aspiring author need a literary agent to represent the book, and if it does, how do you find a great agent? What role do publicity and public relations play in the success of a book? How much does it cost to self-publish? What are the risks and benefits of self-publishing versus signing a deal with a publishing company? What does copyright mean and how do you obtain one?

These questions are just the tip of the iceberg. Discovering answers to them can prevent you from being immersed in a confusing ocean without a life vest.

As a publishing industry veteran of nearly thirty years, I know firsthand the rewards of good agent and publishing decisions, and the heartache accompanying uninformed decisions. Experience as a book publicist (fifteen books on the New York Times Bestseller List, five at number one), literary agent, author of New York Times bestsellers, and educator (instructor at New York University and the University of Chicago) has confirmed my belief that aspiring authors need guideposts to assist them during the publishing process.

In *How to Become a Published Author,* my friend and colleague Mark Shaw tells it like it is, straight and to the point. Deftly combining literary acumen with legal experience, he helps you to navigate the path to becoming an author. Whether you yearn to be published by a traditional company, or traditionally self-publish, Mark explains the options and suggests criteria for deciding the one best suited for you.

When Mark asked me to write this Foreword, I was honored since I know whoever reads this book will be forever empowered. So curl up, start reading, and get ready for a remarkable journey regarding the publishing industry and how you can become a published author or poet.

Jodee Blanco
Author, *The Complete Guide to Book Publicity, The Evolving Woman,* and *Please Stop Laughing at Me*

Author's Note

Welcome to *How to Become a Published Author.* Before we begin, here is a question for you: What do these authors and her/his books have in common?

Fred Dunlap – *The Dunlap Rules*

W. A. "Bill" Cornell – *Tell the Whole World I am Real*

Christine Montross – *Body of Work; Falling Into the Fire*

Jan Chalfant – *Rare Coins, Rare People*

Dave Bego – *The Devil at My Doorstep*

Nancy Spears – *Buddha: 9 to 5: The Eightfold Path to Enlightening Your Workplace and Improving Your Bottom Line*

Patti Lawson – *The Dog Diet: What My Dog Taught Me About Shedding Pounds, Licking Stress, and Getting a New Leash on Life*

Dawn Knight – *Taliaferro, Breaking Barriers from the NFL Draft to the Ivory Tower*

Frances Jewel Dickson – *The DEW Line Years, Voices from the Coldest Cold War*

Sam Drash – *Reaching Paradise Through Intercourse: American Towns with Unique Names*

Marilyn Price – *Machu Picchu, an Artist's Journal*

Charles Pearson – *The Last Expedition*

Ron Lowry and Mary Walker – *Chasing Lewis and Clark Across America: A 21st Century Aviation Adventure.*

The answer: three answers really – each is a first-time published author, each was published within the past few years, and each was mentored or consulted with using the guidelines and strategies featured in this book. I hope that their success story, and that of many others who have used the book, will be an inspiration for you as to embark on a journey toward becoming a published author.

Of course, completing a book and having it traditionally published is like visiting Paris in the springtime: Many say they will—most never do. This is unfortunate since I am certain anyone who works hard at becoming a professional writer can achieve this goal through proper planning and hard work.

Why listen to me? What do I know that hundreds of authors of books on writing and publishing don't? Good question, but one with a ready answer: During the course of having multiple books published, I have learned many lessons and have been through the wars like few others since I possessed no background or education in the field when I began writing for publication in 1992. This means How to Become a Published Author is unique because it provides practical advice about How to Become a Published Author from someone who achieved success in the trial and error trenches of traditional publishing.

Along with my writing adventures, I have consulted with hundreds of aspiring authors through my previous work as creative director for Books For Life Foundation, the not-for-profit organization that assisted writers of all ages and skill levels. I have also presented How to Become a Published Author seminars at libraries, colleges, universities and at seminars in the United States as well as France and Taiwan. This has helped me to appreciate the frustration encountered while attempting to become published. Many talented writers give up, believing the odds are too prohibitive. This isn't true if they follow a few simple rules and a proven strategy.

No less an authority than Charles Dickens said that authors write, "half from experience and half from imagination." Certainly, both authors and poets are a reflection of their experiences. Mine include, among others, being a criminal defense lawyer specializing in murder cases, a newspaper publisher (co-founded the Aspen Daily News), a network television correspondent and host (ABC's Good Morning America, CBS's People, CNN, ESPN, BBC, and Entertainment Tonight), a film producer (two feature motion pictures), a television producer (Fox Broadcasting), entertainment attorney, a radio talk show host, and earning a Master's Degree in Theological Studies from San Francisco Theological Seminary at the ripe young age of sixty-two. Based on my checkered background, some conclude that I am an interesting fellow. Others categorize me as a roustabout who can't hold a job! More about me is included in the Appendix or can be learned at my website, www.markshawbooks.com.

These adventures have provided memorable moments adding to the education of a small-town (Auburn, Indiana, population 5,000) youngster whose first brush with publishing was selling TV Guide door-to-door. Along the way, I have resided in Chicago, Los Angeles, New York City, San Francisco, Sausalito, and Aspen while traveling to France, Italy, England, Scotland, Switzerland, Luxembourg, Taiwan, and Germany. Doing so has permitted me to witness many different cultures, providing a background rich in history.

Memorable experiences broadening my horizons include a terrifying flight in an F-4 Air Force fighter jet, walking the streets of London with actor Ben Kingsley, riding with actor/driver Paul Newman in his race car, interviewing rock singer Cyndi Lauper in a dumpster outside the Hard Rock Café in San Francisco, meeting my look-a-like, John Denver and becoming friends with beloved actor James Stewart. I also have chatted with Larry King about the infamous Jonathan Pollard case, visited the famed Cannes Film Festival, lunched with astronaut Neil Armstrong, and interviewed Miss Nude California (keeping eye contact was difficult). Most recently, these adventures and more were captured in the book, Road to the Miracle chronicling my discovery of a daughter and two grandchildren I never knew existed.

More than anything, I love books, including the Bible, the greatest book ever written, but I didn't begin to write professionally until reaching the age of forty-eight. Prior to 1992, the only professional writing I had attempted was the first draft of a novel. When one literary agent read the manuscript and sent me a terse letter stating that my writing was "sophomoric," I cursed the agent, tossed the manuscript out a window, and decided writing was for literary geniuses, not me. Little more than a decade later, I am proud of my published books. Topics have ranged from exploring the mysterious death of media icon Dorothy Kilgallen in the bestselling "The Reporter Who Knew Too Much" to the JFK assassination to former Nazi youth leader Ursula Martens to spiritual guru Thomas Merton to famed attorney Melvin Belli to boxer Mike Tyson to championship golfer Jack Nicklaus, from famed aviator R. A. "Bob" Hoover to golf course designers Pete and Alice Dye, from basketball star Larry Bird to controversial spy Jonathan Pollard, and from perfect game pitcher Don Larsen to Holocaust survivor Cecelia Rexin and the magnificent Clydesdale horses. Collaboration on a music anthology called Let The Good Times Roll with musical historian Larry Goshen was most rewarding.

Publishers of my books have included large companies (Pocket Books/Simon and Schuster, Ballantine/Random House, Palgrave Macmillan, HarperCollins, Contemporary/McGraw Hill), medium-sized houses (Post Hill Press (Distribution by Simon and Schuster), Skyhorse, Addison Wesley, Sagamore/Sports Publishing, Taylor, Paragon House, Barricade Books), and small companies (Guild Press, People's Press). I've learned much from observing their varied methods of operation.

To date, more than thirty editions of my books, including one translated into Japanese, have occupied bookstore shelves around the world. Publisher research and discussion with numerous fiction writers has confirmed the basic guidelines outlined in this book pertaining to becoming published apply to all genres of writing. Along the way, there are a few tips for poets even thought publishing poetry is a far different game that publishing either fiction or non-fiction.

During my author journey, most critics have been kind, but my first review was shocking. On the morning after my book, Down for the Count, The Shocking Truth Behind the Mike Tyson Trial, was released, a radio talk show host telephoned. "Mark," he began, "nice to have you on the program, but do you want to know the crux of the review of your book in the morning newspaper?" Sure, I said, believing it couldn't be that bad.

"All right," the host said, "here's the headline, 'Shaw's Book On Tyson Worthless.'"

As my Adam's apple slid to the pit of my stomach, I attempted to muster a response. I mumbled something that made no sense, fumbled through the interview, and hung up. Resisting the temptation to hang myself, I glared at my sleepy-eyed dogs, rose to my feet, and let out a roaring expletive that could be heard in three neighboring states.

Excellent reviews from USA Today, the The Boston Globe, and the Los Angeles Times soothed a bruised ego, but the path to becoming an author had begun on a sour note. Nonetheless, it had begun. Instead of moping about the first reviewer's nasty critique, I used it as inspiration and followed book one with book two and book three, and so forth. When book number five, The Perfect Yankee, the story of New York Yankees pitcher Don Larsen's perfect game in the 1956 World Series was published, a New York Times book reviewer proclaimed the book, "informative and entertaining." Columnists have dubbed me a "prolific writer," a phrase characterizing those who write at a quick pace and manage to publish books on a yearly basis.

The release of Down for the Count provided a thrill like no other. When I teach at seminars about the publishing process, I never fail to mention how wonderful it felt to hold a published book in my hands. What satisfaction.

My journey to How to Become a Published Author could fill volumes. Having no professional training as a writer, no college courses on the subject (during five-and-a-half years at Purdue, I majored in golf and partying!), no writing workshops, and no knowledge of the publishing industry, I did what came naturally—I winged it!

This applied to writing skills as well. Only after having written several books did I begin to better understand what good writing was all about. My savior was a tiny book called Elements of Style, by professors William Strunk, Jr. and E. B. White.

Like me, you too can wing it when you begin your quest to be traditionally published, but based on my publishing experiences; I've learned there is a logical progression toward the publication process. The key is to create a terrific book idea, develop a sound strategy toward publication alternatives, and then work hard to implement your game plan. No one can guarantee success, but the odds for it occurring can be substantially improved.

To assist your efforts, this book features an appendix with sample forms for, among others, Query Letters, Book Proposals, Agency and Publishing Contracts, and Promotion Ideas. There are also examples of terrific writing from the masters and grammar/punctuation exercises to test your writing skills. Throughout the book, charts outline writing tips, how to evaluate a book concept, proper manuscript form, and the main steps involved with the publishing process.

With careful planning and the guts to stay the course despite rejection, you can become a successful published author or poet. By being attentive to Mark's Ten Steps to Publication, a roadmap of sorts based on my experiences, you can savor the moment you will never forget—holding a copy of your published book for all the world to see.

With this in mind, let's unfold the map, consider several useful tips that have proven worthy, and begin the journey so you too can shout to the world: "I am published."

Mark Shaw

A man is known by the company his mind keeps.

THOMAS BAILY ALDERICH

Step #1

Analyze The Publishing Industry
To Gain Confidence

Why Writing?

Let's begin with inspiration. Please repeat after me: I Will Be Published! Once again—I Will Be Published!

Thank you. Keep the promise in mind while reading this book. In addition, remember—authors are the most important people in the publishing world. Without them, publishers don't exist.

"Being published" assumes many forms. They include binding several copies of a personal memoir or journal entries for family and friends, writing a magazine or newspaper article, penning a short story or essay for publication in magazines or writer's journals, writing a short article to be published on an Internet site or the company newsletter, crafting a poem to be included in a magazine or anthology collection, writing several poems for inclusion in a poetry book or chapbook, or completing a fiction or non-fiction manuscript that will be self-published or released by a traditional publisher in hardcover, paperback or ebook.

This said, whether you have created a book idea, a few sentences, a paragraph or two scribbled on a torn sheet of paper, a chapter outlining characters, partial text ripe for a short story, essay, or magazine article, half of a non-fiction book revealing that Neil Armstrong did not walk on the moon, the first draft of the great American novel, or several pages of poetry—STOP. Before proceeding, enter the real world of publishing.

To confirm that the quest to become a published author or poet is a priority, ask a basic question: What is your motive for writing? The answer is critical, since the journey generates a wide range of emotions including elation, loneliness, excitement, and frustration.

There are many possible motives for writing. Some people write to prove they can with no desire to have others read their work. Many write with profit in mind even though the creative arts are not about earning huge sums of money. Others want to deliver an important historical message through poetry or non-fiction while still others wish to write a work of fiction to provide escape or entertainment.

Whatever the motivation, the literary profession is based on a special relationship—the writer and his or her words. On paper, or a computer screen, you will create word after word producing stanzas, sentences and paragraphs, pages, and ultimately, a book. Along the way you may encounter writer's block, tear up pages, threaten to throw your computer into the nearest dumpster, attempt to kick the loyal dog, and hate the fact you ever decided to write.

Each individual's experience varies, but writing is not for the meek. It's no surprise that many authors and poets become alcoholics, junkies, or lunatics. "The mind is a precious thing," the saying goes, "so don't disturb it." But you will disturb it, and it will disturb you. When problems surface, you may feel that ANYTHING is better than facing a keyboard or writing another word.

Despite these obstacles, if you accept the challenge to write professionally, then a logical strategy is imperative. To maximize the odds of becoming published, gather information about the publishing industry, improve your writing skills, learn how to professionally submit material, and conduct research to discover literary agents or publishers who are most likely to represent or publish particular genres of work. Completion of these tasks won't guarantee a published book, but the chances of it occurring will be increased a hundred-fold.

Book Store Research

Whether you can define the book genre you contemplate, have no clue as to subject matter, or have already written several stanzas, a chapbook, short story, chapters, or a manuscript, understanding the publishing world is critical. By examining the current state of affairs in the publishing industry, you can learn much about whether your book idea is commercially viable. If it is not, then the evolution of new ideas, or a different slant to an idea already conceived, may be warranted.

A common error committed by many aspiring authors and poets is to complete a manuscript or collection of poetry while possessing little knowledge of the inner workings of the publishing industry. Writing for publication without researching the literary marketplace is akin to listing a home before assessing its market value. Lack of information decreases the chances of selling the house just as lack of expertise about the publishing industry hinders the potential to be traditionally published by a company that will cover all costs of releasing a book.

Laborious reading or extensive research isn't required to begin a sojourn into the publishing world. Instead, visit a large bookstore or an independent outlet. This scouting mission is guaranteed to enlighten, since bookstores are packed with written works published in many forms and through many means, often involving writer ingenuity and alternative publishing strategies.

Upon entering the bookstore, note the rectangular table or tables positioned within twenty-five feet of the door. Multiple books are stacked on them, carefully positioned to attract attention.

Welcome to the "head tables"—sometimes called the "front-of-store tables." They feature books released by the crème de la crème of the publishing industry such as those published by what is known as the "Big Five." They are Simon and Schuster, Penguin Random House, HarperCollins, Hachette and Macmillan. These companies and others who have hit the jackpot with a book invest promotion and marketing funds so their books will receive maximum exposure. Because the books are chosen by the bookstore buyers and not by publishers (who nevertheless pay for the space), there may be successful books from smaller publishers mixed in.

Studying the head tables (in some stores they are marked "Bestsellers," "New Hardcover," or "New Paperback,"), permits you to determine what genre of books are being marketed at different times of year, what authors are writing them, and what publishing companies have released them. This provides an overall understanding of the machinations of the publishing industry.

Publishing Industry Overview

While circling the head tables, note the ambience of the bookstore—the whispering of customers discussing which book to purchase while reading snippets from jacket covers or the first pages of the text. At the store's café, people read, flip through magazines, write in notebooks, or type away at a laptop as the aroma of cappuccino drifts through the air.

Remember that those meandering around the store are potential customers for your book. They are the very people who may pay as much as $29.95 for a hardback edition. If enough of them can be convinced it is a must-read, a bestseller results.

Pick-up the books on the head tables, feel their texture, and note the colors, the graphics or photographs, and the style of print. During one visit, the table might reveal such books as The Stolen Heir by Holly Black, The Girl on the Train by Paula Hawkins, The Boys from Biloxi by John Grisham, Hello Beautiful by Ann Napolitano, The House of Wolves by James Patterson, and Dark Angel by John Sandford.

Many of these authors are the generals in the current army of contemporary books. Most of the well-known fiction writers could write a book about the disappearance of a lamppost and sell 500,000 copies. They enjoy a following of loyal fans awaiting their next book with heart-stopping anticipation.

While glancing at the books on the head tables, check the titles to reveal which is fiction or non-fiction. It will approximate two to one, fiction to non-fiction, but the ratio varies from week to week. Celebrated authors corner the fiction market, but non-fiction books such as the classic Tuesdays With Morrie provide inspiration since sports personality Mitch Albom was a virtual unknown before this book was published. No one could have predicted that it would be on the New York Times bestseller list for more than 300 weeks and counting.

Before departing the head tables, open a few books. Read the inside jacket cover text, the author biography, and the back cover text. On the second or third page, the name and location of the publishing company is provided.

When glancing at the books, become familiar with the major players in the publishing industry, especially those who may be involved in a specific genre. With this in mind, scribble a note or two listing publishers that have published the type of book envisioned. As the writing process continues, add to the list. When the time arrives to seek publication, the list will be helpful.

To learn more about the team who collaborated to publish a book similar to one under consideration, check the "Acknowledgments" page. Besides the publishing company and the author, the team may include the writer's agent and an editor or editors who championed the book. Note these names for future reference.

Notice the titles and subtitles on the book covers. Jot a few down, since the title is as important to marketing the book as the words written within. Publishers develop ulcers worrying about titles guaranteed to hook the reader.

Book Genres

Within a few minutes, you have learned more about the publishing process than you realize. Since there are few courses teaching the basics of real world publishing, self-education is a necessity.

Being informed is crucial. Doing so will help with creation of the type of book publishers must add to their list for fear of missing a bestseller.

Further your learning process by walking through the bookstore to view the enormous number of book subjects available. This may trigger book ideas or reveal that a book has already been written on the very subject being contemplated.

Book categories abound and vary somewhat from store to store. They include Self-Improvement, Cooking, Relationships, Wine and Spirits, Diseases, Addiction/Recovery, Diet, Woman's Health, Teen Series, Beauty and Grooming, Humor, Biography, Games, Sports,

World History, Metaphysics, Travel, and Military History. There are also sections marked Music, Study Aids, Religion, Language, Philosophy, Fiction/Literature, Juveniles, Architecture, Art, Science Fiction, Mythology, Personal Finance, Computers, and more.

Surveys vary, but become aware of publishing trends when considering a book idea. Most industry experts agree children's books, published in hardcover and trade paperback, occupy the top two or three spots on the pecking order. Romance novels follow. These usually account for nearly one-half of the mass-market paperbacks (smaller and less expensive than trade paperbacks and hard covers) purchased each year. Non-fiction books, biographies, autobiographies, self-help, inspiration, and so forth are among the best sellers, with fiction (general trade paperback and hardcover, general fiction, mass-market paperback, and mystery, mass-market paperback) completing the list. To gain a current understanding of which books are selling, consult bestseller lists in various publications.

If you are interested in children's books, concentrate on these sections while roaming the bookstores. Children's books enthusiasts will discover that companies like Simon and Schuster feature divisions specializing in books for young readers. Children's books enjoy a long shelf life whether they are picture books, books specifically for babies and toddlers, young readers, middle readers, or young adult readers.

Travel books and cookbooks may be potential publications for the budding author. Everyone loves a travel book to aid vacation or business plans. Hundreds of cookbooks are published each year. As with any category researched, pay close attention to current books on the store bookshelves.

Religious books are a popular venue for first-time writers. There is a huge market for religious novels and inspirational books. To date, Rick Warren's The *Purpose-Driven Life,* a book that has changes many a life, has sold more than thirty million copies. Revered Trappist Monk Thomas Merton's spiritual book, New Seeds of Contemplation continues to be a great seller more than fifty years after its initial publication.

Thousands of new works of fiction and non-fiction are released every year based on more than half-a-million or more submissions to publishing companies. The number of poetry submissions is astronomical, as well. No wonder many would-be authors and poets are intimidated. Don't be.

While touring the bookstore, remember your mindset is one of an *aspiring author or poet, not a customer.* This is a research mission involving investigation. Plan to spend an afternoon or even a full day or two browsing the shelves. Consider what is being written, how the books look and feel, their length, and how they are presented. Each book has its own self-contained marketing program designed with one thing in mind: sell the damn book!

With this goal in mind, examine the packaging, the cover, and how the author or poet is showcased. Reading the author biography on the inside back jacket cover will provide insight as to his or her background and their previous publications. Inspiration is garnered from first-time authors and poets who have been published.

The type of writing contemplated—fiction, non-fiction, or poetry will dictate the amount of time you spend in that particular area. Focus on books released in recent years. With so many books published, and so little space, only books that sell remain on the shelves. Many *front-list* books (recent releases) become *backlist* assets that will sell year after year. Others have their "fifteen minutes of fame," and are returned to the publisher or banished to the "remainder" bin marked at two bucks a copy.

Nobody can predict exactly what book will become a bestseller. Some books appear to have *bestseller* stamped on them, but many times the so-called experts don't know and are guided by "hunches." Who could have predicted that my book, The Reporter Who Knew Too Much about celebrated journalist Dorothy Kilgallen would become a bestseller? Some publishing company rejected the book since Kilgallen was little known when the book was published.

Another unexpected bestseller was *Quiet Strength* by Indianapolis Colts coach Tony Dungy. Comedian Stephen Colbert also provided a sign of inspiration when his book, I Am America (And So Can You) reached number one on the New York Times bestseller list.

Checking the fiction bestsellers provides a few surprises. There are the predictable names—John Grisham, Tom Clancy, James Patterson, Mary Higgins Clark, Anne Rice, and Stephen Coonts. But among the bestsellers is the *Left Behind* collection by Tim LaHaye and Jerry B. Jenkins, little-known authors before their breakthrough books, and A Girl Named Zippy, by first-time author Haven Kimmel.

Inspiration may certainly be gained by considering the spiraling career of Khaled Hosseini. His first book, The Kite Runner, was successful with the second one, A Thousand Splendid Suns, even more so.

Reference Magazines

To learn more about book publishing and outlets for publishing articles or short stories, check the magazine section. To complete the first day's "training" regarding the book business, select publications such as Publisher's Weekly, The New York Times Sunday Edition, Writer's Digest, and Poets and Writers Magazine. Just as those immersed in the financial world consult Forbes to stay abreast of developments in that field, these publications are a guidepost to what's occurring in the book world.

Other sources of knowledge about the publishing industry are publications by chain bookstores and Book Sense, a directive of books recommended by independent outlets. Each provides insight regarding current trends in the publishing industry.

Publisher's Weekly

Publisher's Weekly is necessary read for aspiring authors and poets. The first half features advertisements for new releases, publishing news detailing sales records, the revolving door shifts of executives from company to company, and the names of authors signed to write new books. These include celebrities who are advanced a million dollars to write about the color of their toothbrush and the epiphanies that surfaced during their rehab. One year, it seemed every issue carried news of yet another body part that actress/author/ fitness guru Suzanne Somers could perfect.

Publishing excesses aside, becoming familiar with the names of those in positions of power in the literary industry is important because they are the ones who consider a book for publication. Even if a book concept is rejected, the person rejecting it may rotate to a new literary agency or publishing company and later consider another book written by the same author. This is why it is wise to never write a nasty letter after being rejected. Accept the decision and move on.

The middle pages of Publisher's Weekly feature interviews with publishing heavyweights or successful authors. Valuable tips emerge based on their experiences.

Several pages near the back of Publisher's Weekly are dedicated to reviews of books being published in the coming months. They are catalogued under the banners of fiction, non-fiction, audio, poetry, and paperback. This section keeps the writer current on the latest news about books being published, while providing insight into reviewer's comments regarding their content and potential.

Another issue of Publisher's Weekly was of special interest to aspiring novelists. Under the banner, "First Fiction For Fall," the magazine lists several publications by first-time authors. The list provided ideas as well as inspiration to those who believe the odds of a first-time author securing a publishing commitment are prohibitive.

Spring and fall editions of Publisher's Weekly are important for authors and poets. They feature multiple pages listing book titles being released during that season. These pages provide insight into publishers and the types of books each company favors. It also presents a glimpse of the varied subject matter that becomes fodder for publication. Keep in mind that one season's hot topics may be cold by the time a new book on the subject is written.

New York Times

The New York Times Sunday Edition supplements Publisher's Weekly. Other newspapers feature book review supplements, but the New York Times Book Review is king. Read it several times to soak up every ounce of knowledge. Advertisements touting books are interesting and valuable, reviews are revealing, and the bestseller list indicates what books people are reading whether in hardcover, paperback or eBook.

Several lists will catch your eye: the bestsellers in Non-fiction and Fiction, Business Books, and even eBooks. Each week the list changes but note what books stay on the list for a lengthy period of time.

For those interested in business books, the Times feature a separate listing in the business section under "Business Bestsellers." Note the variety of book topics with some touting investment tips and others memoirs of interesting personalities such as Alan Greenspan.

Often the Times includes two other lists of interest to aspiring authors. They are bestsellers for "Advice, How-To and Miscellaneous," and "Children's Paperback Books." Both are excellent reference sources.

Reading these lists and those in Publisher's Weekly provides hope for the beginning writer. No idea is sacred. It doesn't take a genius to discover a unique concept for a book that can be worthy. Imagination is the key. Never doubt your ability to create an exciting book that can be a bestseller.

Writer's Digest

Writer's Digest is a required reading for any beginning writer. No reviews or bestseller lists are featured—just pertinent information about writing and writers. The articles are valuable, since many contain tips concerning the craft of writing.

Various articles in Writer's Digest have included: Craft a Killer Query, What Works, What Doesn't, How To Build A Novel Proposal, Inspiration 101, 100 Best Book Markets For New Writers, How Not To Be A Paperback Writer, The Dos and Don'ts Of Writing Dialogue, and How To Set Your Writing Goals.

Another feature of Writer's Digest may be a list of popular reference books for writers. Among them are Discovering the Writer Within, Grammatically Correct, Fast Fiction, The Writer's Guide to Character Traits, Novel Writing, Get Organized, Get Published, Keys To Great Writing, and The Writer's Idea Book. These books provide information regarding every facet of the writing profession.

Several examples of book text are featured in the magazine as are tips regarding selling manuscripts. There is information about writing workshops conducted by professional authors and advertisements for writing competitions.

Poets and Writers Magazine/Poetry Magazine

Poets and Writers Magazine is a prestigious publication packed with useful information for aspiring writers and poets. Founded in 1970 to "foster the development of poets and fiction writers and to promote communication throughout the literary community," the magazine presents vital facts about every aspect of the writing process. Published bi-monthly, one issue featured 8 Editor's Tips On Getting In The Glossies, as well as sections detailing News and Trends, The Literary Life, and The Practical Writer. Special notices and advertisements for awards, grants, conferences, and residencies are also included.

An excellent source of information for poets is Poetry Magazine. Checking their Web site at www.poetrymagazine.com provides current information about the poetry-publishing world. The magazine sponsors the Ruth Lilly Poetry Prize, an annual competition awarding a deserving poet $100,000.

Publisher's Lunch.com

Michael Cader Books publishes Publisherslunch Deluxe, a free newsletter providing an overview of the publishing industry on a day- to-day basis. It also features job openings, articles on various industry personalities, and industry trends.

The companion publication to Publisherslunch Deluxe is Publishers Marketplace. For a low monthly fee, Cader emails details about all of the deals completed each day by publishers large and small. Most important besides the name of the book sold, the tagline describing it, author information, and the publisher that has optioned the rights is valuable information regarding the literary agent who represented the author. Watching who is making deals in the genre of book you are writing permits you to list agents who should be interested in your book idea. This will assist your efforts when it is time to submit your query letter and book proposal.

Publishers Marketplace also lists the names of agents and the names of the authors and poets they represent. More about both publications can be learned at www.publisherslunch.com

BookExpo America

To expand publishing industry education, consider a trip to the annual BookExpo America convention. Locations have included Chicago, New York City, and Los Angeles. More information is available at www.bookexpoamerica.com.

Colorful booths spanning several halls house the majority of the publishers across the country. Large publishers occupy the largest, most expensive space. Medium sized and smaller publishers, including university presses, are also well represented.

Walking amongst the booths is electrifying. Large placards promoting books by the famous and not so famous drape booth walls. Long lines snake around corners as fans line up to meet, greet, and obtain the autographs of famous authors.

Publishing company representatives mingle with retailers, their authors, poets, the media, and distributors from around the world. An event or one-day admission price permits writers to frolic with those who are the publishing industry. During the event at Chicago's McCormick Place, several social events were held to permit those who love books to chat with those who love books. A local book fair was featured so book enthusiasts could locate a rare copy of Steinbeck for a buck-and-a-half.

BookExpo America presents the perfect arena for aspiring authors and poets to meet independent booksellers from around the world. Even though chain stores rule the industry, there are superb independent outlets. Knowing the owners and their sales force can prove invaluable, since independents champion first-time authors and poets.

Each BookExpo America registrant is provided a convention guide that is a great resource for any aspiring author or poet. Included are the listings of the exhibitors. Inspect it, discover who is appearing and where, and then visit exhibits, meet people, and note what books are being promoted. Display posters highlight major marketing campaigns being planned.

Most BookExpo America publishing company booths are piled high with catalogs focusing on future releases. Galleys (review copies of soon-to-be-released books) are sometimes available although many publishers attempt to limit these "freebees" to retailers. Studying various writing styles and storytelling variations for future books can be most helpful.

The point of attending BookExpo America is to meet and greet while exchanging business cards. Networking with agents, publishing executives and others immersed in the industry is essential. After the convention, add the names of those met to ever-growing lists compiled in anticipation of submitting material to the marketplace.

If attending BookExpo America is impossible, consider visiting an American Bookseller (sponsor of BookExpo) regional book show. These are great venues to meet smaller and regional publishers.

For those interested in the potential to meet industry professionals at consumer book shows, research such venues as LA Book Fest, NY is Book Country, and the Miami Book Fest. All provide opportunities to soak up the atmosphere of the book business.

The Internet

To supplement knowledge you gained through bookstores, publications, and BookExpo, check the Internet web sites where books are marketed and sold. Look at Amazon.com and BarnesandNoble. com in particular. This is another source of bestseller information as well as information regarding how books are being promoted online. It is also a good way to search for other published books that may compete with the book being contemplated.

Education is Power

Knowledge regarding the business end of the publishing industry is power for those who dream of writing professionally. Instead of pursuing the dream half-cocked, those who investigate the publishing world can make their dream come true. They bear allegiance to Mark's Step #1—Analyze The Publishing Industry to Gain Confidence.

With this understanding, and an understanding of the writing process, it is logical for you to ask, "How may I become published?"

There are several alternatives, but the path to becoming published by a traditional publisher is quite logical. In its simplest form, a writer first generates an idea for a book. Based on an outline, at least a partial manuscript developing the idea is created.

Using this material, a Query Letter and Book Proposal are completed. Either through their own efforts or those of a literary agent or entertainment attorney, the Query Letter and/or Book Proposal is submitted to one or more publishers. If a publisher says the magic word, "Yes," a deal is negotiated.

The author then revises the book in tandem with an editor at the publishing company. A release date is set, usually months or even a year ahead to provide time for editing, book layout, and a marketing and promotion campaign. The completed book is then published amidst a grand celebration.

Getting from point A (idea) to point Z (publication) is a magical mystery tour filled with adventure. Regardless of whether you choose fiction or non-fiction, the journey begins with a search for what literary material is marketable in the publishing world.

Step #1 Summary

- Visit chain bookstores or independent outlets to research the book industry.
- Check book covers, inside jackets, and Acknowledgments for publisher, author, agent, and editor information.
- Compile lists of agents, editors, and publishers that may be interested in your book genre.
- Review publishing industry reference publications such as Publisher's Weekly, New York Times, Writer's Digest, etc.
- Read the Internet publication Publishersmarketplace every day.

What is a book? Everything or nothing. The eye that sees it is all.

RALPH WALDO EMERSON

Step #2

Write A Story You Are Passionate About—
But One that is Marketable

Short Stories, Magazine Articles, Essays

"Damn the torpedoes, full speed ahead" is one way to begin the writing process. But just as a baseball player with dreams of playing in the major leagues begins his quest in the minors, a bit of seasoning is warranted before you plunge into the world of writing for publication.

This seasoning involves writing short stories, essays, magazine or newspaper articles, or poetry for mainstream publications. Doing so teaches the discipline of writing with space and word constraint to produce good beginnings, middles, and ends to stories. For poets, it is the opportunity to test their mettle in a single poem or two.

Another benefit of writing short-form material is the ability to test linguistic skills and begin developing a personal writing style. The process may also help you decide whether to write fiction, non-fiction, or poetry.

Most importantly, publication of short stories, essays, newspaper articles or poetry provides a showcase for your talent while earning you a publishing credit. The latter will prove helpful when you seek publication for long-form fiction or non-fiction material.

Many celebrated authors began by writing magazine and newspaper articles, and short stories. Among them was Ernest Hemingway. His talent was recognized while he wrote for publications such as Atlantic Monthly and *The Toronto Star.*

Several modern-day magazines, including Esquire, GQ, Harper's, Playboy, Seventeen, and Zoetrope, print short works of fiction. Publications like Vanity Fair, Atlantic Monthly, and Ladies Home Journal, among others, will consider short works of non-fiction.

One author who gained exposure by writing short stories is Terry McMillan, best-selling African-American author of How Stella Got Her Groove Back. She began reading literary works by African-American writers while shelving books at a Port Huron, Michigan library at age sixteen. While majoring in journalism at UC Berkeley, she wrote The End, her first short story. When it was published, it provided a springboard for her long-form efforts.

Mary Higgins Clark, author of several best-selling mysteries, jump-started her career by writing short stories. The first sold for $100 to Extension Magazine after six years and more than forty rejection slips. This modest success stimulated Clark, who wrote Aspire To The Heavens, a novel about the life of George Washington. It was a dismal failure, but her second effort, Where Are The Children, proved successful. This book paved the way for such bestsellers as Before I Say Goodbye, Deck The Halls, and The Street Where You Live.

J. K. Rowling, famous for the Harry Potter series, began her career by writing short stories. While attempting to complete two novels, she conceived a "what-if" idea. It focused on a young boy who didn't realize he was a wizard. The skills she had honed writing short stories enabled her to complete Harry Potter and the Sorcerer's Stone. It was published a year later to wide acclaim, catapulting Rowling to international fame.

Charles Dickens garnered experience as a newspaper reporter before turning to long-form writing. He then wrote short texts to accompany a series of humorous sport illustrations. Next came The Pickwick Papers. It led to Oliver Twist, Nicholas Nickleby, the first of Dickens' successful Christmas stories, A Christmas Carol, A Tale of Two Cities, and David Copperfield.

Poets gain credentials through publication of their poetry in reputable magazines and journals. Publishers scan these publications searching for new talent.

For me, seasoning occurred when I wrote several columns for

USA Today during the Mike Tyson trial. The credit led to a publishing commitment for Down for the Count. To those who scanned my manuscript, I wasn't a novice writer with little credibility, but one who had been published in a national newspaper.

If you decide to write short stories, educate yourself about this form of writing. The easiest way is to return to the bookstores and focus on the classics. Look for anthologies of short stories by a variety of famed authors. These will expose you to several examples of good writing. Pay attention to how the authors formulated the beginning, middle, and end of their stories.

Celebrated author Elmore Leonard stated "Read and study what the writer is doing. Find a writer you have a rapport with and study the paragraphing, study the punctuation, study everything." William Zinsser, author of On Writing Well, echoes Leonard's comments. He wrote, "Writing is learned by imitation. If anyone asked me how I learned to write, I'd say I learned by reading the men and women who were doing the kind of writing I wanted to do and trying to figure out how they did it."

Resource Material For Short Stories, Magazine Articles, and Poetry

Marketplace information for short stories or magazine articles is easily obtainable. Several books listing publications accepting unsolicited submissions are released each year, but Writer's Market is the most inclusive. The cover of one edition promised, "75 Literary Agents, 1000+ All New Publishing Opportunities, 1400 Consumer Magazines, 450+ Trade Magazines, 1100 Book Publishers." There is also Writer's Market—Online, Children's Writer's and Illustrator's Market, Christian Writer's Market Guide, and The Writer's Handbook.

Submitting written work to the outlets in the proper form is critical. Writer's Market provides battle-tested suggestions. Following the guidelines suggested is key since editors seek professionals who know the rules.

Once you've conceived a short story or magazine article, compile a list of publications most likely to accept it. There are several with outstanding reputations, including The Paris Review, Rosebud, The

Magazine For People Who Enjoy Good Writing, Poets and Writers Magazine, Ploughshares, Stone Soup, The American Scholar, and The New Yorker. Being published by them is an honor. A former editor at Simon and Schuster ordered his underlings to scour such publications scouting for potential writers.

Depending on your area of interest, read the above-mentioned magazines as well as Vanity Fair, Atlantic Monthly, Harper's, Omni, Rolling Stone, Seventeen, Reader's Digest, PC Computing, Esquire, Gentleman's Quarterly, Cigar, Ms., O, Ladies Home Journal, Washingtonian, and Ellery Queen's Mystery Magazine. Reading good writing helps you develop good writing skills, and ideas for books abound in the pages of top magazines. From an article in Vanity Fair, I developed an idea for a book about a teenage computer wizard employed by the government to slay cyberspace terrorists.

For those interested in poetry, publications of note include Poets and Writers, Poetry Magazine, the Kenyon Review, Glimmer Train, Atlantic Monthly, and the Atlanta Review. Libraries are good sources for these publications.

Be selective when choosing publications for submission of material. It is unprofessional to submit an article to a magazine that does not publish that genre of material. Sending an article on raising Argentine llamas to Architectural Digest is embarrassing and signals to the publisher that you have not done your homework.

Newspaper Experience

Writing newspaper articles or columns provides another source of education and exposure for aspiring authors. Writing with word-count restrictions forces one to be brief and to the point. Journalists face deadlines, providing a helpful discipline when publishers demand revisions within a certain timeframe.

The journalist hones editorial skills and investigative methods that prove worthy when writing long-form. Becoming a competent reporter, columnist, or freelance writer provides credentials that impress publishers, since the successful journalist has name recognition, a proven track record, and a readership that may purchase books.

To gain notice for your writings, consider an op-ed column, letters to the editor, or other means to gain publication. Every time your words reach a readership, you add to your writing credential.

One misconception in literary circles is that writing short stories or articles is inferior to writing long-form. There is an expertise to both, but being restricted by a word count may prove more challenging than writing a book the length of *Gone With the Wind.*

Fiction Or Non-Fiction

Whether to write fiction or non-fiction is an important decision for the author with publishing aspirations. If you have inclinations toward both, try both. Write a few chapters, a short story, or an article portraying a true-life event. Then let your imagination flow. Decide which provides more satisfaction, since writing with passion is essential to future success.

The decision to write fiction or non-fiction should not be made without considering an important question: Is it easier to become a published author by writing in one genre or the other?

There is no clear consensus as to whether fiction or non-fiction provides a better stepping-stone to a career as an author, but far more works of fiction are presented to literary agents and publishers than non-fiction. With so much competition, the odds of success for a first-time author of fiction are diminished. This is because publishers realize it is normally the author who is the star since readers return to purchase books by authors whom they have enjoyed before.

Non-fiction may provide more opportunity. First-time authors with a "platform" (expertise in a particular subject) abound, since generally the *subject matter* is as important as the name of the author on the book cover. Publishers recognized that the true story focusing on discharge of chemical waste by a large corporation portrayed in A Civil Action was the star, not the unknown author, Jonathan Harr. A similar situation occurred following the terrorist attacks on the United States when several books by unknown authors about the Taliban, Osama bin Laden, Afghanistan, and chemical warfare became bestsellers.

As with all rules of thumb, there are exceptions. Non-fiction is a broad genre including how-to, self-help and instructional books, biography, inspirational books, humor, and what is known as "narrative non-fiction"—true stories unfolding in much the same storytelling pattern as fiction. Authors of narrative non-fiction can also become superstars with a dedicated readership, as did Jon Krakauer, author of Into Thin Air and Into The Wild, or Stephen Ambrose, author of Undaunted Courage. Editors reviewing narrative non-fiction submissions look for many of the same qualities they seek with fiction—a compelling story with unforgettable characters written in page-turning style.

An exception to the author being the star of fiction may occur when the subject matter of the novel focuses on a headline-making topic. During the period following the January 6 insurrection, novels featuring themes in this arena were popular.

Marie Butler-Knight, former publisher of Alpha Books, an imprint of Penguin Group USA, believes the genre of non-fiction can make all the difference regarding publishing potential. "Generalizations can be dangerous because there are different types of non-fiction," she says. "How-to/informational books are easier to break in with if you have subject matter expertise. If you're a generalist author, you'd better have a subject matter expert as a co-author or you'll have a hard time convincing a publisher to publish you."

Regarding biographies and narrative non-fiction, Butler-Knight disagrees with those who believe the genres are totally story-driven. "In order to succeed, these types of books need to tell compelling stories," she states. "They require the same sort of writing skills as fiction. To a publisher, this sort of work is totally author-driven and every bit as risky as publishing fiction."

The publishing world's view toward fiction and non-fiction is symbolized through the comments of Jane von Mehren, former executive editor of Penguin Books. She told Writer's Digest, "Non-fiction has become a strong, sophisticated area . . . In many ways, non-fiction is easier to publish than fiction because it targets a very definable audience, and it's easier to package books and target them to specific readers." She added, "It's a booming area. In non-fiction, we look for books that will have a long shelf life, offering solid information and advice useful for years to come. It really helps when a non-fiction author is already an expert in his or her field, and the book builds on an existing platform."

Von Mehren stated, "In fiction, we're looking for a breakthrough story that will have a long life in trade paperback . . . Trade paperback fiction is gaining momentum, with excellent literary titles getting broader exposure . . . An unknown writer can break through with a great story. For an editor, that discovery is still an incomparable thrill."

Whether to attempt to dent the traditional publishing industry with works of fiction or non-fiction is the writer's choice, but John Baker, a fixture at Publisher's Weekly for years and a noted expert on the book industry, reveals interesting statistics he learned from a top literary agent. "I'm told that 95% of the material that agents receive is fiction," he said. "And that they sell 5%. Of the 5% of non-fiction that lands on their desk, they sell 95%."

The First Book

Launch of a first book is critical to planning a professional writing career. Combining passion for the subject matter with marketability is a key.

Developing a work of fiction demands that you investigate the marketplace. Your story must provide a unique perspective on a topic that will titillate the reader. "What if" scenarios are a popular launching pad for aspiring novelists. They permit creative speculation that can stir a reader's imagination.

One author in favor of this method is John Irving. Creator of such classics as Hotel New Hampshire, The Cider House Rules, and The World According to Garp, Irving discusses the "What if" scenario in the Acknowledgments section of The Fourth Hand, a fascinating tale about a television newscaster whose left hand is eaten by a lion. After stating that it was his wife Janet who asked the compelling question, "What if the donor's widow demands visitation rights with the [donated] hand?" Irving admits, "Every novel I have written has begun with a 'What if . . .?'"

A common thread in successful novels is the inclusion of a love story. It can be between man and woman, man and man, woman and woman, parent and child, human and animal, or patriot and country. Writers are strongly advised to include this element because few novels prove successful if they don't weave a terrific love story into the mix.

A staple for aspiring authors to consider in the non-fiction arena is the biography. Well-researched books chronicling the lives of famous people have launched many a writing career.

If the subject is still alive, permission may be required unless this person is a public figure. Publishers prefer "authorized biographies" of living subjects as preferable, but "unauthorized biographies" are commonplace.

Before proceeding with a biography, or any book, consult Books in Print, Amazon.com, publisher's websites, and other sources to discover whether a similar book on the same topic has been published. If it has, read a copy to explore storytelling methods and determine how you can differentiate your book from others already on the market.

If a novel or biography on your subject has already been published, don't be deterred from pursuing the subject if you can present a fresh slant on the story. Attempt to provide a fresh look at the subject, one that provides a new twist perhaps – one not targeted in any other book published. There may have also have been a time lapse between publications on a certain subject, or perhaps a personality has not been written about for many years triggering a new focus about that person.

Remember, passion for the material you write is paramount, but understanding publishing trends will enhance the opportunity for you to secure the first publishing commitment. Write from the heart, but with an eye toward marketability.

Book Scope

Many beginning writers with traditional publishing aspirations decide to write a book about a subject too small in scope. One writer told me his book idea about a cyberspace killer stalking fellow players of a video game. The idea was unique, but the stakes weren't high enough to garner interest from agents or publishers. I suggested one of the players be the son of the Secretary of Defense. The twist elevated the story to provide a national scope, one affecting an official of the United States government.

The non-fiction arena provides similar challenges. Whether your work is a biography, chronicle of an event, or debate of an important issue, the scope must be of significant importance to gain national interest. Otherwise, agents or publishers will pass, believing the book audience is limited.

Many aspiring authors want to write an autobiographical story about special events occurring in their life. There are exceptions, but most often the scope of such a story is too limited to interest a literary agent or publisher. One writer focused his book on a youth summer camp he attended where a tragic death occurred. The story was important to him, but too personal to interest a broad readership. I suggested he write about another topic. When he becomes well established, perhaps the summer camp story will have a greater chance of success. Once again, uniqueness is the key—will readers really be interested in your story?

Assessing the market potential for any book you contemplate is essential. Literary agent Caroline Carney suggests aspiring authors estimate anticipated sales before contacting a literary agent or publisher. "One of the easiest benchmarks," she states, "is to look at the size of the most popular association in your field (or, in the case of fiction, in a field reflecting the enthusiasm of your main character)." Carney further advises writers to visit the library and consult Bacon's Magazine Directory to discover the circulation size of the largest magazine catering to their primary reader's particular interest, or to note sales figures listed on paperback reprints of popular titles in a particular genre.

Carney believes the aspiring author must pay attention to guidelines within his or her field of interest. "Those contemplating a sports book," she explains, "should adhere to the old saying, 'the smaller the ball, the higher the sales.'" This means literary agents and/or publishers, based on past sales figures, will be more interested in books about golf, tennis, and baseball than they will about football or basketball.

Book Ideas

Book concepts spring into the mind from all directions. Remember Muhammad Ali's famous quote, "The man who has no imagination has no wings."

Writers must develop strong antennae to avoid missing an idea or event that may provide fodder for a book. Ideas are everywhere (H. L. Menchen wrote, "There are no dull subjects. There are only dull writers."), and success can strike like a lightning bolt out of the blue.

Asked how he decided to write Ragtime, E. L. Doctorow stated, "[Inspiration] can be anything. It can be a voice, an image; it can be a deep moment of personal desperation. With Ragtime, I was facing the wall of my study in my house in New Rochelle, and so I started to write about the wall. Then I wrote about the house that was attached to the wall. It was built in 1906, you see, so I thought about the era . . . And one thing led to another and that's the way the book began."

William Faulkner's classic, The Sound and the Fury was inspired, he swore, "with a mental picture." The picture, he wrote, "was of the muddy seat of a little girl's drawers in a pear tree, where she could see through a window where her grandmother's funeral was taking place."

Author Simon Garfield provides a good example of someone birthing a unique idea. His book, Mauve, is the history of the purplish color invented by English teenager William Perkin in 1856. Another is the writings of Richard Hamblyn. His book, The Invention of Clouds, surveys the landscape with a passionate tone.

Bestselling author James Patterson (Along Came A Spider, Kiss The Girls), a former advertising executive at J. Walter Thompson, uses a creative pattern. He told Writer's Digest, "I have a big folder of ideas, and when it comes time for me to write a new book, I'll pull it out and go over everything that's in there." Patterson then picks two or three ideas from the folder and writes them down. "Then I write a page or two on each to begin to see if there is a story I like," he says.

In addition to an "idea folder," I keep a small green notebook in my pocket. It contains a "book idea" page, and pages listing books in progress. When an idea pops into my head, I write it down. In August of 2001, I was consumed with a "what if" idea regarding an invasion of the United States. I note it in my notebook. A month later, much to my sorrow, the terrorist attacks at the World Trade Center and the Pentagon occurred. The "what if" had become reality.

Some ideas take longer to develop than others. I met the legendary San Francisco attorney Melvin Belli in the mid-1980s. He was a swashbuckling character right out of a romance novel— the Ernest Hemingway of the legal profession. Even though we lost contact after I left California, I was fascinated with "The King of Torts" and his role in defending Lee Harvey Oswald's killer, Jack Ruby. The idea to write about Mr. Belli and the Ruby case ruminated for fifteen years, but finally the time was right and Melvin Belli: King of the Courtroom, was published.

The search-for-the-truth path to non-fiction presents many great opportunities for the writer. The book can be investigative, featuring little known, fresh facts about a subject. Other non-fiction areas of interest might be "How-To" books, inspirational material, straight interview books, and satirical material poking fun at politicians or sports figures.

Novelists, such as young Sam Spahn, author of Krill-Guy, The Adventures of an Invincible Penguin, discover ideas from true stories, personal experiences, or the "what if" scenarios. Although personal experiences may fuel your inspiration, remember to give your story a universal twist so others can relate to it. A useful reference is Novel Ideas, penned by Barbara Shoup and Margaret Love Denman. The book features information about the creative process and the thoughts and ideas of twenty-four prominent authors.

For young writers, Writing For Children & Teenagers by Lee Wyndham is a useful reference book. The book promises to "tackle the special problems of writing for the young, and of writing for the look 'n' listen age."

All aspiring authors will benefit from a daily dose of Publishers Lunch, the Internet publication that details every deal completed in the publishing industry. By perusing the featured blurbs that include a short overview or synopsis of the book, ideas are generated for similar themes or messages that are marketable. Taking an idea and giving it another angle or twist can proved successful for many authors.

Person

Books can be written in first, second, or third person. When you are deciding which writing tool to employ, the question is whether you will be the participant in the story (first person: "I ran down the street after the dump truck"), an observer (third person – "Alfred directed the motion picture based on the bestselling book."), or speak directly to the reader (second person – "You should never try this at home."). Using more than one person can be confusing, particularly in fiction or narrative non-fiction.

There should be Unity to your presentation. Utilizing a mix of first, second, and third person as is this book, is most common in instructional writing. Since writing a book is like having a conversation with the reader even though you are not present, decide how best to "address the reader" with the message being conveyed.

If you write in first person, you must portray the actions of subordinate characters through the voice of the main character. Third person permits you to describe the action as the characters interact. Second person is good for advising or instructing the reader directly, as if you are speaking intimately, one-to-one.

Celebrity memoirs are normally written in first person. Biographies and books chronicling events or issues generally employ third person.

Positive and negative factors affect the "person" chosen. Writing novels in first person lets you spin a tale and display a distinctive voice similar to that utilized by well-recognized author Elmore Leonard. Employing this method is often suggested for seasoned writers, since weaving the story through the main character is challenging.

Writing in third person allows you to write "about" characters, an event, or an issue. Many authors of non-fiction are inclined to choose this method.

The choice of a person for writing poetry is only restricted by your imagination. Deciding on a particular person dictates word usage, but you are free to spill your words on the page as you choose. Once again, a distinctive voice is the key.

Built-In Promotion

Writing short stories, magazine articles, or a book linked with a memorable event provides a built-in promotional angle. An example might be releasing a book about landing on the moon in 2009, the 40th anniversary of Neil Armstrong's remarkable achievement.

Providing a promotional angle increases your chances of being published. Instead of having to create a marketing strategy, the publisher is presented with a ready-made publicity campaign.

A reference book titled The Timetables of History: A Horizontal Linkage of People and Events is helpful to any aspiring author. The book, written by Bernard Grun, presents information about history-making events in chronological order. It offers useful information under such headings as History/Politics, Literature/ Theater, Religion/ Philosophy, Visual Arts, Music, Science/Technology, and Daily Life.

Reading The Timetables of History or similar publications may trigger book ideas. Those who decide to pursue writing non-fiction as a career should consult the latest edition on a regular basis.

Two of my books, The Perfect Yankee (released during the 40th anniversary of Don Larsen's World Series perfect game), and Nicklaus, A Biography (published on the 25th anniversary of Jack's greatest year), received additional media coverage by being linked with an event. Testament To Courage, the memoir of Holocaust victim Cecelia Rexin, was released on the Day of the Holocaust. In 2013, The Poison Patriarch: How the Betrayals of Joseph P. Kennedy Caused the Assassination of JFK was published during the 50th anniversary of the assassinations.

In future years, books chronicling the tragic events of September 11, 2001, will be released on various anniversary dates. They will include tributes to those who lost their lives in the attacks on the World Trade Center and the Pentagon, portrayals of New York City police and fire department heroes, and biographies of President George W. Bush, Osama bin Laden, Rudy Giuliani, and other historical figures.

Literary agent Susan Gleason warns that publishers may be leery of "event-oriented" books believing that once the event has passed, interest in the book will wane. But many of these books have proven worthy, providing a strong shelf life long after the event.

Motivation and Writing Credentials

Before choosing a book topic, ask yourself a critical question: Why am I the one person in the world to write this book? The answer is relevant whether you are contemplating a novel, writing non-fiction solo, or considering collaboration and ghostwriting opportunities.

Being qualified to write a book is linked with motivation. Literary agents and publishers are curious about why you believe you can provide a fresh voice or unique information. You must convince the agent or publisher of your passion for the material and that you possess the credentials to write a book that will succeed.

Motivation appears in many forms. James Baldwin (Go Tell It On The Mountain) stated, "[The subject] must be something that irritates you and won't let you go. That's the anguish of it. Do this book, or die. You have to go through that. Talent is insignificant. I know a lot of talented ruins. Beyond talent lie all the usual words: discipline, love, luck, but most of all, endurance."

Prospective agents and publishers will assess whether you possess the endurance Baldwin mentions to complete a book. Many aspire to write a novel, a work of non-fiction, or a collection of poetry, but many fail since they cannot sustain momentum through the rigors of the writing process. Publishers want those who are "finishers," writers who will fight the fight to complete a book on schedule.

Agents and publishers seek authors possessing proper credentials (a platform). Credibility is the issue. A history professor will be more likely to write a credible Civil War epic than will a heart surgeon. And an investigative reporter for the New York Times is more qualified to write about the Iraqi war than the owner of a health food store in Topeka.

With this in mind, review your credentials and consider a subject that will impress an agent or publisher. While submitting the manuscript chronicling the Mike Tyson trial, publishers were reminded that I was a former criminal defense attorney; head of the media committee assigned to oversee coverage of Tyson's trial, had been a legal analyst for major networks, and had written several columns for USA Today. Answering the question as to why I was the one person in the world to write a historical book about Tyson and the trial was easy.

An aspiring novelist client faced a significant challenge since he had not been published. He was a business lawyer and intended to use this credential in his Query Letter to agents and publishers. After some probing, I learned he was born in Nova Scotia. He also told me he was an amateur astrologist and a stamp collector. More important, he stated that the novel he had written was based on a nightmare incident he experienced while playing an Internet video game. His Book Proposal and Query Letter incorporated these unique characteristics into the text. He had been transformed from being a business lawyer to a writer with a fascinating background and experience with his chosen genre, one intriguing to any agent or publisher.

An example of writing about an experience involves the book, A Trial By Jury. D. Graham Burnett, a Princeton historian of science, was the jury foreman for a murder trial in New York City. Though his expertise had not been seeded in the law, experience as a juror permitted him to be an authority. In the tone of Twelve Angry Men, the great film directed by Sydney Lumet, A Trial by Jury is a compelling book.

John Grisham used his credential as an attorney to advantage while writing his first novel, A Time To Kill. Deciding it was important to chronicle a case disturbing to him, Grisham began to write. With his wife as editor, he completed the novel and promoted the book himself. Selling it out of the trunk of his automobile, Grisham was determined to succeed. The book was a modest success, but it led to The Firm, an international bestseller later produced as a film. A multitude of bestsellers followed, but none would have been published if Grisham had not possessed the credibility of having been an attorney with a talent for storytelling.

Stephen Coonts, author of multiple New York Times bestsellers, was an Ensign in the United States Navy. After receiving his flight wings in 1969, he served aboard the USS Enterprise during the final few months of the Vietnam War. This was followed by two years as a flight instructor aboard the USS Nimitz.

The result of Coonts' love for aviation and recollections of his days as a Naval aviator provided a publisher with sufficient credentials to interest them in his first novel, Flight of the Intruder. Final Flight, The Minotaur, and Under Siege followed, rocketing Coonts to international acclaim.

The renowned author Tom Clancy earned his credentials through old-fashioned hard work. When the Maryland-based insurance broker heard the story of a Russian frigate attempting to defect to Sweden, he was mesmerized. Though he possessed no background as a naval or intelligence officer, or writing experience, he researched the subject and began to write a novel. The result was The Hunt For Red October, a spellbinding thriller. Future bestsellers Patriot Games and Clear and Present Danger followed, causing Clancy to become a frequent guest aboard jets, submarines, and destroyers.

Being qualified to write a story provides confidence, an essential characteristic for any aspiring author. Knowing your subject matter will help you to press ahead on those days when your brain refuses to cooperate and the page is empty.

Above all, agents and editors at publishing companies seek qualified writers with the imagination to create a fresh idea resulting in a book that will entertain or inform like none before it. Your challenge is to provide that concept, one causing the agent or editor to throw their hands in the air and shout, "Yes!" When that occurs, you will hear the magic words, "We will publish your book."

Copyright

To ensure no one steals your book concept, copyright the material. This is essential even if you believe it will never be seen by anyone but Aunt Myrtle.

First consider copyrighting your material when you have a satisfactory draft of your book. Book Proposals and Query Letters may also be copyrighted.

A copyright protects literary work under United States law for the life of the author or poet plus seventy years. Copyrighting material is easy. For details, consult the Library of Congress website. The necessary documents can be downloaded.

Proper authentication of the literary material is required. After a few questions are answered, the completed document and a copy of the literary material, accompanied by a filing fee, are mailed to the address provided. Within weeks, a letter is forwarded designating a copyright number. File this document in a safe deposit box.

A terrific reference source regarding copyright is Kirsch's Guide To The Book Contract, by attorney Jonathan Kirsch. In simple language, he explains why you should protect your writings.

When a book is traditionally published, the copyright continues in the name of the author even though the publishing company obtained specified rights to publish it. The book will be assigned an ISBN (International Standard Book Number) to distinguish it. Internationally recognized, this ten-digit number (1st digit—country of origin, 2nd digit—publisher designation, 3rd set of digits—title of book, last digit—self-check) or a thirteen-digit number used since 2007 identifies the book for purposes of commerce and supply chains. If you self-publish, you can obtain, for a fee, an ISBN number at www. bowker.com. Once it is issued, you should register the number with Books in Print to ensure the book information is available to major retailers, librarians, and independent booksellers across the country. Book titles can be registered at www.bowkerlink.com.

A barcode used by bookstores and other retailers to record sales and price will be printed on the book. Other barcodes may be printed on the cover or jacket, including UPC and EAN numbers. A traditional publisher will handle this for you.

There is one barcode per book. More information can be obtained at the Bowker web site.

Protecting your writings is essential. You have worked hard to conceive a terrific book idea, one that is marketable. Now you are ready to make certain the writing is the very best it can be.

Step #2 Summary

- Hone writing skills by penning short stories, magazine articles, newspaper articles, essays, short poems, etc.

- Read prestigious magazines to understand the literary marketplace.

- Consider whether fiction, non-fiction, or poetry is your passion.

- Research the genre and category of the book being contemplated to discover similar books.

- Provide a wide scope for your book to attract a broad potential audience.

- Decide whether to write in first, second, or third person.

- Choose a book subject with a built-in promotion.

- Ask yourself—"Why am I the one person in the world best qualified to write this book?"

- Copyright your material for protection.

Checklist to Evaluate
The Merit of a Book Concept

Questions
1. Is the subject matter of the book unique?
2. Are you passionate about writing this book?
3. Can you describe your book concept in fifteen words or less, preferably less?
4. Is there broad readership for the book?
5. Why are you the one person in the world who should write this book?
6. Is there a built-in audience for the book?
7. Do you have a unique slant on a subject matter?
8. Is the book promotable?
9. Can you name five successful books similar to yours?
10. Why is your book unique?
11. Does the book cover a timely subject?
12. Does your book provide the answer to a question or solve a problem? (Agents and Publishers seek books providing solutions.)
13. Can you link the release of the book to an anniversary of an event of note to aid promotion?
14. Is the book about a notable subject?
15. Do you have a unique credential or "platform" from which to write the book?
16. Do you have a competent game plan to promote the book?
17. Can you convince a literary agent or publisher your book will sell more than 10,000 copies or more?

Tip—Answers to these questions permit you to evaluate the potential success of your initial book. Be objective, and if your concept doesn't appear to be meritorious, consider another book topic. Perhaps the initial one will become a future book once you are established as a published author.

There is no such thing as a moral or an immoral book. Books are well written or badly written, that is all.

OSCAR WILDE

Step #3

Your Passport to Publication
Is Good Writing

The Writing Process

There is nothing more personal than writing. Thoughts originating in the deep recesses of the intellect are unique. When these ideas are reduced to writing, they become a direct reflection of one's spiritual and intellectual being.

Those who choose to write professionally must do so with passion and a sense of responsibility since their words will affect the reader's mindset. Thoughts and ideas expressed verbally flutter through the air like multi-colored butterflies and seldom are accurately recalled. A famous psychologist once stated that people don't comprehend the substance of spoken words unless they are repeated six or seven times. Written words expressing thoughts and ideas are more likely to be recalled since readers choose quiet time to enjoy the very essence of published works. **Authors have the opportunity to inspire, inform, challenge, and entertain whether they write fiction or non-fiction.**

For those choosing to pursue a writing career at an early age, the battle plan is clear: keep an open mind and absorb everything life has to offer. For suggestions on how to be more creative, read *Pencil Dancing* and *New Ways To Free Your Creative Spirit* by Mari Messer.

Formal education is available through writing classes, books on writing, seminars, and college courses. Search for competent instructors with traditional publishing credits or outstanding academic skills.

To bolster the ability to write with sufficient knowledge, the aspiring writer must garner a sense of history, of what occurred to alter the course of mankind and why. Course study in psychology, philosophy, history, and classical literature provides a solid foundation.

Extensive travel is the comrade of good writers. Spanning the globe opens the door to a rich heritage. Sojourns to Greece, Egypt, Italy, England, France, and many other countries are valuable. Asked his advice for young writers, William Faulkner stated, "Travel and read."

While visiting foreign countries, learn about the people, the history of the country, and the customs. Working in a foreign country provides a wealth of knowledge. Don't shy away from what might be considered taboo employment. Faulkner wrote, "The best job ever offered to me was to become a landlord in a brothel."

Writing workshops, seminars, and writers' conferences are meat and potatoes if writing professionally is your goal. This is the perfect environment in which to gather valuable tips and nuances from those who have achieved the goal of being published. Many such events are publicized in independent, creative arts-oriented newspapers such as The Village Voice.

If you decide later in life that writing is a profession of choice, the alternatives differ. Workshops, seminars, and conferences are valuable tools for learning, but a crash course on writing professionally is a prerequisite if you have not exercised this skill in many years.

Having no formal training, I relied on others to assist me when I began to write Down for the Count, the book investigating the Mike Tyson trial. Colleagues with backgrounds in literature and English perused the manuscript as well. I did the best I could with what I knew at the time.

Education is essential to learning the craft of writing, but those who proclaim that someone with no formal literary training cannot succeed should recall the background of no less a "scholar" than William Shakespeare. While he was schooled in Greek and Latin literature, rhetoric, and Christian ethics, there is no evidence that the Bard was ever taught the art of writing. History indicates he left school at age fifteen, never pursued further formal education, and was not considered a learned man. This did not prohibit him from writing what many experts consider to be the most extraordinary body of works in the history of literature.

Poet Walt Whitman further proves that formal training is not linked to literary success. His formal education ended at age eleven. Unlike other writers of his time who enjoyed structured, classical educations at private schools, Whitman learned about writing in the local library. He then joined a newspaper, The New York Mirror, where he wrote his first article in 1834. Less than two decades later, after dabbling in short-story fiction, Whitman wrote the classic, Leaves of Grass.

Regardless of the success enjoyed by authors such as Shakespeare and Whitman, my path toward becoming an author would have been less cumbersome had I spent more time learning the craft. At the time, my sole intent was to have book after book published to earn a living and avoid traveling far from home. This was a goal since I had become the stepfather of four young children, including triplet boys, at the ripe age of forty-four. Writing professionally was the link to spending quality time with the kids as they grew up.

If you are the "I just decided to take up writing and I want to be published" type as I was, then become an avid reader and practice writing. Best-selling romance writer Nora Roberts echoes King's sentiments. She began her career as a stay-at-home mother who wrote ideas in a notebook during a snowstorm in 1979. Pleased with her efforts, she continued to write. The result was her first published work, Irish Thoroughbred. Since then she has written several bestsellers, all because, as she says, "I don't believe in waiting for inspiration. It's my job to sit down . . . and write."

Whether you are interested in writing fiction or non-fiction, you should read both. Read the classics—Hemingway, Joyce, Dickens, and Steinbeck. Poets can learn from Whitman, Frost, Edgar Allen Poe, and Edna St. Vincent Millay. Each of these great writers admits their education about writing was influenced by the books they read. Asked what authors he enjoyed, Hemingway listed more than thirty-four before confessing that to list them all "would take a day to remember." Among them were Mark Twain, Bach, Tolstoy, Dostoevsky, Chekhov, Kipling, Shakespeare, and Dante. Hemingway admitted he also gained education from artists and composers. "I learned as much from painters about how to write," he stated, "as from writers . . . I should think that what one learns from composers and from the study of harmony and counterpoint would be obvious."

Competent authors are superb storytellers. While reading the classics, note how the canonized authors weave a story. Whether the choice is fiction or non-fiction, the story must be clear, have a good beginning, middle, and end, and never be boring. Reading well-written books helps you realize how others have accomplished the feat. In On Writing, Stephen King states:

Good writing ... teaches the learning writer about style, graceful narration, plot development, the creation of believable characters, and truth-telling. A novel like Grapes of Wrath may fill a new writer with feelings of despair and good, old-fashioned jealousy—I'll never be able to write anything that good, not if I live to be a thousand—but such feelings can also serve as a spur, goading the writer to work harder and aim higher. Being swept away by a combination of great story and great writing . . . is a part of every writer's necessary formation. You cannot hope to sweep someone else away by the force of your writing until it has been done to you.

In Bird by Bird, by Anne Lamott, the author presents an interesting strategy regarding fiction storytelling. Lamott quotes Alice Adams from a lecture about short story writing. The excerpt reads:

[Alice] said that sometimes she uses a formula when writing a short story that goes ABDCE, for Action, Background, Development, Climax, and Ending. You begin with action that is compelling enough to draw us in, make us want to know more. Background is where you let us see and know whom these people are, how they've come to be together, what was going on before the opening of the story. Then you develop these people, so that we learn what they care most about. The plot – the drama, the actions, the tension – will grow out of that. You move them along until everything comes together in the climax, after which things are different for the main characters, different in some real way. And then there is the ending: what is our sense of who these people are now, what they are left with, what happened, and what did it mean.

Fiction writers can learn from Scott Turow, author of several bestsellers, including Presumed Innocent. An excerpt reads:

> *The atomized life of the restaurant spins on about us. At separate tables, couples talk; the late-shift workers dine alone; the waitresses pour coffee. And here sits Rusty Sabich, thirty-nine years old, full of lifelong burdens and workaday fatigue. I tell my son to drink his milk. I nibble at my burger. Three feet away is the woman whom I have said I've loved for nearly twenty years, making her best efforts to ignore me.*

Besides being a terrific storyteller, character description was Jack Kerouac's specialty. An excerpt of On the Road reads:

> *He was a gray, nondescript-looking fellow you wouldn't notice on the street, unless you looked closer and saw his mad, bony skull with its strange youthfulness – a Kansas minister with exotic, phenomenal fires and mysteries. He had studied medicine in Vienna; had studied anthropology, read everything; and now he was settling to his life's work, which was the study of things themselves in the streets of life and the night.*

In Balzac and the Little Chinese Seamstress, author Dai Sijie sweeps the reader into his novel portraying life during China's Cultural Revolution. An excerpt reads:

> *The room served as shop, workplace, and dining room all at once. The floorboards were grimy and streaked with yellow-and-black gobs of dried spittle left by clients. You could tell they were not washed down daily. There were hangers with finished garments suspended on a string across the middle of the room. The corners were piled high with bolts of material and folded clothes, which were under siege from an army of ants.*

Providing a good beginning, middle, and end to a story by doing so with each paragraph provides excellent storytelling. In Down and

Out In London and Paris, George Orwell presents a worthy example. The excerpt reads:

> *The Jew delivered the cocaine the same day, and promptly vanished. And meanwhile, as was not surprising after the fuss Roucolle had made, the affair had been noised all over the quarter. The very next morning the hotel was raided and searched by the police.*

While Woody Allen may be better known for his comedic films, one of his books, Without Feathers, is a classic. A short stories he weaves is called The Whore Of Mensa, a great "what-if" detailing one man's search for intellectual companionship instead of the usual sexual gratification. An excerpt reads:

> *One thing about being a private investigator, you've got to learn to go with your hunches. That's why when a quivering pat of butter named Word Babcock walked into my office and laid his cards on the table, I should have trusted the cold chill that shot up my spine.*
>
> *"Kaiser," he said. "Kaiser Lupowitz?"*
>
> *"That's what it says on my license," I owned up.*
>
> *"You've got to help me. I'm being blackmailed. Please."*
>
> *He was shaking like the lead singer in a rumba band. I pushed a glass across the desktop and a bottle of rye I keep handy for non-medicinal purposes.*
>
> *"Suppose you relax and tell me all about it."*

In the non-fiction bestseller Seabiscuit, author Laura Hillenbrand captured the reader's attention by providing visual and dramatic scenes propelling the reader into the middle of the action. An excerpt reads:

> *A minute later the field bent around the far turn and rushed at the grandstand. There was one horse in front and pouring it on. His silks were red. It was Seabiscuit. The crowd roared. Pollard [the jockey] and Seabiscuit*

glided down the lane all by themselves, reaching the wire in track-record-equaling time. Kayak was right behind them. It was Pollard's first win since 1938.

Journals and Idea Books

Learning the craft of writing is a continuing process. One of the best means to hone the craft is by writing in a journal or diary. It promotes discipline while providing a chronology of your life.

Author John Fowles (The French Lieutenant's Woman) stated, "I am a great believer in diaries, if only in the sense that bar exercises are good for ballet dancers; it's often through personal diaries that the novelist discovers his true bent." This comment is applicable for non-fiction writers as well.

One exercise to consider requires writing in a journal each day for a week. Content and length are optional, but the goal is to complete the task. Then cast aside the journal for a few days before reading it. If you're satisfied with the text, and the process involved, then you have the potential to write professionally. If you hate what you wrote, and the discipline of having to write each day, then consider basketry, modern art, or some other means of expending creative energy.

Another useful exercise is to organize a folder containing observations about others. Good writers are people watchers. Whether you do so in a park, at sports events, or at a bus stop, chronicle your thoughts and observations. Vivid description and words evoking emotion are the earmarks of the good writer. To enhance this skill, study speech patterns, how people move, what habits they possess, and face and body features. Make lists of these characteristics; then add other elements. A fat notebook I often refer to includes pages listing names (Avon Privette, Paris Wolfe, Tootie Witmer, Audrey Wink, Holly Furfer, Bobby April, David Duck), smells (bug spray, moth balls, fresh strawberry pie, chemical fertilizer), descriptions (salty, speckled, overripe, furry), hair style (butch, raggedy, ponytail, mousy), and body parts (webbed feet, spindly toes, stubby arms, firm butt, limp face, spidery fingers, slumping posture, drooping eyes, artificial eyes, whiskey nose, parched lips, dead legs). Another list includes weather descriptions (gray drizzle, sideways rain, Oklahoma wind) and sky descriptions (primrose, veined with dry lightning, streaky blue).

In another section of my "help" book, one added to on a daily basis, I list "useful phrases." Included is soft laughter, hushed giggle, black scuff marks, pocket change, replied indifferently, fork patrol, pigeon toed, steady gaze, shimmered in the moonlight, and crumpled pompadour.

Before beginning the writing process, consult your lists and permit words and ideas to fill your brain with creativity. Clever words and phrases spice up the text, providing the reader with the all-important asset that E. B. White emphasizes: visualization. Learned author John Cheever endorsed White's viewpoint when he stated, "The books you really love give the sense, when you first open them, of having been there. It is a creation, almost like a chamber in the memory. Places that one has never been to, things that one has never seen or heard, but their fitness is so sound that you've been there somehow."

Having gained the essential skills necessary to write well, the aspiring author is in pursuit of a realistic goal: being published. A good book idea plus an excellent strategy plus hard work permits this goal to be realized.

Word Usage

While reading, note the author word choice. There are those who love the vocabulary and appreciate hundred-dollar words that claim, "I'm a literate son-of-a-gun with a graduate degree in Webster's." But language must never be vague, elusive, or downright inaccessible. A story loses much of its flow and meaning if the reader spends too much time opening a dictionary. Phrases like "revelatory episodes," "epigrammatic prose," and "diorama of American plenty" will confuse and dismay ninety-five percent of the population.

Throughout my tenure as an author, readers have provided feedback indicating that my books are "easily read." Little highbrow language exists in my books because I purposely exclude words preventing the flow of the language. I want to make them stop and think or enjoy the text, not be impressed with my use of big words.

Doing so is essential if you want to reach a broad readership, because writing is personal, not only for the writer, but for the reader. As the writer, you are conveying information regarding a story intended to captivate the reader. You want your words to leap off the page and infiltrate the reader's brain to entice, excite, entertain, or make them stop and think. When readers purchase a book, it will be successful if they ask, "Who is this author or poet and what is he or she trying to show [not tell] me?"

Punctuation Usage
[See also – Punctuation Points in the Appendix]

No matter how good the book, magazine, or article idea may be, punctuation errors diminish the chances of becoming published. No literary agent, editor at a publishing company, or editor at a magazine or newspaper has the time to wade through punctuation flaws. Noting them produces an instant feeling that the writer is unprofessional.

Glaring errors such as locating a period or comma outside quotation marks in a sentence are commonplace and embarrassing. Ninety-nine times out of a hundred, the period or comma will be positioned inside the final quotation mark.

A common error occurs when writers don't realize that all numbers up to a hundred are written out. Also—no numerical number ever begins a sentence.

Proper use of hyphens, semicolons, colons, and commas is a must for aspiring authors and poets. Be aware of the rule regarding when to capitalize the first letter of a word following a colon.

Writers should italicize the names of films, books, screenplays, operas, plays, and magazines. Quotation marks are permitted for book chapters, poems, articles, songs, and short stories. Underlining any of the above is not necessary for emphasis.

Learning basic rules ensures that writing mistakes will not prevent literary agents or publishers from casting aside submitted material due to blatant errors. The author's best friend is a competent line editor, or a book complete with grammar and punctuation tips.

Modern-day study guides for the aspiring writer abound. The Chicago Manual of Style is a dense book, not exactly vacation reading. Set aside ample time so you can focus on its contents. A better idea is to consult the book in spurts, take notes, and then refer to it again and again like a close friend who tells the truth.

Publishers prefer that authors and poets adhere to the rules presented in this publication, but Elements of Style, by William Strunk Jr. and E. B. White, is ninety-five pages long, the perfect length for obtaining good, solid information about writing. Spending less than ten dollars for the book is one of the best investments an aspiring author or poet can make.

Professor Strunk published the classic for his students in 1919. It soon became known as "the little book that could." Over the years, White, most famous for writing Charlotte's Web, has revised it for modernization purposes, but this gem features Strunk's brilliant mind, probing the depths of writing and what is proper and correct. Under titles such as "Elementary Rules of Usage," "Elementary Rules of Composition," "A Few Matters of Form," and "Words and Expressions Commonly Misused," the Cornell professor provides simple, clear, and brilliant guidelines. Among the jewels are warnings against overuse of adverbs and adjectives, advocacy of active voice and positive words, and rules for positioning pronouns. Elements of Style explains the whys and wherefores so even a dunderhead can understand. I recommend putting the book under your pillow while you sleep with the hope that the knowledge will seep into your brain.

While the first four sections of the book are a must-read, E. B. White added Book V titled, "An Approach To Style." He writes, "Up to this point, the book has been concerned with what is correct, or acceptable, in the use of English. In this final chapter, we approach style in its broader meaning: style in the sense of what is distinguished and distinguishing. Here we leave solid ground. Who can confidently say what ignites a certain combination of words, causing them to explode in the mind?"

Regardless of the caveat, White's suggestions are on solid ground. Sections include: "Placing yourself in the background," "Write in a way that comes naturally," "Work from a suitable design," and "Write with nouns and verbs, not with adverbs and adjectives."

White discusses the need to revise and rewrite, not to overwrite, and not to overstate.

After discovering Strunk and White's book and consulting the Chicago Manual of Style, I was pleased to note that much of what they suggested had somehow been incorporated into my writing style. This stemmed from reading what other good writers had written . . . and perhaps some bad writers' work as well, since I learned to discern the gibberish many believed necessary to tell their stories.

Absorbing the lessons outlined in the "little book" provides a basis for developing writing skills. Each author or poet chooses a storytelling method, but proper usage of language guarantees that errors won't signal lack of talent. Editors at publishing companies dismiss a manuscript or collection of poetry if there are misspellings and grammatical errors, but they also pay close attention to word usage.

Learning good writing skills at an early age will benefit aspiring authors and poets. Parents interested in supplemental materials to improve children's writing skills may consider the Shurley English method. More information is available at www.shurley.com.

Clarity

In On Writing Well, author William Zinsser states, "Good writing has an aliveness that keeps the reader reading from one paragraph to the next, and it's not a question of gimmicks to 'personalize' the author. It's a question of using the English language in a way that will achieve the greatest clarity and strength."

On my end, readers through the years have commented that my books are easily read. I take this as a complement but in reality, I don't have a large vocabulary to choose from. Being from a small Indiana town, I never developed a great grasp of the English language. Using simple words so that clarity is never an issue has become a special friend.

Fiction writers must ask themselves several questions regarding clarity. Is the story time-oriented so the reader understands the time frame being presented? Are the characters well defined and do they act in a manner consistent with the background provided? Is there a believable backdrop for the story, one that is vivid? Have I written a clever dramatic story with a ticking clock to add suspense?

Non-fiction writers face a comparable question—will a story that is quite clear to the writer be as clear to the reader? Will the reader understand the message being conveyed by the text? This applies to poets as well.

Author John Updike provided a guidepost regarding clarity. He wrote, "When I write, I aim in my mind not toward New York, but toward a vague spot a little to the east of Kansas. I think of the books on library shelves, without their jackets, years old, and a countryish teenaged boy finding them speak to him." Author Zinsser suggests, "Clutter is the disease of American writing. We are a society strangling in unnecessary words, circular constructions, pompous frills, and meaningless jargon."

As the writing process continues, writers must be certain they are telling the story they intend to tell, and with accuracy. Many times we read what our brain wants to read instead of what is on the page. In a final draft of this book, I credited Robert Frost with writing Leaves of Grass. I knew better, but had Frost on the brain. When an editor pointed out the mistake, I was embarrassed.

One method of determining clarity while proofreading for errors is to read the material aloud. By inspecting and hearing each word, meaning becomes clearer and mistakes are revealed that would otherwise have been overlooked.

Writing Skills

Information about how to write and writing style are referenced in many books, including Elements of Style by professors Strunk and White. White was correct when he wrote that no one understands why a certain group of words carefully joined produce magic on the sheet of paper for one author while resulting in gobbledygook for another. Each writer's composition of words will differ according to his or her skill and experience.

In his book, On Writing, Stephen King offered a simple explanation for what he believes is important when considering writing style. He wrote, "Book buyers want a good story to take with them on the airplane, something that will first fascinate them, then pull them in and keep them turning the pages." Mystery writer Tony Hillerman (Hunting Badger) told Writer's Digest, "I feel my first priority as a writer is to entertain the audience."

Never forget every book is an adventure—Write it like one. This is true whether you are creating a tortoise and hare story, a book about the inner workings of the latest computer, a chronicle of the evolution of Red Lobster restaurants as an American success story, a biography of the gifted poet Etheridge Knight, or a collection of poetry about why birds fly south for the winter.

Author James Patterson espouses a unique perspective of writing. In *The Writer's Handbook,* he states, "In the beginning, I really worried a lot about sentences in my books. But at some point . . . I stopped writing sentences and started writing stories. And that's the advice I give to new writers. Sentences are really hard to write. Stories flow. If you've got an idea, the story will flow. Once you have the story down you can go back and polish it for the next ten years."

No one doubts that clear, concise storytelling featuring language that shows, but does not tell, is paramount to success. Some writers sprinkle flowery language throughout their manuscripts. Others write like Hemingway and produce some sentences that are never-ending. Regardless, the finest writers, whether they are writing fiction, non-fiction, or poetry, are brief and visual, two great talents gained through experience. Being visual means to flavor your writing with the five senses—sight, smell, touch, taste, and hearing—so the reader consumes and is consumed with the text.

In The Elements of Style, Professor Strunk wrote, "If those who have studied the art of writing are in accord on any one point, it is this: the surest way to arouse and hold the reader's attention is by being specific, definite, and concrete. The greatest writers—Homer, Dante, Shakespeare—are effective because they deal in particulars and report the details that matter. Their words call up pictures." Strunk added, "Vigorous writing is concise. A sentence should contain no unnecessary words, a paragraph no unnecessary sentences, for the same reason that a drawing should have no unnecessary lines and a machine no unnecessary parts."

Author Nora Roberts believes visualization means proper selection and description of characters whether the book is fiction or non-fiction. She told Writer's Digest, "Your characters, have to jump off the page. They have to appeal to the reader in some way . . . They need to be appealing, humorous and human."

Literary agent Julia Castiglia echoes Roberts' words in Writer's Digest: "What we really look for are books that are well written, with a certain zing to them that climbs off the page and wraps itself around our brains, that so entrance and seduce us that we just can't say no."

Word Choice

The requirement that the writer show the reader and not tell cannot be over-emphasized. Word choice is key. Mark Twain wrote, "The difference between the right word and the nearly right word is the same as that between lightning and lightning bug."

To improve a story, use active words portraying concrete images instead of abstractions: avoid crutch-words ending in "ly;" avoid "not" and "no;" use active verbs like "clawed," "swatted," and "pawed," instead of linking verbs like "is" and "was;" avoid overuse of gerunds (verbs used as nouns by adding "ing"); and use stronger nouns instead of adjectives. Regarding the need for active verbs, author William Zinsser wrote, "Verbs are the most important of all your tools. They push the sentence forward and give it momentum. Active verbs push hard; passive verbs tug fitfully."

Avoid words such as "a little," "very," "kind of," "pretty much" or "really," qualifying other words. They are often unnecessary and make your writing sound trite.

Concise word usage translates to paragraph length. Reader attention span may be short, so use of a few sentences separates the text and keeps the flow of the story at a steady pace. Long paragraphs are bulky and can bog down the reader. Avoid them.

Strong word usage is essential at the beginning of a chapter, or a verse. Words completing a chapter or a verse must tantalize and urge the reader onward.

Adverbs and Adjectives

Stephen King's book, On Writing, provides several important tips. One suggests a writing mantra to be repeated again and again: "The adverb is not your friend." He believes if the word chosen cannot stand on its own, replace it with one that does.

Word choice signals the distinctive voice writers convey in conversation with the reader. How they manipulate certain words into the story dictates the tone of that voice. William Zinsser states, "Bear in mind, when you're choosing words and stringing them together, how they sound. This may seem absurd: readers read with their eyes. But in fact they hear what they are reading far more than you realize. Therefore such matters as rhythm and alliteration are vital to every sentence." Zinsser adds, "Develop one voice that readers will recognize when they hear it on the page, a voice that's enjoyable not only in its musical line but its avoidance of sounds that would cheapen its tone: breeziness and condescension and clichés."

Never one to discount the advice of an author like Stephen King, who has sold more books than there are people in China, an "adverb hunt" was commenced during the final edit of my book *Miscarriage of Justice*. To this end, we scoured the manuscript and eliminated ninety-five percent of the adverbs.

The "word surgery" performed on the adverbs in the book was successful, and the patient lived. Some adverbs can be helpful, but removing the malignant language improved the book considerably.

While editing, we also concentrated on "word brevity," eliminating words not advancing the story. Any time we saw "they were," "they are," "there is," "it is," or "it was," we crossed them out along with dreaded clichés.

Many authors develop an affinity for one word. Mine is "that." I love the word, but often it is not required. During editing of this book, I attempted to eliminate as many "that's" as possible. I'm sure I could delete others, but at least I have spared readers many of my unnecessary pet words. Be careful, though: non-use of a word where it is required can be as bad as overusing it.

Brevity is essential. Without exception, less is better. When Ernest Hemingway was chided for the short length of his classic Old

Man and the Sea, he answered critics by saying, "[It] could have been over a thousand pages long and had every character in the village in it . . .That is done excellently and well by other writers . . . So I have tried to do something else. First I have tried to eliminate everything unnecessary to convey experience to the reader so that after he or she has read something it will become part of his or her experience and seem actually to have happened. This is very hard to do and I worked at it very hard."

Author Zinsser echoes Hemingway's thoughts. He states,

> *[The] secret of good writing is to strip every sentence to its cleanest components. Every word that serves no function, every long word that could be a short word, every adverb that carries the same meaning that's already in the verb, every passive construction that leaves the reader confused as to who is doing what— these are the thousand and one adulterants that weaken the strength of a sentence.*

Historians recall that brevity was a key to Abraham Lincoln's speeches. During his Second Inaugural Address, he utilized just 701 words. Five hundred five of them were of one syllable; 122 contained two.

To realize that short books are jewels of the writing profession, recall such classics as The Great Gatsby, The Red Badge of Courage, Turn of the Screw, and A Lost Lady. Tuesdays With Morrie is another. A helpful book for those who love to use run-on sentences is The Dictionary of Concise Writing: 10,000 Alternatives to Wordy Phrases by Robert Harwell Fiske.

Run-on sentences permit readers little time to breathe. Early in my career, every paragraph seemed to feature the dreaded run-on. Only by weeding them out, splitting up thoughts, and focusing on being concise have I become a better writer.

Style of writing is an individual matter. It is important to know the standard rules for writing, but many successful authors have broken the rules. Lori Foster, a noted romance author, wrote in Writer's Digest, "What really sells your book is your individual voice, not the rules that you obey." Elaborating, she stated, "Just about everyone has heard the dozens and dozens of rules listed as a criteria for getting published in romance. They include: no hopping from one character to another's head, one point of view per scene, no exotic settings, and no athletes or television personalities. In truth, there are very few definite rules."

Truman Capote's thoughts on rules are right on point. He said, "Writing has laws of perspective, of light and shade, just as painting does, or music. If you are born knowing them, fine. If not, learn them. Then rearrange the rules to suit yourself."

Keys To The Writing Process

If you decide to write an entire manuscript before completing a Query Letter and/or Book Proposal, remember one important rule: Once you start, don't stop. The main reason most people intending to write a book never do is because they encounter a stumbling block regarding word choice, punctuation, or grammar usage. Before they know it, the creative juices turn sour.

Author and literary writing guru Natalie Goldberg speaks to this in her book Writing Down The Bones. She believes initial thoughts "capture the oddities of your mind." Goldberg writes, "First thoughts have tremendous energy. It is the way the mind flashes on something." Goldberg provides a list of exercises in her book to inspire writers toward creative thinking.

Author John Steinbeck (The Grapes of Wrath) spoke to the importance of completing what you begin. He stated, "Write freely and as rapidly as possible and throw the whole thing on paper. Never correct or rewrite until the whole thing is down. Rewrite in process is usually found to be an excuse for not going on. It also interferes with flow and rhythm which can only come from a kind of unconscious association with the material."

In a 1947 letter to Jack Kerouac, writer Neal Cassady, upon whom Kerouac based the character Dean Moriarty in On The Road, wrote to Kerouac:

I have always held that when one writes, one should forget all rules, literary styles, and other such pretensions as large words, lordly clauses and other phrases as such…. Rather, I think one should write, as nearly as possible, as if he were the first person on earth and was humbly and sincerely putting on paper that which he saw and experienced and loved and lost; what his passing thoughts were and his sorrows and desires. . .

Actor Sean Connery, playing the part of fictional author William Forester in Finding Forrester, addressed the subject in an interesting manner. He stated, "You write the first draft with your heart. You re-write with your head."

Instead of worrying about mistakes or lapses in the text, plow ahead. There will be time later to fill in the blanks or correct errors. To aid your efforts regarding manuscript form, a Manuscript Techniques list follows this chapter.

Writing Regimen

There is no definitive answer to how much text a writer should complete each day. Stephen King states in his book On Writing, "I like to get ten pages a day, which amounts to 2,000 words. That's 180,000 words over a three-month span, a goodish length for a book."

Esteemed author John Updike (The Power and the Glory) writes 1,000 words a day, six days a week. This process has resulted in more than fifty books, two of which have earned Pulitzer Prizes.

Ernest Hemingway, who never began writing unless twenty sharpened pencils were close at hand, described his daily routine by stating:

> I write every morning as soon after first light as possible. There is no one to disturb you and it is cool or cold and you come to your work and warm as you write. You read what you have written and, as you always stop when you know what is going to happen next, you go on from there. You write until you come to a place where you still have your juice and know what will happen next and you stop and try to live through Until the next day when you hit it again. You have started at six in the morning, say, and may go on until noon or be through

before that. When you stop you are as empty, and at the same time never empty but filling, as when you have made love to someone you love.

Poet Maya Angelou's regimen is classic. "I have a hotel room in every town I've ever lived in," she stated. " . . . I leave my home at six, and try to be at work by 6:30. To write, I lie across the bed, so that [my] elbow is absolutely encrusted at the end . . . I stay until 12:30 or 1:30 in the afternoon, and then I go home and try to breathe."

Tom Wolfe (A Man In Full, The Right Stuff) sets page goals. He stated, "I set myself a quota—ten pages a day, triple-spaced, which means about eighteen hundred words. If I can finish that up in three hours, I'm through for the day."

Many writers believe they deserve a magnum of champagne in celebration if they can write four to six pages a day. Others write less, some more. It all depends, but never let anything prohibit progress toward the appointed goal. This means the telephone, loved ones, pets, door-to-door salespeople, radio, television, grammar problems, spelling miscues, mosquitoes, or children. All are the writer's enemies since they obstruct completion of the task. My black Labrador's name is Black Sox, but I could name him "Procrastination," since playing ball with him is a tempting diversion to writing.

Block out these enemies, begin to write, then write and write, and write some more. Be sure to "save" the material paragraph by paragraph while working; and then save it on a disk when you have completed the day's task so computer "crashes" won't eliminate your text. Mother Nature is another enemy of the writer, and her electrical storms are computer killers.

When words are dashing out of the brain, there is exhilaration beyond comprehension. While the juices are flowing, the fingers can't work fast enough. The rush is better than any chemical "high."

Every writer discovers a time and place to write, but my regimen is quite consistent. Being a morning person, I write from just after 5:00 a.m. until 7:30 or so. Breaking up the writing period is a quick break to eat a bowl of Rice Krispies with fruit.

Some days, I was tempted to read my composed material to Black Sox when he was still alive a la John Steinbeck. He wrote,

"I've always tried out my material on my dogs first. You know, with Angel, he sits there and listens and I get the feeling he understands everything. But with Charley, I always felt he was just waiting to get a word in edgewise. Years ago, when my red setter chewed up the manuscript of Of Mice and Men, I said at the time that the dog must have been an excellent literary critic."

Once breakfast is completed, I walk outside, take a few deep breaths, and then return to the writing table until eleven o'clock or so. By then, my brain is empty.

Afternoons are set aside for research and a wretched duty: editing. Most weeks I write every day except for Saturday when I attempt to break par against a great group of buddies at the local golf course. Even then, I carry five-by-seven note cards in case an inspiring thought or observation leaps into my mind.

A proposed regimen is as follows: The writer decides on Sunday to complete the first fifty pages of a manuscript. He or she writes ten pages on Monday and Tuesday, and ten more each on Wednesday, Thursday, and Friday. This night is reserved for celebration, Saturday for recovering from any Friday night hangover, and Sunday for the Sabbath. Poets can adapt a similar regimen for their work.

By not touching the manuscript, the writer will have a fresh perspective on Monday. Bestselling author Truman Capote (In Cold Blood) was a proponent of this method. After describing himself as a "horizontal author [who] can't think unless I'm lying down," he stated, "when the yellow draft is finished, I put the manuscript away for a while, a week, a month, sometimes longer. When I take it out again, I read it as coldly as possible, then read it to a friend or two, and decide what changes I want to make."

Revisions

When people ask what I do, I tell them that I am a "re-writer," not a writer. This emphasizes how much time is spent revising text.

The process of rewriting is complex. Pulitzer Prize-winning author Elie Wiesel stated, "Writing is not like painting, where you add. It is not what you put on the canvas that the reader sees. Writing is more like a sculpture where you remove; you eliminate in order to make the work visible. There is a difference between a book of two hundred pages from the very beginning, and a book of two hundred pages, which is the result of an original eight hundred pages. The six hundred pages are there. Only you don't see them."

When you are in the revision stage, as opposed to when you are rushing through a first draft to complete it start to finish, speed is the enemy of quality. To be sure the work is the finest it can be, take your time. Columnist James Kilpatrick wrote, "Edit your copy, then edit it again; then edit it once more. This is the hand-rubbing process. No rough sandpapering can replace it." William Zinsser stresses the importance of revisions. He concludes, "Rewriting is the essence of writing well; it's where the game is won or lost."

Author Dean Koontz might seem obsessive to some, but according to the Los Angeles Times, "The man doesn't just write at a breakneck clip, he edits each page at least 20 to 30 times immediately after he writing it. When the chapter is finished, he prints it out and starts editing those same pages all over again."

Every time text is revised, it improves. Many times writer's return to words they've written and are amazed at the flow and clarity. Other times the material embarrasses them. How I wish I could re-write many of the first books I had published using the skills learned over the years. Nearly every published author or poet I know feels this way.

Revising material is a constant process. In On Writing Well, William Zinsser proclaims, "Writing improves in direct ratio to the number of things we can keep out of it that shouldn't be there. Examine every word you put on paper. You'll find a surprising number that don't serve any purpose." He adds, "Most first drafts can be cut by 50% without losing any information or the author's voice."

Laurie Rosen, editor of thirty-seven bestsellers, advises novelists to follow ten basic steps while considering revisions. Among the ones she listed in Writer's Digest are: "Revise toward a marketable length (Average novel length is between 60,000 and 100,000 words. Manuscripts exceeding 100,000 words are a tough sell), torque the power of your scenes (emphasize the purpose of the action), tease the reader forward into the next chapter, give your antagonist some depth, and dramatize, dramatize, dramatize."

Some authors or poets set page counts or deadlines for completion of revised drafts. Meeting them is an excellent form of discipline. Setting reasonable deadlines is suggested. No writer should create or edit when the brain is weary.

Critique

When an acceptable draft is completed, let others review it. It doesn't matter if your reviewer is a spouse, a relative, or a friend down the street. If you can find someone with perhaps more of an objective view, this is preferred.

Writers need a variety of people to provide objective opinions. Being removed from the material, reviewers can spot flaws and misinformation, and correct mistakes. They may even suggest an alternative means of telling a story.

The key is locating people not afraid to say what they think. Then, when criticism is leveled, swallow your ego and be receptive. While writing one book, a longtime friend that was an English major in college reviewed the manuscript. I cringed while perusing her comments since every page was saturated with red ink. On one page, she circled two paragraphs free of error and printed beside it, "Did you write this?" Her questioning my ability made my face turn red in anger, but I knew in some ways it was an offhand compliment. At least I took it that way. When the book was completed, I knew I had become a better writer because of her stern comments.

Good writing requires dedication and perseverance since words are the writer's communication with the world. Only through hard work will the message be strong. For aspiring authors and poets attempting to impress literary agents and editors, good writing is their most important calling card.

To test the competence of your writing skills, interactive exercises targeted at excellent use of grammar and punctuation are presented in the Appendix. Take some time to see how your skills measure up.

Step #3 Summary

- Read the classics to understand good writing.
- Keep an "idea book" of word usage.
- Don't overwhelm the reader with "highbrow" language.
- **Read *The Elements of Style*—then re-read it. Keep a list of language "Do's" and "Don'ts."**
- Read self-help books on proper use of punctuation.
- Discover a writing regimen that works for you.
- Remember, good writing is clear and concise.
- When you start writing a manuscript or collection of poetry, don't stop until your first draft is completed.
- Re-write and edit. Every time a re-write occurs, the text is better.
- Solicit objective critique of your writings.
- Remember—there may not be a "right" word to use, but there is a "best" word.

Writing Tips Checklist

- Purchase and read grammar and punctuation books including Elements of Style by Professors Strunk and White.
- Use strong, active words. Nouns and verbs are preferred.
- Avoid overuse of adverbs and adjectives. Look for nouns and verbs that stand on their own.
- Eliminate clichés.
- Be brief. Avoid run-on sentences.
- Avoid superlatives. Don't exaggerate. Let facts speak for themselves.
- Use strong verbs that move the story forward.
- Don't overuse obscure words to impress.

- Avoid weak words such as probably, maybe, something, anything, awhile, several, lots, get, a lot, almost, perhaps, and so forth.

- Construct clear, concise sentences. Don't use too many "ands."

- Attempt to use positive words and avoid "not."

- Don't use "etc." or abbreviations.

- Write out the numbers one to ninety-nine and numbers beginning sentences.

- Avoid exclamation marks unless called for in dialogue.

- Remember the general rule that quotation marks are positioned outside periods and commas.

- Use single quotes for a quote within a quote.

- Avoid phrases such as "It is interesting that," or "I really believe that."

- Italicize book titles, CDs, films, operas, and plays; quotation marks are acceptable for poems, short stories, articles, songs, and book chapters.

Manuscript Techniques
Format Do's and Don'ts

- **Do** use 8 ½ x 11—20 unlined bond paper.

- **Do** use black type.

- **Do** use Times New Roman print.

- **Do** type on one side of the paper.

- **Do** use a one-inch margin on the left side of the paper.

- **Don't** worry about the right margin. Leave it undefined.

- **Don't** staple the pages together.

- **Do** double-space the lines, utilizing 12 font.

- **Do** average 250 words per page—(twenty-five, sixty character lines).

- **Don't** provide extra spaces between the paragraphs.
- **Do** indent and single-space lengthy quotes or excerpts.
- **Don't** use quotation marks when indenting quotes or excerpts.
- **Do** provide Chapter titles and subtitles using 18 and 16 point font size respectively.
- **Do** center chapter titles and subtitles.
- **Don't** leave subheadings at end of page.
- **Don't** provide address, telephone number, fax and e-mail information on cover page.
- **Do** include address, telephone number, fax, and e-mail information in Query letter.
- **Optional—Do** type first letter of your last name and keyword from title at left margin on each page.
- **Do** type page number in lower right hand corner of page.
- **Do** provide running number of pages.
- **Do** check to make certain no pages are left out.
- **Don't** submit manuscript until it has been edited several times. Perfection is required.
- **Don't** trust your computer to do the work for you—check the dictionary.
- **Don't** type "The End" on the final page of the manuscript.
- **Do** reduce illustrations or photographs to 8 ½ x 11 paper if they exceed that size.
- **Do** print, if at all possible, on a laser printer.

The reading of all good books is like conversation with the finest men of past centuries.

RENE DESCARTES

Step #4

There Is No One Right Way To Tell A Story, But There Is A Best Way

The Writer's Persona

Being an author has several advantages. George Bernard Shaw, a distant kin I'm told, stated, "My main reason for adopting literature as a profession was that, as the author is never seen by his clients; he need not dress respectably."

Here's another—an author schedules his or her own hours—no nine-to-five requirement. Most important, "creative" people can be "strange." If they dribble food, slosh beer around in their mouth before swallowing, or drive a purple Volkswagen bus with tinted windows, society excuses the behavior. As a creative person, writers may change their mind as often as the television weatherman.

Above all, the opportunity to tell stories that force people to stop and think is a main attraction. There also is considerable satisfaction with a process where you begin with nothing, no written words, just an idea, and then, through hard work and perseverance, end up holding a manuscript and later, a published book in your hands. Realizing your story will be read by many others makes all the tough days sitting in front of a computer worthwhile.

Authors experience different levels of satisfaction when their books are published, but I consider them to be "children" that have been scattered across the universe. Books are extensions of the human mind, and the power of the written word must never be underestimated. To date, I have heard from more than 5000 people who've read my books. I answer ever email from them.

Storytelling

Authors' experiences regarding storytelling abound. Creativity is a key, but so is organization. It is crucial since any story fiction, non-fiction, or even poetry should progress in an organized manner. The story doesn't have to be told chronologically, but it must have a logical progression. Otherwise, the reader is lost.

Telling stories through the written word requires a different talent from verbal expression. A dear departed friend, Jack Leer, was the finest storyteller I ever knew. He could stand in front of a group of people, and they would be howling in no time even if what he said wasn't that funny.

Jack's talent did not extend to the written page because he could not write like he spoke. A different expertise was required, and he did not possess the dedication to learn the craft.

Storytelling methods differ as much as the colors of the rainbow. Truman Capote stated, "Since each story presents its own technical problems, obviously one can't generalize about them on a 'two times two equals four' basis. Finding the right form for your story is simply to realize the most natural way of telling the story."

Ernest Hemingway, when asked about the talent for writing fiction, said, "You invent fiction, but what you invent it out of is what counts. True fiction must come from everywhere you've ever known, ever seen, ever felt, ever learned."

The aspiring author or poet should examine as many books as possible to learn various storytelling methods. Note how each writer has chronicled the story he or she wishes to tell. This is essential whether the story is contained in a magazine or newspaper article, a short story, a Query Letter, a Book Proposal, collection of poetry, or a manuscript.

To provide examples of storytelling alternatives, please consider the following experiences with my books. Perhaps they will trigger a thought or two in your mind as to the storytelling method that will work best for you.

Down for the Count
(re-printed as Falsely Accused?)

Storytelling was a learning experience for me, but speaking to judges and juries when I was a criminal defense lawyer provided the perfect training ground. Arguing the innocence of a client to twelve souls charged with life-and-death matters required organization of the evidence so the jury heard the story I wanted them to recall when they deliberated. Years of preparing those speeches permitted me to hone my skills as a storyteller.

My education in speaking to juries began with the very first case assigned me when I was a public defender. My client was a young man charged with killing his 300-pound girlfriend with a shotgun from six feet away in front of her children. When I visited James in jail, he told me his defense was that he was trying to shoot over her head to scare her. My job was to defend him according to the facts he provided, and I argued his version to the jury. It only took the jurors ten minutes to convict him of first-degree murder, but the final argument was my first experience with storytelling in front of an audience.

As the years passed, I continued to speak to juries, honing my storytelling abilities. When I first considered writing a book, I relied on the storytelling methods used in criminal trials.

To tell the stories that became my first book, Down for the Count, I began by dramatizing the courtroom scene as boxer Mike Tyson awaited his fate after a grueling rape trial. The jury returned and the judge announced the guilty verdict. This was featured in the Prologue.

Chapter One, aptly titled, "Guilty" began with a strong sentence. It read, "When Mike Tyson first heard the word 'guilty' spoken by Judge Patricia Gifford, his head cocked to the side as if he had been hit with a thunderous right cross. He whispered, 'Oh, man,' and slumped down in his seat."

Readers' feedback told me I had captured their attention, triggering a desire to read further. In On Writing Well, author William Zinsser expresses the need to do this better than anyone. He wrote, "[Your] lead must capture the reader immediately and force him to keep reading. It must cajole him with freshness, or novelty, or paradox, or humor, or surprise, or with an unusual idea, or an interesting fact, or a question. Anything will do, as long as it nudges his curiosity and tugs at his sleeve."

The vivid portrayal of Tyson's reaction led back in time to the investigation of his crime. Chapter One recounted the circumstances under which the prosecution decided whether to seek an indictment against the former heavyweight-boxing champion of the world. The story then continued in chronological order through the months leading up to the trial. This was most important since much of what happened to Tyson at trial was directly due to what occurred before trial. This was especially true when his promoter and self-proclaimed mentor Don King hired Washington D.C. highbrow lawyer Vincent Fuller, an attorney with no experience in the criminal courtroom, to defend the accused rapist. This caused Tyson to virtually be defenseless.

Once pre-trial matters were considered, the trial unfolded. Events were chronicled with two goals in mind: to permit readers to judge for themselves if the boxer was guilty and to let them decide whether a black celebrity could gain a fair trial in a Midwestern city (Indianapolis, Indiana) in the early 1990s.

The publication process for Down for the Count was a great learning experience regarding the workings of the publishing industry. Like others who dive in with no research, I did not have a clue as to how it operated.

The original title for the book, I'm a bit embarrassed to admit, was Beauty and the Beast. It featured no Prologue. Chapter One began with the incident between Tyson and the alleged rape victim, Desiree Washington. It proceeded in real time.

When a competent draft of the manuscript was completed, I forwarded it to several prospective literary agents whom I had selected from a reference book. One agent responded, believing he could sell the book. At his request, I made several revisions.

The agent was so certain he had a bestseller on his hands that he conducted an "auction." He notified publishers of his intent to provide them with manuscript pages. Once editors had read them within a twenty-four hour time limit, they could telephone with bids for the rights to the book.

The literary agent requested that I stand next to the telephone so we could discuss the various offers as the day passed. I did so for eight hours, but he never called. To his amazement, and my chagrin, no one wanted the book. The consensus was that the world knew everything it wanted to know about the Tyson trial.

Reeling from defeat, I tossed the manuscript aside. I still believed in the book, but no one else did. Being a stubborn cuss, and not one to give up, I kept thinking about how I might improve the text to attract a broader audience interest in the social impact of the Tyson case. What drove me was a character trait important to any aspiring author or poet: perseverance.

Two months later, I had the idea to include in the text the relationship between the issues involved in the Tyson case and several significant legal events surrounding the trial. They included the Rodney King beating by California police, the Anita Hill-Clarence Thomas Senate hearings, the William Kennedy Smith rape trial in Florida, and the racially motivated Bensonhurst murders in New York City.

Armed with a new title, Down for the Count, and a new theme for the book, I completed another round of revisions before the manuscript was submitted. I did not include a Book Proposal or a Query Letter since I had no knowledge of the form.

By revising the storytelling method to reflect how the Tyson trial compared with the legal events surrounding it, I found a publisher. An open-minded approach to storytelling alternatives had paid off.

Assisting my quest to discover a marketable concept for the book was a question I asked myself: What provocative thought did I want readers to examine? To be provocative, good non-fiction must leave readers with a question they had not answered before. With Down for the Count, I wanted readers to stop and think about whether justice had been served. Using this theme tantalized the publisher as well.

Forever Flying

In the 1970s, I had the opportunity to work with the famous attorney, F. Lee Bailey (Boston Strangler, Dr. Sam Sheppard and O. J. Simpson murder cases). He chose me as local counsel for a case involving a diabolical physician suspected of beheading an undercover D.E.A. agent who suspected the doctor of drug dealing. I assisted Lee with the defense and we kept in touch thereafter.

Some twenty years later, Lee's agent telephoned, asking if I would be interested in collaborating on a book with the legendary aviator, R. A. "Bob" Hoover, on a book. Lee represented Hoover in connection with FAA attempts to deny him a license to fly because of his advanced age. I flew to Washington D. C., watched Lee in a Court of Appeals hearing, and met Hoover. Impressed with his background and fighting spirit, I agreed to the collaboration.

Organizing the storytelling order for the book that became Forever Flying was difficult. R. A. "Bob" Hoover was a true renaissance man who had been successful with several careers. Besides being a World War II hero shot down by the Germans, a prison camp survivor who stole a German plane and flew to freedom, a terrific experimental pilot who was a finalist along with Chuck Yeager to break the sound barrier, Hoover was the greatest aerobatic pilot who ever lived.

To hook readers, Chapter One featured an encounter between Hoover and the Russian government during a Moscow international air race competition. When the Russians refused to allow him to perform certain aerobatic maneuvers in a new experimental airplane, he did so anyway. Tense moments occurred as embarrassed Russian officials decided whether to arrest Hoover. They didn't, but the episode showed that he was a courageous aviator.

After the Russian incident, the story backtracked to Bob's early days. The book then proceeded in chronological order to include Bob's successful fight with the FAA.

To compare how Forever Flying evolves, and the means by which Chuck Yeager's own story unfolds, read his bestseller, Yeager. The storytelling method differs, since interspersed with Yeager's recollections are reminiscences quoted from those who knew him well.

When Paul McCarthy, a senior editor at Pocket Books, an imprint of Simon and Schuster, read the Book Proposal, he was smitten with Hoover's story. An aviation enthusiast, Paul purchased the rights to the book, realizing Bob was a hero known to thousands of aviation fans. This provided two important elements toward securing a publisher: a built-in audience and tremendous opportunities for promotion of the book.

Literary agent Richard Pine's decision to present the book to Paul McCarthy was based on his personal knowledge of Paul's love for aviation. Writers can learn from Richard's example. When attempting to decide which literary agents or editors would welcome submission of a book idea, homework is required. By specifically targeting the book idea to match with agents or publishers who have been involved with books of the same genre, the chances of securing agency representation or a publisher commitment can be maximized.

The Perfect Yankee

The Perfect Yankee provides an example of discovering little known information others had avoided. While reading Mickey Mantle's bestseller, *My Favorite Year, 1956,* I noted a chapter titled *Perfect*. It chronicled the magical performance on October 8, 1956, by journeyman New York Yankee pitcher Don Larsen. Against the defending champion Brooklyn Dodgers, Larsen pitched the only perfect game in World Series history—no hits, no runs, and no errors.

Convincing the unassuming Larsen to write a book was difficult. For years, he had been reticent to tell his story. Don had even refused accomplished author David Halberstram.

Telling Don Larsen's story required focusing on his incredible achievement. After several fruitless attempts to do so in a chronological manner, I conceived the idea to weave his life around the miracle nine-innings he pitched in the World Series.

Predictably, publishers were dubious. Writing a book about one game didn't register with most. Many passed on the Book Proposal before the same one that had published *Down for the Count* agreed to publish it. The editor realized the storytelling method was imaginative.

Richard Ben Cramer's book, *Joe DiMaggio, The Hero's Life*, illustrates an alternative storytelling method. After presenting a Prologue packed with personal memories of the great ballplayer, Cramer tells his story while commentating on the life and times of Joltin' Joe. A unique voice emerges as if Cramer is sitting in the reading room spewing out facts while revealing his insight into their merit. The author is quite effective with this method.

Aspiring writers should remember that rejection of material might be based more on storytelling method than on content. Being creative is essential. Consider alternative methods and then decide which one will provide readers with a unique perspective of the story you want to tell.

Testament to Courage

Belief that the world should read Cecelia Rexin's remarkable story of hope and love spurred my interest in the Holocaust memoir of a Christian German woman who loved others more than herself. This memoir became the book, *Testament to Courage*.

Cecelia's story began when she was an aspiring medical student in Berlin. Opposed to Adolph Hitler's Nazi regime, she assisted the underground. Her roommate turned her in, and Cecelia was imprisoned. After three years, she was sent to Ravensbruck, and then to Auschwitz.

While incarcerated, Cecelia kept a journal she sewed into the hems of her dresses. Throughout her stay, she hid pages chronicling the horrors of Nazi brutality. Among the stories was her account of saving the life of a young orphaned Russian girl named Laddie. At great risk, Cecelia enlisted the assistance of two German prison guards. Laddie was taken to a pig farm where she spent the rest of the war. After the war, she and Cecelia met in an emotion-filled moment in a hospital.

My personal interest in Cecelia's story is an example of another important characteristic a successful writer must possess: curiosity. Without a yearning to learn, to explore, to discover, the writer is doomed. Whether it is fiction, non-fiction, or poetry, the aspiring writer must probe for the truth, for the story no one else can tell, or that no one else seems to feel is important enough to document.

No other writer has expressed the need to probe life's experiences better than Frank McCourt. He wrote the bestseller Angela's Ashes at age sixty-six. He told The Writer's Handbook, "If you keep your ear cocked, you'll discover treasures of significance."

Tom Wolfe wrote of his pursuit of a book that became the bestseller, The Right Stuff. "This book grew out of ordinary curiosity," he said. "What is it, I wondered, that makes a man willing to sit on top of an enormous Roman candle, such as a Redstone, Atlas, or Titan rocket, and wait for someone to light the fuse?"

With Testament To Courage, this mindset triggered a storytelling method that revealed events during World War II while Cecelia Rexin was incarcerated in the concentration camps. My education regarding the events was provided through a thick book titled The Second World War, A Complete History, by Gilbert Martin. It documented every aspect of Adolph Hitler's attempt to rule the world. In it, I marked sections coinciding with the dates Cecelia had noted in her journal.

Weaving events throughout the war with the diary proved worthy. Through Cecelia's eyes and snippets of major events as the war progressed, readers are provided with a sense of historical significance.

The editor, fascinated with Cecelia's story, also appreciated the storytelling method. It distinguished Testament To Courage from other Holocaust books.

As the years passed, I was intrigued with turning this non-fiction book into a fictional story. This was based on extending the story to include a war crimes trial that would test the courage of Cecelia concerning her desire to save the life of one of the German prison guards who helped save her life and that of the orphan. [Note: later on I published Courage in the Face of Evil based on Testament to Courage.]

Miscarriage of Justice

Keeping an open mind about the storytelling process resulted in Miscarriage of Justice, The Jonathan Pollard Story. The Pollard case has always been controversial. A Naval Intelligence Service analyst who spied for Israel in the mid-1980s, he received a life sentence after having pled guilty to espionage. The severity of the sentence was shocking to many, since others convicted of the same offense received lighter sentences. Supporters alleged anti-Semitism; others believed he should have been shot.

Through the years, the Pollard case became a political football. Several times it appeared he would be released, but it never occurred.

After interviewing Dr. Morris Pollard, Jonathan's father, on a radio program I hosted, there appeared to be the need for an unbiased book presenting the true facts in the case. This would permit readers to stop, think, and make up their own minds.

Key to telling the Pollard story was capturing the reader's attention by first outlining the dramatics of his spying escapades. These had occurred from his first meeting with an Israeli contact named Colonel Aviem Sella to the moment when Pollard was arrested. Once this was chronicled, the text reverted back to his early years so readers could gain a sense of who Pollard was and why he acted as he did.

The next section dealt with the events leading to Pollard's sentencing. Details of the sentencing of Jonathan's wife, Anne, provided the reader with a sense of her background and the love affair that blossomed with Jonathan.

Pollard's harsh imprisonment and supporters' efforts to free him were also chronicled. The final section featured an analysis of the spy's case, including comparisons with the prison sentences imposed on spies for both allies and enemies of the United States. The title reflected my belief that Pollard's sentence was disproportionate to his crime.

The long road to publishing the Pollard book spanned more than two and a half years. More than 300 drafts of the book were written. Staying the course proved worthy, as it did for Ernest Hemingway, who re-wrote the ending to Farewell To Arms thirty-nine times.

The publisher of Miscarriage of Justice was impressed with storytelling presenting the facts devoid of the author's opinion. Too often writers mesh personal feelings with facts, restricting the reader's ability to stop and think.

Melvin Belli, King of the Courtroom

The idea for a biography of one of the greatest attorneys who ever lived (Belli died in 1996) evolved from a friendship I enjoyed with the San Francisco legend in the mid-1980s. A swashbuckling character out of a Damon Runyan novel, Belli was labeled "The King of Torts" by Life Magazine due to his pioneering efforts in the field of personal injury law.

While Belli represented such celebrities as Errol Flynn, Mae West, Muhammad Ali, the Rolling Stones, and Jim and Tammy Faye Baker, his most famous client was Jack Ruby. Initially, the plan was to weave Belli's fascinating story around the events at trial, but the publisher wanted a straight biography. With this in mind, the book opens with a thrilling radio program conversation between Belli and the infamous Zodiac killer who terrorized the San Francisco bay area. The aim was to captivate readers before the book moves to Belli's early years, his maturation as a noted civil lawyer in the area of personal injury, and then to his tumultuous private life including his six marriages. Along the way, Belli's interaction with celebrities and famous cases in chronicled with the Ruby case one of them.

Since the intention was to portray Belli, the good, the bad, and the ugly while noting his contribution to revolutionizing the legal profession, the final portion of the book permits readers the inside story as to how the great lawyer fell from grace into bankruptcy and failing health. To end the book on a high note, Belli's final trial is presented indicating that he was still a skilled trial lawyer at he neared the age of ninety.

Feedback regarding the storytelling method was positive especially from those who knew Belli during his glory years. They realized the challenge of deciding what information about him was critical to presenting a balance portrait of this controversial character. My plan was to also use Belli's story as a conduit to chronicling many of the most important events, especially in the legal arena, of the mid-twentieth century. This provided the historical angle I was seeking.

Beneath the Mask of Holiness: Thomas Merton and the Forbidden Love Affair That Set Him Free

During my three years at San Francisco Theological Seminary studying theology, I learned about the gifted spiritual guru Thomas Merton. The most famous monk in the world during the period 1950-1968, he wrote more than seventy books including his bestselling autobiography, The Seven Storey Mountain. Other books by Merton include New Seeds of Contemplation, No Man Is An Island, Wisdom of the Desert, and Zen Birds of Appetite. (See Merton.org for more about Merton).

When I became interested in writing a new biography of Merton (ten-plus had been written by 2008), I knew I needed a fresh approach. Writers had already covered his pre-monastic years when he was a true scoundrel of sin who had fathered an illegitimate child, been a drunkard and womanizer, and committed adultery just prior to entering Gethsemani, a Cistercian monastery located south of Louisville, Kentucky. The question was how I was going to portray Merton since so much had been written about him.

The answer was apparent once I discovered that Merton fell madly in love with a student nurse half his age in 1966 when he was fifty-one-years old. This led me to research the question a curious author always has about such things, "Why?" Soon I was deeply immersed in reading Merton's private journals and everything else I could locate about the love affair. I soon realized no one had completed the puzzle as to why Merton loved a woman named Margie Smith.

Bits and pieces existed but I was determined to fit all the pieces together and complete what I believed would be the first true, complete biography of Merton, warts and all with the main theme his lack of ever understanding pre-Margie the meaning of loving and being loved. The result was Beneath the Mask of Holiness since there was no doubt Merton had hid a dark side of his life, one where he was tormented and suffering while trying to be something he was not. The result was a provocative, controversial book about Merton that Palgrave-Macmillan decided to publish. All because I found a niche for telling a story about one of the great writers and spiritual mentors of the twentieth century, the story I believed he wanted to be told.

The Vicker Punch Mystery Series

This fictional series. A work in progress, presented multiple challenges regarding the storytelling process since each book is based on a true story, providing ample opportunities to mix fact with fiction.

Use of the "ticking clock" storytelling theme is a proven path to good fiction and this was a goal when I began the series. The race against time permits the writer to grab readers and keep their attention as the drama builds. While writing, think of the best books, and the best films ever read or seen on the big screen. Many, if not most, build suspense so the reader or viewer is right alongside the main characters as they fight to save themselves from doom.

The Vicker Punch Mystery Series features legal thrillers wrapped around the exploits of controversial Southern attorney Punch and his band of erstwhile investigators, 18th Street Irregulars. Together with Vicker's sexy wife Alex, and a legal guru named "Dutch" Banderman, they represent high profile clients around the world. For a retainer fee of one million dollars, their exploits include cases involving an Aspen lawyer whose trial involves a not guilty by reason of hypnotic trance defense, a California widow charged with killing her husband with poison toothpaste, a famous New Mexico physician whose charged with "surgically" removing the head of a Drug Enforcement Agent, and a Florida gospel singer whose defense involves passing a lie detector test.

Key to the series (book titles are Guilty Conscience, Chinatown Capers, Under the Santa Fe Moon, South Florida Melodies and Justice by Jury) is Vicker and his crew's dedication to fighting injustice at every turn. Through innovative defenses, and true-to-life courtroom drama based on my experience as a criminal defense lawyer, the books are designed to educate as well as entertain.

Stations Along the Way
The Spiritual Transformation of Former
Hitler Youth Leader Ursula Martens

When I first heard of the story about Ursula Martens, I was intrigued since she had kept a diary chronicling her experiences as Nazi Youth Leader in Germany during World War II. Optioning the rights to that diary, I began to consider alternative storytelling methods that would bring the compelling story alive since it was truly a slice of history.

After some consideration, I decided to carefully edit the diary so as to not lose Ursula's "voice" since it was important to present her story in an unblemished manner. From age 10, when she was forced to join the Hitler Youth forward, the story evolves as she experiences the horror of war while being brainwashed by Hitler and the Nazis. Finally, as the war ends, she begins to realize that she had been used like millions of other Germans who did not realize the full extent of the Holocaust. Besieged with guilt and shame, Ursula marries an American soldier and travels to the United States where she encounters the same sort of prejudice she inflicted on the Jews. It is only when she is shown forgiveness and love by three Holocaust survivors that Ursula may shed her shame and experience a spiritual transformation where she traded in her devotion to the Swastika for devotion to the Cross.

To present the story in its rawest form, the book became an autobiography within a biography with Preludes utilized in an Appendix to give readers a sense of the events occurring during the war while Ursula is a member of the Hitler Youth. This storytelling method worked well and the result is a terrific "stop and think" book about the dangers of singling out people for being "different," unfortunately a common occurrence today.

The Poison Patriarch

To distinguish this book about the JFK assassination from more than 2000 already in print was quite a challenge. But I had an advantage since I had written Melvin Belli: King of the Courtroom, the biography of Lee Harvey Oswald's killer, Jack Ruby. While researching that book, I learned of Belli's connections to the Mafia and this led my questioning how and why Belli became Ruby's attorney when there were many others much more qualified that the famed San Francisco lawyer.

After much research, I decided to focus for the first time on why Bobby Kennedy WAS NOT killed instead of why JFK WAS. This provided me with the ability to consider motive and when I did, I realized how fault for JFK's assassination fell at the footstep of Bobby and their father Joe. The latter, the powerful, wealthy patriarch of the family wanted to be president but when this was denied, he catapulted John into the presidency by making certain promises to underworld figures that they would be left alone once John was in office.

In a true double-cross, Joe forced John to appoint Bobby attorney general, and after this occurred, he was obsessed with prosecuting Teamsters boss James Hoffa, and Mafia Dons Santo Trafficante and Carlos Marcello. Each detested the Kennedy's with the latter the desperate one who hated Bobby with a passion.

By focusing on why Bobby WAS NOT killed instead of why John WAS, I was able to present a common sense, logical scenario regarding who masterminded the assassinations, who was responsible for the cover-up, and who had the ultimate responsibility for JFK's demise, father Joe. This is why the book title is The Poison Patriarch: How the Betrayals of Joseph P. Kennedy Caused the Assassination of JFK.

The Reporter Who Knew Too Much "Circumstances Undetermined" and the "Mysterious Death of What's My Line" TV Star and Media Icon Dorothy Kilgallen

From a single quote in an interview conducted during the writing of Melvin Belli: King of the Courtroom, this book was born. One of Belli's friends told me during my research that when Belli learned of famed journalist, investigative reporter and What's My Line? television star, Belli said, "Well, they've killed Dorothy, now they will go after Jack Ruby." When I completed writing *The Poison Patriarch*, I decided to discover why Belli had made that comment about Kilgallen.

The road to writing the book was a circuitous one begun when I read a Kilgallen biography and a magazine article written in 2007 that included more information about her death. However, the big break happened when I learned of two researchers who were obsessed with Kilgallen's death and actually tracked down several friends and acquaintances of hers who were eyewitnesses to the events surrounding her death.

Best of all, the researchers had videotaped and audiotaped interviews with these eyewitness and after obtaining the rights to included the interviews in the book, it was full speed ahead with portraying the life and times of Kilgallen from her birth in 1913 to her death in 1965. Along the way, I became enamored with the remarkable achievements by the first female media icon, whose success overshadows that of even current day media personalities such as Oprah, Diane Sawyer and Barbara Walters.

Once the research on my end was complete, I chose a storytelling method detailing first Kilgallen's accomplishments and then details of her death before launching into an investigation of how she actually died and why. Then it was on to naming suspects based on the interviews and ones I conducted on my own before drawing conclusions as to why Kilgallen was in all likelihood murdered instead of dying accidentally of a drug overdose combined with alcohol as reported by a corrupt New York City Medical Examiner's office. In the end, I had created a true "whodunit" murder mystery while providing a fresh look at one of the most remarkable women of the 20th century.

Denial of Justice, Collateral Damage and Fighting for Justice

During the research and writing of *The Reporter Who Knew Too Much*, I became much more interested in Dorothy Kilgallen and the JFK assassination. Writing Denial of Justice emanated when I found a copy of the Jack Ruby trial transcripts. Doing so permitted me to better understand what Kilgallen had learned at his trial and why she had been silenced based on her continuing realization that Lee Harvey Oswald did not act alone. Weaving more personal information about her determination to expose the truth, I was able to better argue that she was denied justice after she died and to present date.

Collateral Damage was possible when I was able to connect the death movie star Marilyn Monroe (1962) with the deaths of JFK (1963) and Kilgallen (1965) for the first time. Along the way, I proved that Marilyn did not commit suicide but was murdered with Robert F. Kennedy complicit in her death.

Fighting for Justice was published based on new facts about each of these 20th Century icon and my having discovered through a primary source corruption having occurred at the Warren Commission. This was a major breakthrough and in addition, provided more proof Kilgallen had been murdered.

In each of these books, I used a chronological method of storytelling although in Collateral Damage, there was some mixing of research due to the different years when the three subjects of the book were connected to each other. More about each of these books at www.markshawbooks.com.

Learning From Others

It may be elusive, but a dedicated writer can discover a formula for clarity, brevity, and writing so visual it leaps off the page. The best advice is to read a wide array of books and pay attention to the methods employed by bestselling authors. Study *In Cold Blood*, Truman Capote's masterpiece, and the writings of Kerouac, Hemingway, and Joyce, among others. Keeping an open mind about the storytelling process produces clever text that titillates the reader.

Fiction writers should also read Presumed Innocent, by Scott Turow. A lawyer and author, he is a creative storyteller who knows how to entertain. John Grisham's books also contain wonderful examples of storytelling. His trademark is weaving a story with very little "fat" to it. Some critics have disdained this method, but who can argue with an author with such an impressive list of best sellers?

Children's book enthusiasts must read J.K. Rowling's Harry Potter series. Her storytelling ability opened her readership to millions of adults.

A Civil Action, Jonathan Harr's book about the evolution of environmental lawsuits in the Boston area, illustrates an effective method of organizing non-fiction. Another writer to learn from is Lauren Hillenbrand, the author of both Seabiscuit and Unbroken. If the genre is biography, read David McCullough's Truman, Theodore Rex by Edmund Morris; Lindbergh, by Scott Berg; or DiMaggio by Richard Ben Cramer.

Each story, whether it is fiction or non-fiction, presents variables as to how it may be told. Read Plot and Structure by James Scott Bell for more information about this subject.

If the story is fiction, consider Susan Sontag's thoughts that, "A novel worth reading is an education of the heart. It enlarges your sense of what human nature is, of what happens in the world. It's a creator of inwardness." Regarding the challenge to write with that passion, Ernest Hemingway said, "For the true writer, each book should be a new beginning where he tries for something that is beyond attainment. He should always try for something that has never been done or that others have tried and failed."

Above all, authors and poets are storytellers, even if the story is not readily apparent, as in some poems. Books can entertain and inform, but perhaps their most important role is to make people stop and think, to consider, or to reconsider an issue. An author or poet has the ability to change minds and influence individuals reading his or her works. What can be more important than that?

Step #4 Summary

- Remember—good stories contain a compelling beginning, middle, and end.

- Research storytelling techniques to become familiar with various storytelling options.

- **Choose a storytelling sequence that immediately captures the attention of the reader.**

- **When considering storytelling alternatives, ask the question—what is the message I am conveying?**

- **Great stories are well paced and keep readers asking for more.**

- **Poets must remember that word space limitations require judicious use of the language.**

- **There is no one *right* way to tell a story, but there is a *best* way.**

A book must be an ice ax to break the frozen sea within us.

ALDOUS HUXLEY

Step #5

Preparing An Outline Is
A Blueprint For Success

Outline Elements

Acommon mistake aspiring authors and poets make is to begin writing before they prepare an outline. **Whether the genre is long form fiction, non-fiction, short stories, magazine articles, or poetry, a roadmap of some sort is essential.** Working without an outline is akin to a builder starting construction without blueprints.

Many fiction and poetry writers swear that preparation of an outline inhibits the creative process. They insist the story flows best if they have no preconceived idea where creative thoughts will lead. This process may be effective for seasoned writers, but beginners should consider preparing at least a "mental outline," if not a written one, to guide organization of the text.

An outline doesn't have to be formal. I scribbled the initial outline for this book (chapter headings) on folded sheets of torn paper while awaiting the arrival of a playwright in Mill Valley, California. Within a few minutes, the backbone of the book was created. Since then, revisions have been made to embellish the text, but the outline has never varied.

An outline should be well defined. Meat from the bones of the outline—manuscript text for instance—will flow more freely when you have an established direction. This requires a clear understanding of the message to be conveyed through the story. Accomplishing this goal will take time and considerable thought.

Jeffrey Deaver, author of the bestselling Bone Collector, is an advocate of outlines. "I sit down with a very rough concept of the story," he stated, "and then over the next eight months, I do a very elaborate outline . . . That's my full-time job doing the outline for six or seven days, eight to ten hours a day."

Once the outline is completed, Deaver permits it to settle in a manner similar ". . . to the ritual with baking a cake." "You let things solidify," he explains, "and then you go back and look at it."

Outline forms vary, but the standard practice is to utilize chapter headings with abbreviated text describing the chapter content. The chapter headings will become chapter titles when the book is completed. They provide readers with a guide to the text.

The outline will dictate the means by which the story unfolds, whether in chronological order or through other storytelling alternatives. Never forget the reader demands entertainment, excitement, and information unavailable anywhere else. The last thing you can afford is to be boring, confusing, or predictable.

The Prologue, if there is one, or the first chapter if there is no Prologue, must be strong enough to hook the reader. When considering storytelling alternatives, determine the most compelling moments within your anticipated text. They may occur in the initial stages of the story, in the middle, or toward the end. This text should be the leadoff man, so to speak, the foot soldier to set up the remainder of the book. Potential purchasers may turn to the Prologue and/or Chapter One to check the beginning of the story. If they're hooked, the book is sold.

Teasing readers with an episode of the story without revealing the entire mix of events or characters has proven successful for many authors. To determine if that style will suffice for you, test it. Consider providing just enough information to hook the reader. Once the material is fashioned, begin the story in chronological order and move forward. Flashbacks are said to be the work of the lazy man, but millions of authors have utilized this mechanism.

Creative revision of the outline, again and again, will produce a solid foundation upon which a successful novel or work of non-fiction can be built. Patience and hard work pays off.

Like fiction writers, many poets view preparation of an outline as akin to blasphemy. They say the words simply flow, and the creative process would be blocked if they took the time to outline their intended message. If this is the case, then there is no need to labor over the blueprint for the poem. But many poets also swear that by jotting down a few thoughts about the intended poem, they can organize their thoughts to better stay on course.

Research

Thorough research precedes preparation of a competent outline. This involves entering the world of the library and/or the Internet. The former is still the staple. The latter is beneficial, though research undertaken in cyberspace should be scrutinized, since much of the information is faulty.

This became apparent to me while I was writing the book, *Miscarriage of Justice: The Jonathan Pollard Story.* On several web sites and in articles discovered through various search engines, miscellaneous material about Pollard was available. When it was cross-referenced, however, contradictions appeared. The saving grace was referencing competent books on the subject but speaking with individuals who possessed firsthand information caused my book to most accurate.

The same sort of inaccuracy happened when I was researching *The Reporter Who Knew Too Much*, the biography of media icon Dorothy Kilgallen. Lazy research and downright disregard of the truth were the call of the day and provided a false perception of how Kilgallen investigated the JFK assassination, one that distorted the truth about how she was killed in 1965. My book and the ones that followed set the record straight based on fresh evidence corroborated at every turn.

Being accurate is essential to works of non-fiction, but a fiction writer must be accurate regarding background material. Credibility is the issue. An aspiring author can't afford to locate an Apache Indian in Sedona area, Arizona, only to discover it was the Hopis and the Navajos who settled there and not the Apache's.

Consider quotes contained in reference material with caution. What someone said is only accurate if the source quoting the reference quoted them correctly. Much misinformation has stockpiled based on one person's misquote being quoted as if it was gospel. To determine accuracy, question, be curious, and tape record interviews with the person being quoted. **Truth** is a wayward child, especially when authors and members of the media are consumed with the trend toward "Infotainment," a questionable blend of news and entertainment.

Readers notice errors. After my book, Bury Me in a Pot Bunker was published, a golf historian in Vancouver wrote a three-page letter questioning certain text. To my chagrin, several of his comments were worthy. I added them to a list of typographical errors in anticipation of a second printing. When mistakes are noted, the author or poet's duty is clear. Admit the mistakes, thank the reader, and make the corrections.

Interviewing

Interviews supplementing research are an art form. Several superb books discuss the subject. There is even a college course titled, "How to Interview."

The key to successful interviewing is the ability to listen. Those who do often gather information others miss. Remember the Bible quotation, "Be quick to listen, slow to speak, and slow to anger."

Observe selected interviewers on television and note a common error. They have a set of questions in mind, often sequenced by number. No matter what the interviewee says, the interviewer asks the next question without following up or deviating from the predetermined order. Inexperienced trial attorneys, I noticed while practicing criminal defense law, fell into this trap thus missing critical evidence time and time again.

The savvy interviewer listens and varies the question order according to the response from the interviewee. The interviewer may return to the question list, but only after a thorough discussion of facts disclosed by the previous answer.

By varying the questions, an interviewer keeps the interviewee off guard. More importantly, good listening impresses interviewees, forming a bond of trust that often results in the interviewee disclosing facts they may have otherwise withheld.

To gain a sense of the art of interviewing, note the tactics employed by those on NPR. Former CNN commentator Larry King was also a master of the follow-up question, since he listened carefully to answers being given by a guest. King leaned toward the person, indicating a genuine interest in the interviewee.

Author John Irving (Cider House Rules) believes listening is essential to the writing process. He stated, "A writer is a vehicle. I feel the story I am writing existed before I existed. I am just the slob who finds it, and rather clumsily tries to do it . . . As a writer, I do more listening than talking. W.H. Auden called the first act of writing, 'noticing.'"

While detailing the essentials of prose, Jack Kerouac also spoke of the ability to listen. He stated, "Be submissive to everything. Open. Listening."

Tape-record interviews whenever possible. Taking notes is important, but tapes ensure accuracy. Tapes are undisputed evidence of the conversation if you are questioned later regarding book quotes.

Finalizing the Outline

Your initial outline may not be the final one. As the process continues, the outline may change several times as you consider different storytelling options.

Beginning writers ask if the outline should be two pages or two hundred. There is no stock answer, since each outline differs according to the writer's preference and the material. Some writers only require chapter headings to guide them; others, several paragraphs of key points to remember.

Within each chapter, include catch phrases that will trigger creative thinking when the writing process begins. As the days pass, you may add or delete material, but unless you completely alter your chosen storytelling method, the overall structure of the book should not change dramatically. Watch the flow of the material and note whether each chapter feeds off the preceding one.

Never be afraid to mix the material around like a good Greek salad. To gain a clear understanding of the essence of the outline, read it aloud. If continuity is a problem, set the outline aside for a day or so. When you read it again, you will have a fresh perspective.

The chapter headings and snippets of anticipated text for the outline for my book, *Melvin Belli: King of the Courtroom,* a biography of the infamous attorney, were a result of numerous rewrites. After more than one hundred drafts, part of the outline read as follows:

Prologue

Frank Ragano meeting with James Hoffa—July, 1963. Discussion of JFK assassination by Hoffa—order from Hoffa to Ragano that mobsters Santo Trafficante and Carlos Marcello oversee plot to kill JFK. Ragano informing Trafficante and Marcello of Hoffa order. Ragano's mention of lawyer Melvin Belli to Trafficante.

Book I

Chapter 1—Preliminaries

Opening of Jack Ruby trial—Dallas—March, 1964. Descriptions of Belli and Ruby. Information on Dallas and trial judge. Discord with Kennedys by labor and mob. Belli participation in Trial of the Century.

Chapter 2—Ruby's Lawyer

Belli famous cases—San Quentin convict, artificial leg trial, breast disfigurement, fattest man in the world, Willie Mays v. San Francisco Giants trial. Description of Belli offices.

Chapter 3—Young Belli

Belli background, Sonora to San Francisco. Years at Berkeley, world traveler.

Chapter 4—Ruby's Lawyer

Belli's famous cases—fireman, Horace Fong, Belli flamboyance, fascination with fashion. Belli relationship with actor Errol Flynn. Adventures in Europe. Belli the lady's man. Belli's first marriage. Belli and the media.

The outline for my work of fiction, No Peace for the Wicked, the fifth in the Vicker Punch series, was a work-in-progress for almost a year. The book was based on a true story so the challenge was to pace the text so the characters hooked readers. This was essential, since the story was character driven.

When the outline was completed, a portion of it read:

Prologue

Art Meadows release from jail. He is hounded by an out-of-control cop determined to send him back to prison. Ike slithers through the streets intent on making it home safely

Book I

Chapter 1—Call For Help
> Embattled attorney Vicker Punch receives call from friend Robbie in Arizona. Must decide whether to return to Ohio or continue his sabbatical from legal woes and personal problems.

Chapter 2—Art's Journey
> Background re Ike—disclosure of Elephant Man's disease, absence of education, family history, trouble with the law.

Chapter 3—The Lawyer
> Background re Vicker Punch, family, law school, rise to prominence as a defense lawyer. Hint of trouble with a case that may lead to disbarment proceedings.

Preparing an outline for a poem or a collection of poetry requires imagination and thought. Like the artist who has a message in his mind, the poet must be creative, innovative, and precise regarding the words that fill a verse. A client of mine decided drafting an outline made sense because she was concerned her thoughts would ramble and lose their potency. Her outline was written in pencil on the back of an envelope. For the poem, *A Day To Remember*, she wrote:

- Where have I come from?

- Where do I want to be?

- Why that is important to me.

- How I will stay the course?
- How I will be remembered?
- Why I care.

When finalizing the outline, be clear and succinct. Referring to it when the story begins to meander is a lifeline to writing success.

Step #5 Summary

- The outline is the blue print of the mind.
- Writing without an outline inhibits the writing process.
- When researching facts, check the validity of the source.
- Interviewing is an art—be a good listener.
- Continually check the outline during the writing process to make certain you are on track.

Some books are to be tasted, others to be swallowed, and some few to be chewed and digested.

FRANCIS BACON

Step #6

Traditional Publishing Is A Writer's Best Friend

Publishing Alternatives

Those with aspirations to become a published author must define the word "published," since **there are publishers *and then there are publishers.***

Publishing alternatives include Traditional Publishing through national/international companies, regional/small presses, university presses, Internet "specialty" Publishing, eBook Publishing, Traditional Self-Publishing, Print-On-Demand Publishing, and Subsidy Publishing (traditional and Internet). For the first-time writer, each possesses advantages and disadvantages.

Writers that are intent on building a publishing career should consider each publishing alternative in light of their goals and the industry perception of each publishing venue. A strategy that has proven most successful is to exhaust the potential to be traditionally published before any type of self-publishing. This excludes other alternatives including, above all else, subsidized publication.

Traditional Publishing

Before committing to any alternative publishing options, why not seek a traditional publisher? These include large, medium, and small publishers, as well as university presses. Most of these companies pay all costs involved in publishing the book.

There are hundreds of traditional publishers seeking the next bestseller. Think positively. If you believe your book is worthy and should be accepted for publication by a traditional house, then give it a try. If this fails, traditional self-publishing is always possible.

Set your sights high. Author Terry Cole-Whitaker's book, *Every Saint Has A Past, Every Sinner Has A Future* is a must read for those who require a daily pep talk about never giving up. She writes, "I decided long ago that it is much better to strive for what seems to be the impossible and fall short than strive for the possible and attain it."

Echoing her thoughts was the revered author William Faulkner. He wrote, "[The writer] must never be satisfied with what he does. It never is as good as it can be done. Always dream and shoot higher than you know you can. Don't bother just to be better than your contemporaries or predecessors. Try to be better than yourself."

This credo is pertinent when you consider what bestselling author Tom Clancy (The Hunt For Red October, The Bear and the Dragon) says about the writing process. He told Writer's Digest, "Writing a book is an endurance contest, and war fought against yourself, because writing is beastly work which one would just as soon not do."

Regardless of your attitude toward the craft, having one book published by traditional means is paramount to launching a career. It can be done. Respected literary agent Richard Pine provided inspiring advice early in my career. When I was upset that several publishers had rejected one of my books, he said, "Mark, it only takes one to say 'Yes.'"

An aspiring author must believe, "Yes, I will be published." As stated before, repeat this mantra on a regular basis. Years ago, Penny Marshall, the Laverne and Shirley television star turned motion picture producer/director, was asked what motivated her. She swore every morning she walked into the bathroom, looked at her image in the mirror, and said, "Today I will produce my film. Today I will produce my film."

This type of never-give-up attitude applies to publishing. Those who believe in themselves become published authors whether their books are releases by the "big boys" (Simon and Schuster, Penguin Random House, Hachette, Harper Collins,), and so forth, or successful small presses continuing to publish terrific books. More about small presses can be discovered in *Writer's Market* or additional worthy websites.

Traditional publishing has several advantages, but one is most significant: The publisher normally pays the author an "advance" so it can publish the book. The amount (usually half up front—half upon acceptance of the manuscript) is based on the number of books the publisher anticipates selling.

Using sophisticated data, the company determines the number, calculates the sum the author would earn under the proposed royalty agreement, and then offers a percentage of the total. Advances range from a small amount to a million-plus. Regardless of the advance, remember that the publisher believes in the potential of the book to the extent they are willing to fund printing and editing costs, disperse upfront money, and permit sharing of royalties instead of asking for money. This is significant since industry statistics confirm publishers earn a profit on fewer than 10 percent of the books they release.

Authors earn revenue from the sale of each copy of the book. The royalty may be based on the retail price or the publisher's net income (wholesale price). In today's marketplace, garnering a percentage of the retail price is rare, since publishers provide the retailer with at least a 40 percent discount. More likely, the royalty will be based on the "invoice price," a term referring to the price indicated on the publisher's invoice to wholesalers (distributors) and retailers (sales outlets).

This figure subtracts the discount from the retail price. Any royalty paid will be based on the "net copies" of the book sold. This refers to the total copies invoiced less those returned to the publisher. Since retailers have the right to return books they cannot sell, the publisher will keep a reserve account (revenues withheld from the author or poet) to cover the anticipated returns.

Typical royalty schedules call for the author to be provided revenue percentages based on increments of books sold. Each agreement will differ, but a standard split may call for the author to garner a 10 percent royalty on the first 10,000 books sold, 12½ percent on the next 5,000 sold, and 15 percent thereafter on the sale of hardcover books. Successful authors who have sold mega-books command percentages escalating to 50 percent and beyond with advances in the multi-million dollar range.

Royalties for the trade paperback edition of a book will vary, but the percentage is less based on a lower retail price. Seven-and-one-half percent is reasonable. For ebooks, the percentage varies dependent on the publisher.

An alternative publication deal may involve the author becoming a "partner" with the publishing company. Here the author and the publisher "share" 50/50 both revenues from the book and the expenses. Again, no up-front funds are required from the author. Research to find legitimate companies who offer this type of arrangement is a must before entering into any agreement.

Authors wonder whether it is advantageous to consider a traditional publisher since the royalty amount is low as compared with traditional self-publishing where the writer keeps all of the revenue. This is a matter of choice, but don't forget that with self-publishing you may have a financial outlay of funds to finance the publication of the book. With a traditional publisher, you do not since they cover all of the costs.

Another question that may be faced by authors is whether to accept a trade paperback publishing offer when they seek a hardcover release. A literary agent or entertainment attorney specializing in the literary field can offer advice. Being published in hardcover is prestigious, but trade paperback can provide the launch for a career.

To a budding author, securing a publishing deal with a traditional publisher, big, medium, or small, is cause for celebration. Drink, eat, and be merry for a week.

Securing a publishing commitment, regardless of the advance amount (the advance for the first Chicken Soup book was $1,000), or lack thereof, is important to building a career. It provides credibility. The first publication can lead to a second, since you are now "publishable."

Author interaction with publishing house editors varies according to the size of the publisher. At a smaller "house," the editor may be responsible for one book or as many as three. This scenario permits them to spend considerable time with the author or poet on everything from final editing to promotion.

Editors at medium-sized or large publishers may not have this luxury, since their job responsibility dictates interaction with several authors. Many times the first-time author is relegated to dealing with an assistant to the editor. Sustaining a good relationship with the editor and his or her assistant is vital to the success of the book.

Never forget that while some editors may not be great writers, they possess terrific instincts. Listen to them, learn from them, and respect them, for they are the foot soldiers regulating the flow of material into the publishing industry.

Internet "Specialty" Publishers

Traditional self-publishing venue are what I call "Internet Specialty Publishers." Two of note are Amazon's Kindle Direct Publishing (KDP), and IngramSpark.

KDP provides the opportunity for authors to publish their own works at no cost except for that expended for printed books ordered. Through the guidelines presented on the website (https://kdp.amazon. com/en_US/), templates are presented that permit uploading of the manuscript and cover art. There is no charge to do so. Within a day or two, the book is available for sale at www.amazon.com and through other outlets that may be chosen by the author. There are fees if the author decides they want to employ KDP to handle additional chores for the book, but the costs are quite reasonable.

IngramSpark (https://www.ingramspark.com/) mirrors KDP but there are differences as well. Minimal up-front costs may prevail and differences exist regarding printing cost and purchase of the books. Regardless, IngramSpark is an excellent publishing alternative

One advantage for using IS is that while most bookstores and libraries that will not stock KDP books due to ill feeling with Amazon, the stores and libraries will stock IS books since it is an Ingram product. One way to make sure a book has the best of both worlds is to publish it first with IS using the author's own ISBN and then publish the book with KDP using the same ISBN so that the book will be listed on Amazon but also be attractive to bookstores and libraries.

Like print-on-demand publishers, books may be printed when the author has use for them. The author selects the retail price and KDP and Ingram Spark take a cut. The author retains all of the rights to the book so that other publishing alternatives may be explored in the future.

Internet eBook Publishing

For those authors who want to join the ever-growing group that publishes their book in eBook form, KDP, IngramSpark, Lulu, Smashwords, and other sites offer this alternative. As noted, these sites offer a simple plan to upload the manuscript and cover art. The author may, as above, select the price for the eBook while retaining the publishing rights to the book. Other factors to consider will be what royalty is paid, when and how it is paid, and how free previews of the book are positioned. The world of the eBook is ever-changing and authors must keep up to date on the latest developments in the publishing marketplace.

Since the sale of eBooks that may be read on Kindle, Nook, iPads or other such devices is growing daily, authors have a great alternative for exposing their book to the marketplace. If substantial sales are the result, this will add to the potential to secure a traditional publisher in the future.

For those authors who have published books that have gone out of print, eBook publishing is a chance to extend the life of the book. This has been handy for me with such books as *The Perfect Yankee, Down for the Count*, and *Larry Legend*.

Traditional Self-Publishing

Traditional Self-Publishing dictates that authors write the book, design and lay out the pages, design and prepare the book cover or jacket, contact a printer and bookbinder, and pay to have the book printed and bound. Using a commercial layout program such as InDesign, PageMaker or Quark ensures a professional appearance for your book. Since keeping the "cost per book" to a minimum is important, obtain several printing and binding quotes. Printing a book of approximately two hundred pages for less than five dollars a copy is possible if sufficient copies are ordered.

On the day your book is delivered, celebrate since you have accomplished a goal others covet. You can give or sell the book to family, friends, and colleagues—whomever you want. You retain any revenue, since no agent or publisher receives a percentage.

When you self-publish, print as many as you wish, whenever you wish. You can sell them at flea markets, on a table in your front lawn, or at book signings organized at bookstores and other outlets.

If you choose Traditional Self-Publishing, you are the writer, editor, promoter, marketer, warehouser, and bookkeeper for your book. If it succeeds, it is because of your efforts.

Since you will not benefit from advice and counsel offered by a publishing company while finalizing your manuscript for self-publication, hire an accomplished line editor to review the manuscript. Doing so will strengthen the writing style and prevent careless grammatical and spelling errors infiltrating the text. Every word written is a reflection of your writing ability, and you want the book to be first rate and professional.

Many self-published authors who do not hire a line editor are embarrassed when their book is released. Careless mistakes ruin good writing.

Remember there are line editors and then there are line editors. Request edited works of fiction or non-fiction to ensure credibility. Choose an editor with experience in the particular genre that you have chosen.

To aid your self-publishing efforts, read credible books on the subject. Beware of those who want to charge up-front fees. Many are unworthy.

Regarding where a self-published author may sell books, be creative. One author discovered a chain store in his area willing to stock a few copies of his book on consignment. To his delight, the store agreed to charge a 25 percent fee, well below standard. Independent bookstores may stock self-published books on a similar basis.

Besides bookstores, consider non-traditional outlets. Depending on the genre of your book and its anticipated target audience, you can locate outlets where potential customers will congregate. For instance, Let The Good Times Roll, a music anthology book I co-authored, was marketed through music outlets including nightclubs, bars, and museums. Many of my books have also sold well in a men's clothing store.

Don't forget the Internet as a distribution outlet. Amazon.com is an excellent way to reach both broad and specialized audiences. Their Advantage program encourages self-published authors to expose their books on the website. Other Internet sites, including Barnes and Noble, are also available.

Most authors that self-publish establish a personal website to promote themselves and their book. If you do so, make certain it looks professional. Sloppy websites with cheap graphics will inhibit your reputation as a budding writer instead of enhancing it. Long ago, I had a webmaster create www.markshawbooks.com. When a new book is published, the cover and info about the book is displayed.

If you decide to sell your book on your website, consider PayPal, the "poor man's credit card" account. Information is available at their website and start-up costs can be kept to a minimum.

Entering your book in reputable competitions, such as those sponsored by Writer's Digest or prestigious poetry magazines, is advisable. You never know who will read your works and decide, "Hey, this is a writer I want to know." A list of selected competitions is available in Poets and Writers Magazine.

When marketing and promoting your book, consider spending funds to hire a public relations company to represent it. This adds a professional edge to your efforts and provides access to media you may be unable to reach otherwise. The Achilles heel for most self-published authors is not permitting enough lead time for their book to be published and not spending enough time and resources for promotion and marketing.

Editor Amy Pierpont believes self-publishing can be a definite asset. In The Writer, a recommended publication for aspiring authors, she stated, "Publishers are always looking for talented writers, and when we find they're already self-published, it is often an added plus because the author comes with a built-in audience."

Success stories abound among traditional self-published authors and poets who write less for monetary gain and more due to an important story they want to tell. Among them is Costa Mesa, California housewife Laura Doyle. She and her husband self-published a book titled, The Surrendered Wife. It detailed how women could transform their marriages into intimate, passionate unions.

To their surprise, the book became a hit on Amazon.com. Scouts at Simon and Schuster learned of the success and offered a contract. The book was a New York Times bestseller.

Gordon Miller achieved success by self-publishing. His book, Quit Your Day Job Often and Get Big Raises triggered a contract with Doubleday for a second book, The Career Coach: Winning Strategies for Getting Ahead in Today's Job Market. "Self-publishing can be a terrific experience!" he swears. "Align everything about the book to your target market. Most of all, have fun with it."

Miller believes self-publishing has earned a brand new reputation. "There is no question that self-publishing has gained more respect," he states, "primarily because there are so many stories of self-published books going on to be national bestsellers."

Each week in Publishersmarketplace, the Internet email publication previously mentioned, there appears another example of an author or poet that traditionally self-published and built up a significant following for their book to attract a traditional publisher. Many are also signed for a follow-up publication based on the success of the first one.

Don't forget an important fact, those who decide to traditionally self-publish wear a badge of courage for their efforts. Traditional publishers certainly believe that to be true.

If you decide traditional self-publishing is the right alternative for you, my suggestion is that you use a mock schedule like the one presented here in order to consider the options open to you. By assessing the choices, you can then decide how to proceed from book idea to publication.

For example, a schedule might look something like this for a book or collection of poetry with an anticipated release date on September 15th of the year following the date of your decision to write a book:

Schedule

Current Year

September 15th – begin consideration of book or collection of poetry you will write based on your passion for the subject matter and potential marketability of the book

October 1 – If you have not already done so, educate yourself about how the publishing industry works, the process toward writing your book, and how traditional self-published books fit in with the multitude of other books being published

October 15 – finalize decision regarding book or collection of poetry to be written and the storytelling method to be used in writing the book

November 15 – finalize book outline and begin writing process

Following Year

April 15 – complete first draft of manuscript or collection of poetry

May 15 – complete final draft of manuscript or collection of poetry

June 1 – organize publishing company if you decide to traditionally self-publish

June 2 – secure releases for quoted text/photographs/illustrations used in book

June 3 – send manuscript or collection of poetry to line editor

June 5 – meet with book designer

June 7 – consider printing alternatives and request quotes

June 10 – investigate book distribution alternatives

June 15 – consider public relations company alternatives

June 20 – consider website alternatives

June 25 – review layout copy and revise

June 30 – secure ISBN number and bar code

July 10 – review revised manuscript or collection of poetry

July 17 – scan author or poet photograph for book and write short biography

July 24 – finalize printer selection – send manuscript or collection of poetry to printer

July 25 – copyright text through Library of Congress website

July 25 – finalize website design – authorize completion

July 27 – finalize promotion and marketing campaign, including viral, for book either through professional company or by author or poet

July 27 – secure person to write Foreword and provide endorsements for book

July 28 – finalize cover and send to printer along with ISBN number

July 29 – set up book signings, personal appearances

July 29 – list book in *Forthcoming Books, Books In Print,* and other publications

June 30 – establish storage area for storage of books

August 5 – receive book proof from printer, review, and give approval

August 14 – website up and running

August 10 – review all aspects of book release,   pr, book signings, etc.

September 10 – receive shipment of books and celebrate when you hold one in your hand

September 15 – distribute books to Amazon, other outlets

September 11 – Full-scale marketing and promotion, including viral marketing

Sept. 15 – book release, more celebrating

Print-On-Demand

Print-On-Demand publishing is an alternative for the first-time author to consider. Trade paperback-sized books are stored electronically and printed one at a time based on the demand. Turn-around time can be less than forty-eight hours. If a greater quantity is requested, shipment is possible within a week.

Fee-based Print-On-Demand companies are not publishers in the traditional sense. They charge "set-up" fees ranging from ninety-nine dollars to a thousand dollars or more. Some also offer marketing packages and other services. You normally submit your book in electronic form on a computer disk.

Writers receive royalties from the sales of the book. Royalties can range from 20 percent for hardcover books purchased directly from the publishers to 10 percent on those purchased by bookstores, libraries, and the author. This may seem advantageous, but investigate what the fee-based Print-On-Demand publisher can do that you cannot do simply by traditional self-publishing.

The main differences between fee-based Print-On-Demand publishers and traditional self-publishing concerns control (when you self-publish, you control all aspects of the book as compared with Print-On-Demand where you choose from the publishing services offered), book revenue (traditional self-publishing permits you to keep all book proceeds while Print-On-Demand outlets only provide a royalty), and book rights (by traditionally self-publishing, you keep all the rights while some Print-On-Demand outlets require you to contract with them for an extended period of time).

If you are determined to print only a few copies of your book for family and friends with no potential for commercial success, fee-based Print-On-Demand has merit. If you are a public speaker interested in "BOR" (Back of Room) sales, or a businessperson seeking publicity for a specific economic issue, POD can also make sense. Reputable companies to assist with this process include Bookmasters, Book Surge, affiliated with Amazon.com and Lightning Source.

If you do choose a fee-based Print-On-Demand outlet, be certain to hire a line editor with experience in your genre to edit the book. Many POD books are released that include typos and grammatical and punctuation mistakes. Make certain that you have the right to check the final version of the book before it is printed to verify printing quality. When you receive your books, check immediately the printing quality and whether the text includes your revisions. If it does not, return the book to correct the mistakes. Your book is a reflection of you and many are released that prove embarrassing to the writer.

Writers attempting to build a traditional writing career should avoid fee-based Print-On Demand outlets. In the true sense of the words, they are simply subsidy publishers and viewed as such by the traditional publishing industry, bookstores, and libraries. Certain stigmas that attach are described in the next section and reviewers will most likely pass when requested to review the book.

Subsidy Presses

The term is often interchanged with Vanity Press, These companies are easy to locate. Author House in Bloomington, Indiana is arguably the most well-known, the most diabolical of the group.

In short, companies like Author House make money by charging aspiring authors for the company services start to finish They accept manuscripts, guide efforts with regard to finalizing proper form and substance for the material and the cover, and then print the book. Editing services and promotional ideas are offered at extra cost.

Similar companies exist on the Internet. All promise your book will get a look-see from the national chain stores, but the promise doesn't guarantee the book will be stocked in those stores. Most times it will not unless the book stirs enough interest to entice the stores to stock it.

One company, for instance, advertises through mailings "monthly specials" akin to a used car dealer. They also hoodwink the author by making the claim that they will "make [your] book available through more than 25,000 bookstores worldwide." This may be true, but the reality is that few will actually stock the book.

Many Subsidy Press outlets promise that authors will keep the rights to their book. This is acceptable, but the Subsidy Press will receive a hefty portion for each book sold at a price that they determine. Website advertisements alert the author that they have a "variety of options regarding payment percentages."

Most offensive is the large fees companies like Author House charge. For instance, on its website, there are different publishing "packages," one costing as much as $15,000 dollars. Before agreeing to such terms, read the fine print before committing and ask, "What can this subsidy publisher or fee-based POD do that I can't do by traditionally self-publishing for instance with Kindle Direct and Ingram where I keep all the revenues?"

In essence, nothing and the best part is not spending much, if any, money on doing so. And, by dismissing the Author Houses of the world, the author avoids a distinct disadvantage: the stigma attached to subsidy publishers.

Those who publish with these vultures and scam artists are marked as rank amateurs who could not be otherwise published. Right or wrong, this is the perception. As self-publishing guru Dan Poynter once said, "The name of the subsidy publisher on the spine of the book is a kiss of death."

One strong example to consider. A longtime friend of mine, so anxious to be published and unaware of the subsidy publisher trap, published a book through a Washington State subsidy publisher. She paid a large upfront fee to do so and even signed an agreement where she earned very minimal royalties for each book sold.

When the book was successful based on her efforts, she asked for the royalty fee to be increased. It was not, and worse, when she tried to find a traditional publisher to consider publishing her next book, nothing materialized since the stigma of having hired a subsidy publisher tainted her reputation.

Without doubt, Subsidy publishers rely on the desperation of aspiring authors and poets who believe there is no other way to be published. As stated, beware of the "publishing trap" and consider alternatives before being sucked in by a subsidy publisher. Investigate before committing.

Contacting Literary Agents and Publishers

If, after considering the options of submitting your book idea to traditional publishers or traditionally self-publishing, you decide on the former, contact literary agents for potential representation. You may also contact publishers directly if you feel this is worthy although many require agented submissions for consideration.

My advice is to attempt to secure a traditional publishing commitment if at all possible before considering any of the other methods of publication. The reason – as noted – what do you have to lose by simply giving it a shot since the worst thing that may occur is for you to be rejected? If you are, it is not as if you have a life-threatening experience. Try, try, and try some more, and if there is not a traditional publisher willing to publish your book, you may then try traditional self-publishing or another option.

Locating publishers is simple—gaining their attention is more difficult. While various publications list publishers and contact names, an author submitting material faces long odds. Estimates vary, but publishers confirm they receive thousands upon thousands of manuscripts, Book Proposals, and Query Letters each week.

Prior to the existence of www.publisherslunch.com, many reference materials existed where information about agents and publishers could be located. A Google search provides access to these materials but none comes close to providing the information Publishers Lunch does. Not only is the up-to-date information what's happening in the publishing world provided but for $25 a month the world of publishing opens up for all aspiring authors to view.

For instance, by hitting the "Dealmakers" icon, the listing of the top 100 literary agents and publishers is provided regarding nearly every book genre known to woman or man. If you are attempting to publish historical fiction or commercial non-fiction, all is needed is to hit that icon and up pops the most likely agents to be interested in your type of book. Included with the information alongside the name of the agent or publishing company editor is the website link, phone numbers and best of all, email addresses where submitted material, normally a query letter or book proposal may be forwarded.

In effect, Publishers Lunch is the bible of the publishing industry, your guide to all you need to know regarding securing an agent or publisher for your book.

Literary Agency Fees

To understand the business acumen of selected agencies, here is the most important information to know. First, the agency will normally receive a 15 percent commission on domestic sales, 20 percent on foreign sales from all revenues provided to the author.

While fifteen percent may seem like a big bite, and it is, the number is standard in the publishing industry. Representing yourself deflects any fee, but having a literary agent supporting you and providing advice is essential to building a career. I've always rationalized the agency fee by saying, "85% of something is better than 100% of nothing."

Also, most publishing companies would rather deal with a literary agent than with the author or poet who is the creative genius that wrote the book. When business matters occur, editors at publishing companies prefer to discuss them with the agent. She or he will assist the author or poet if a conflict occurs between them and the publisher. Having an agent act as a buffer can prevent hard feelings.

One reminder about literary agents—never forget that they work for you, not vice-versa. If you feel the agent isn't acting in your best interest, let him or her know. Good communication is essential to a long-term relationship, since agents represent many other clients. When agents are upset, it is usually more about them than it is about you. Exercise patience and understanding.

Remember that top literary agents have an on-going working relationship with the same publishing company editors. When conflict occurs, don't hesitate to question the agent about decisions being made. The agent must act in your best interest. If this does not occur, you should part company.

Contacting literary agents by telephone or e-mail after representation has been finalized is proper, but consideration is suggested. Agents earn revenue by selling books and do not have time to chat on the telephone or through Internet instant message. Agents should not be considered counselors, therapists, or even editors. They can enhance a career, guide it, and provide support, but their main job is to sell as many books as possible.

Understand that telephone calls are often not returned. If literary agents have news to report, they will contact you. Otherwise leave them alone, especially on hectic Mondays, getaway Fridays, or during August when New York literary agents and editors flock to the Hamptons for sun and surf.

Choose a literary agent with a vision for a lasting career. Before selecting one, discuss long-term goals and the type of material of interest. Planning book two while book one is being readied for publication is essential for fiction, non-fiction, or poetry. Work with your agent to form a team that plans ahead in accordance with trends in the marketplace and book subjects that will be timely.

Book ideas originate with the author and the poet, not from the agent. One poet requested a meeting with an agent so he could learn of ideas for alternative poetry books. I explained that researching the marketplace was his job.

To help you understand the author/poet/agent relationship, a sample agency agreement is featured in the Appendix of this book. Also featured are tips regarding the agent and publisher listings featured in Writer's Market.

Securing a literary agent is terrific, but you must continue to be a cheerleader for your book. Check in with the agent on a frequent basis. Remind them your book is the best one ever written and request updates on publisher progress. Most agents represent many books and it is a must to keep yours on the front burner.

Literary Agency Warnings

If a literary agent or agency requests that you pay them a fee for representation in addition to, or as an alternative to a percentage, run away.

Well-established literary agencies never charge an upfront fee. Be wary if an agent or agency requests a "reading fee" or "an evaluation fee." Recouping reasonable expenses for copying and mailing is proper, but make certain there is a cap on the amount spent without your written authorization. If there are questions regarding the conduct of a literary agent, contact the Association of Author's Representatives. Legitimate literary agents are members and subject to the AAR Canon of Ethics.

Hiring one literary agent to represent your works is appropriate, but some agents or agencies are better at handling particular types of books than others. Searching the AAR listings guarantees that you are contacting literary agents who will be most interested in your genre of writing.

Literary agent contracts can be written or verbal. When entering into a written agreement, beware of hidden clauses binding you to the agent for a lengthy period. Attempt to work on a project-by-project basis. If the relationship doesn't work, the agreement can be terminated.

Literary Agent Research

A most common question among aspiring authors is: "How may I find a literary agent that will be interested in my book?"

A prelude to this question is whether you need a literary agent at all. If you intend to publish your works for a regional magazine, a literary journal, or independent presses, you probably don't need one.

But if you decide that submission to the larger publishing world is worthy, an agent is essential since most of the prestigious companies will not accept unrepresented books.

To discover the right agent for your book, strategy is a key. When you decide on the exact book you want to write, check literary agency listings ones at Publishers Lunch to determine which ones represent that genre. List the "usual suspects" in a notebook and then visit the nearest bookstore.

Just as the initial visit discussed in Chapter One provided education about the workings of the book industry, this one will narrow the field of potential agents to be contacted. It requires checking the Acknowledgments pages of books similar to the one under consideration to discover if any of the names you have collected from Publishers Lunch coincides with those listed in the Acknowledgments. Also note agents listed on the AAR website and at www.literaryagents.org.

This exercise lets you formulate a list of top agents who are candidates to handle the type of book you contemplate. As previously mentioned, the Acknowledgments may also provide the names of editors at the publishing company who collaborated with the author.

A tip for unpublished authors suggests seeking what has become known as an "early-career agent." This means that although all budding writers would love to have John Grisham or Mary Higgins Clark's agent represent them, this is unlikely and probably a mistake since they are too busy representing their big guns.

Organizing a list of agents and publishers who should be interested in your book narrows the field for submission. A separate Word document listing of those names is warranted. When you are ready to submit your Query Letter and Book Proposal, the list will serve as a guide. Contacting those individuals will cut the odds, since you will know that these agents or publishers have shown interest in the type of book you are considering. Otherwise, you waste time and effort submitting material to agents who will have no interest.

Don't be afraid to use non-traditional means of contacting literary agents and/or publishers. Anyone can discover names, but if you are dedicated to being published, you will not only hone in on the "usual suspects" interested in the contemplated book, but use friendships, acquaintances, or the bartender down the street to advantage. Remember that any agency will consider Book Proposals and/or manuscripts in the following order: those submitted by clients and former clients, those referred to the agency by other agents or clients, and those arriving unsolicited.

If you know someone who has been represented by an agent, ask for a referral. Don't be afraid to approach published authors or poets since the worst that can occur is for them to say "no."

Meeting literary agents at writers' conferences or conventions is a terrific way to begin a relationship. Resist the temptation to overwhelm the agent with ideas for several books. Simply make the acquaintance and then follow up with a letter or telephone call at a later date.

To attract attention to your Book Proposal and Query Letter, be clever. On the packages I sent out while seeking representation for Down for the Count, I imprinted the cover with a red stamped outline of two dogs barking. I hoped an animal lover at the agency might place my material on the top of the pile.

Remember that most agents and publishers are not receptive to receiving a completed manuscript. Instead they welcome a Query Letter and a Book Proposal. Some make it clear that if a manuscript is submitted, it will be deposited in the nearest receptacle.

A reminder—the fiction writer should have a completed manuscript ready for submission at the time their Book Proposal and/or Query Letter is submitted to agents, since they are less interested in works-in-progress. Remember to indicate a readiness to forward the manuscript upon request.

Literary agents are looking for new writers. They make their money by selling books and are on the lookout for terrific book ideas. As noted agent Kimberly Cameron told Writer's Digest, "I am always optimistic every day that I am going to discover a wonderful voice."

Entertainment Attorneys

If you decide to hire an attorney instead of a literary agent, or in addition to an agent, use caution: there are entertainment lawyers and then there are entertainment lawyers. Many general practitioners and business lawyers have read a book or taken a seminar regarding the entertainment field. They describe themselves as savvy in that arena. Beware of such animals. Check the lawyer's credentials before retaining him or her. Request references and inquire as to their knowledge of the publishing industry.

Publishers relish the opportunity to negotiate with competent attorneys, but those unschooled in the literary world inhibit deal-making. "The worst thing that can happen," explains Marie Butler-Knight, former publisher of Alpha Books, an imprint within Penguin Group USA, "is for the author to be represented by an attorney who isn't knowledgeable about literary contracts."

The Publishing Process

Publishing a book should be an exhilarating experience, but there will be bumps along the way. Adhering to Mark's Step #6—Traditional Publishing Is A Writer's Best Friend will help stem the tide of disappointment.

With this in mind, do your homework—the book you believe in deserves it. Choosing the right literary agent and/or publishing alternative guarantees that you are using a strategy optimizing your opportunities for a career as a published author or poet.

Step #6 Summary

- Research alternative means of book publishing.

- Beware of Subsidy Publishers or other non-traditional publishers who promise distribution to major bookstores and libraries.

- Poets beware of publishers promising publication if a certain number of books are purchased.

- Instead of subsidy publishers, consider Self-Publishing alternatives.

- **When searching for literary agents, check *The Guide To Literary Agents*, *Writer's Market*, and *Poet's Market*.**

- Beware of literary agents who request payment in advance for their services.

- Once you have compiled a list of likely agents and publishers, check guidelines to see what form of submission is proper.

Self-Publishing Concepts

- Assess the marketplace to be sure your book concept is unique.
- Read a competent book on the subject of self-publishing to ensure your understanding of the concepts outlined here.
- Complete the manuscript including:
  » Prologue and epilogue, if any
  » Copyright page (copyright statement, disclaimers, ISBN, publisher Information)
  » Table of contents
  » Acknowledgments page, if any
  » Appendices, if any
  » Bibliography, if any
  » Index, if any.
- Hire a competent line editor to edit the manuscript.
- When the manuscript is edited, file for copyright protection from the Library of Congress.
- Secure an ISBN number (R.R. Bowker is one source).
- Prepare the cover or jacket, including:
  » Front cover artwork, if any
  » Back cover artwork, if any, text, and barcodes
  » Front and back jacket, including artwork, if any, and text
  » Inside back cover material, and author photograph, if any.
- Investigate alternative printing costs.
- Establish storage space for books if you plan to distribute them yourself.
- Complete your book printing and binding.
- Set release date for publication of book.
- Position your book for sale at bookstores, Internet outlets such as Amazon.com, and your website.

- Consider contacting independent distributors listed in various industry publications.
- List your book in Forthcoming Books and Books In Print.
- Read The Complete Guide To Book Publicity by Jodee Blanco.
- Begin promotion campaign including media exposure, book signings, and mailings.
- Celebrate release of your book with an expensive bottle of champagne.
- Begin writing a new book while the current one is being promoted.

All the world knows me in my book,
and my book in me.

MICHEL DE MONTAIGNE

Step #7

Market The Query Letter and Book Proposal, Not The Book

Book Proposals

To maximize the potential to become traditionally published, prepare a professionally written Book Proposal. Why so? New York-based literary agent David Black, discoverer of, among other books, the bestseller, *Tuesdays With Morrie*, states, "While it's possible that an unknown writer will be discovered by a top literary agent, it's a challenge. The number of books published each year is getting smaller. Make sure you send a proposal of the highest quality, and that it's designed to get respect."

In The Insider's Guide to Getting Published, author John Boswell provides compelling facts regarding Book Proposals. He writes, "Today fully 90% of all non-fiction books sold to trade publishers [sale to consumers] are acquired on the basis of the proposal alone."

The percentage of works of fiction sold through Book Proposals is subject to conjecture. Offered the choice of reading a concise, exciting Query Letter or Book Proposal or a 400-page novel submitted by an aspiring author, agents and editors will choose the former. If the Book Proposal material indicates promise, they may contact the writer and request that a manuscript is forwarded to them.

Aspiring authors and poets wonder whether they should write the Query Letter or the Book Proposal first. Methods will vary, but I suggest writing the Book Proposal first since you will use portions of the information formulated in the proposal in the Query Letter. Remember that the Query Letter is simply a "mini-proposal" setting up readers for the extended information about the book contained in the Book Proposal.

The journey toward completing a draft of the proposal begins with understanding what a Book Proposal is and what it is not. Above all, the Book Proposal is a sales tool. Within the scope of thirty to forty pages, less in many cases, the "written pitch" outlines the author or poet's game plan so an agent or editor at a publishing company can consider its merits.

What the Book Proposal is not relates to the style of writing. It should not be promotional, boastful or pompous. A well-conceived Book Proposal doesn't tell the reader the book is the greatest one ever written. Instead, the text shows them through good writing and interesting facts that the book has merit.

Being enthused about your book's potential can color your objectivity. Before long, the proposal takes on the aura of a used car salesman attempting to convince Mr. Jones a chartreuse Plymouth has great resale value. Heed the advice of Jack Webb, Sergeant Joe Friday on the television program, Dragnet. Confronting a perplexed witness to a crime, Joe would bellow, "Just the facts, ma'am; just the facts."

Literary agent David Black's perception regarding Book Proposals is accurate. He says, "I can usually tell in 10-30 seconds if the [book] proposal I'm reading is promising, and my instincts are usually correct."

Ten to thirty seconds—that's not much time. If the writer hasn't hooked readers after they've scanned the cover page, the tagline, and the first few words in the Overview or Synopsis' first paragraph, the book idea is deader than dead.

Agents and editors don't have time to waste. Either the Book Proposal sparks the immediate brainwave, "Wow, this can be a great book," or the material is headed for the dumpster.

Sample Book Proposals for fiction, non-fiction, and poetry are presented in the Appendix. Use these proposals as guideposts, noting the proper form. Self-help books vary about the components of the Book Proposal, but the Appendix samples follow a form that has proven successful.

Many writers abhor the idea of writing Query Letters or Book

Proposals. The process appears difficult and time-consuming. But with a well-planned strategy, writing the letter and proposal can be completed without actual loss of life. And doing so will pay off. Over the past few years, I have been amused when an author or poet telephones and says, "You'll never guess what happened. I actually received a letter from an agent or an editor asking to read my manuscript based on the query letter and book proposal."

Even more satisfying is notice that a writer who composed a Book Proposal using this book as their guidepost has secured a publishing deal. This occurred for Christine Montross, a Brown University medical student client of mind whose book about laboratory experiences during her first year, Body of Work, was sold by her literary agent at ICM to Penguin Group USA. That book became a bestseller and she has followed it up with two more publications.

Writers like Christine seem amazed at the good fortune, but the response is to be expected. Plain and simple—forwarding a professionally written Query Letter and Book Proposal gains the attention of literary agents and publishing company editors. Believe it.

Taglines

Any book, whether fiction, non-fiction, or a collection of poetry may be described in ten to fifteen words or less, preferably less. If this is not possible, then the book idea should be discarded, since the Tagline will be an essential part of any Book Proposal.

The Tagline, a/k/a "hook for the book," or "handle," is akin to "pitches" made to motion picture studios by producers and screenwriters attempting to convince executives to produce a film. For The Perfect Yankee, the story of Don Larsen's perfect game in the 1956 World Series, the pitch was, "It's Bull Durham meets The Natural with a touch of Major League thrown in." If you are familiar with those films, you know exactly what The Perfect Yankee is about.

Examples of great taglines abound. Pearl Harbor, the film, gained the connotation, deserved or not, of "Titanic with a love story." Steven Spielberg's motion picture, A. I. (Artificial Intelligence), utilized the tagline, "E. T. Grows Up." The film Rock Star was dubbed, "The Story of a Wannabe Who Got To Be."

The publishing industry also relies on Taglines to sell and promote books. A book may be described as "It's Into Thin Air meets The Perfect Storm" or "It's My Friend Flicka set in the Colorado Rockies." Comparisons stretch to the author as well. "He writes like John Grisham," "She can write mysteries like Mary Higgins Clark," and "He's a cross between Hemingway and Woody Allen," are examples.

Perhaps the best illustration of a Tagline for a book that became a bestseller is Grisham's The Firm. It read, "It's a book about a recent law school graduate who is offered a job at a law firm that seems too good to be true—and it is." He may have used more than fifteen words, but it works.

Book advertisements such as the ones featured in the Thursday Life Section of USA Today provide inspiration for Taglines. Each is designed to convince the public that the specific book is a must read.

Consider this advertisement for the book Hostage by author Robert Crais. The Tagline read, "Three fugitives with a desperate plan. Three hostages with a deadly secret. One battle-scarred cop with no way out." For Ross Lamanna's Acid Test, the tagline was, "High tech weaponry. Humans beyond humanity. And the world at their mercy." Adding to the lure was the endorsement, "Thrill-a-minute writing... like Tom Clancy on speed." A Love Worth Giving, by Max Lucado, bore the Tagline, "Love Never Fails (You Just Have To Do It Right)."

For Iyanla Vanzant's Living Through the Meantime, the advertisement featured the Tagline, "Leads you step-by-step to a greater understanding of your motivations and your desires, helping you to break the patterns of the past and begin the healing process." A Los Angeles Times quote followed stating, "Vanzant is the author people want to hug and thank." Hank Hanegraaff's The Covering featured the daUnitng words, "24/7/365, Protection From Evil."

The advertisement for Turn Off The Hunger Switch was clever. It read, "What's Really Keeping The Weight On? Chocolate? Pasta? Chips? Actually, It's All In Your Head. Literally."

The New York Times Book Page provides a bestseller list of interest each week. Alongside the name of the book, the author and the publishing company is the description that reflects the book's Tagline. Checking these out on a weekly basis can be most helpful.

Taglines for poetry books are as varied as the material

submitted. Since most collections of poetry have a common theme, the poet must present a snappy hook providing the reader with a clear indication as to the message being conveyed. One poet intended to write a chapbook designed to enlighten divorced fathers regarding their responsibilities toward their children. When asked by an editor what the theme of the collection was, he simply answered, "Dads, Don't Be A Dope." Another whose collection featured the "dark side" of religion used the Tagline, "Christ's Underbelly."

Book Titles

Book titles for fiction, non-fiction or poetry must be snappy, concise, and descriptive. A rule of thumb is that they should be six words or less. Above all, they must pique the reader's curiosity.

With non-fiction, the subject matter is a star and the title will depict a certain person, event, or issue. Titles such as Fifty Shades of Grey, Tick Tock, The Girl with the Golden Dragon, Marrying Daisy Bellemy, The Golden Compass, T is for Trespass, Three Cups of Tea, Water For Elephants, Playing for Pizza, Shadow Dance, Quiet Strength, Age of Turbulence, Ghandi, MacArthur, Truman, Dolly (Dolly Parton), In Cold Blood, DiMaggio, and Hoffa, are examples. One Hundred and One Ways To Invest, Race and Responsibility, A History of National League Ballparks, Suzanne Somers' Eat, Cheat, and Melt Away The Fat, and Gay Men In The White House provide instant recognition regarding subject matter.

For works of fiction, clever word usage provides clues to the book's content. Stieg Larsson's The Girl with the Golden Tattoo, Hemingway's The Old Man and the Sea, John Dunning's The Bookman's Wake, and Scott Turow's Presumed Innocent reflect recognition of the themes presented.

Titles for my publications are the result of extensive consideration. Down for the Count described what occurred to boxer Mike Tyson when he was convicted of rape. Bury Me in a Pot Bunker might have caused people to think it was a book about death and dying, but it depicted the life and times of golf course designer Pete Dye, famous for golf courses featuring deep pot bunkers.

Forever Flying described the adventures of aviator R. A. "Bob"

Hoover. The subtitle, "Fifty Years of High-Flying Adventures, from Barnstorming in Prop-Planes to Dogfighting Germans to Testing Supersonic Jets," added zest.

The Perfect Yankee portrayed Don Larsen's World Series perfect game achievement. Testament To Courage described the "angel of mercy" persona of Holocaust survivor Cecelia Rexin. Larry Legend chronicled the life of NBA superstar Larry Bird, and Miscarriage of Justice, The Jonathan Pollard Story summed up the plight of the most controversial spy in American history.

Beneath the Mask of Holiness: Thomas Merton and the Forbidden Love Affair that Set Him Free set the stage for my controversial biography of the spiritual guru. Use of the word "forbidden" in the title certainly caught the eye of many readers.

Certainly the titles for my six books relating to Dorothy Kilgallen and the JFK assassination are original in nature. The Poison Patriarch vividly describes Joseph P. Kennedy, The Reporter Who Knew Two Much the life and times and deaths of celebrated journalist and media icon Dorothy Kilgallen, and Denial of Justice captures the theme of proof that she was denied that justice when she die and to present day. Collateral Damage details what I proved in that book, that the deaths of Marilyn Monroe, JFK and Kilgallen may all be connected to the actions of not only Joe Kennedy but especially Robert Kennedy who was complicit in Marilyn's death and whose actions against Mafia Don Carlos Marcello resulted in the assassination of JFK. Most recently, Fighting for Justice fits with the theme of the book, that I have fought against distortions of history seeking justice for Marilyn and Dorothy Kilgallen.

Where do titles originate? Inspiration is everywhere, but mine have originated straight, I believe, from the Holy Spirit that guides my life since I am awakened in the middle of the night with the title embedded in my brain. I write that title on note cards kept by the bed.

Bottom line: Aspiring authors and poets must create a title so strong it will catch the attention of an agent or publisher. If this is accomplished, it kick-starts a mindset that says, "I must read this material."

Book Proposal Components

If you have decided traditional book publishing is your first choice toward becoming published, determined the book contemplated is marketable, completed the research necessary to ensure accuracy of the text, finalized an outline, written at least three sample chapters, conceived a book title, and described your intended publication in fifteen words or less, you are ready to attempt a first draft of the Book Proposal. It should include:

- Cover page title, subtitle and author name
- A second page featuring a snappy quote that will hook the agent or editor
- Contents page, (optional)
- Book Tagline (Hook)
- Overview (Non-Fiction) or Synopsis (Fiction) of the book concept (Also called Brief Description or Content Summary)
- Author Biography
- Book Audience
- Similar Successful Books
- Book Promotion Ideas
- Format/Manuscript Status, (optional)
- Book-To-Film Potential
- Book Outline
- Sample Text (two or three sample chapters (dependent on length)
- Appendix

Some authors decide to submit only the Query Letter and Sample Chapters, but including the additional information mentioned above guarantees that the writer has provided all of the essentials about their book idea. Take the extra time to prepare material for each section listed. It will pay off.

Examples of Book Proposal formats are featured in the Appendix. Remember: the first page will provide the title, a subtitle if there is one, and your name. The second will present the snappy quote. The third page provides a Proposal Table of Contents. This is optional.

Beginning on the fourth page, with the title of the book at the top, are the components of the Book Proposal. They are: the Tagline followed by the Overview or Synopsis, Author Biography, Book Audience, Similar Successful Books, Promotion Ideas, Format/Manuscript (optional), and Book To Film, if appropriate. The Outline, Sample Text, and Appendix follow these compartments. There is no need to separate the compartments on individual pages—they should flow from page to page.

If the Book Proposal concerns children's books, poetry, essays, or other material that is not long form, the sample material should be representative of that genre. Length is less important than ample presentation of material showcasing your talent. When mentioning photographs, you should indicate "photographs available on request." Some publishers shy away from books requiring an extensive number of them due to cost factors.

Regardless of the genre of the book, the Book Proposal must be adapted to the material being presented for consideration. Emphasis should be placed on the merits of the book that you believe are most important. Providing the literary agent or editor with concise, well-organized information is a key.

Book Proposal Form

As stated, sample Book Proposals for fiction, non-fiction are provided in the Appendix, but your proposal will be uniquely yours. Write it in your best, succinct prose in accordance with proper form: easy-to-read typeface, double-spaced, and printed on one side of the page with margins of one inch. Laser-print the text on 8 1/2 x 11 inch white paper (no onion skin). Do not staple it so copies can be made. Many software packages provide the proper format.

Opinions vary among literary agents and publishers, but the basic general format for the Book Proposal is simple. I suggest that you open a new computer file and list the various components in continuous order. The cover page will only include your book title in 36 font, the subtitle, if any, in 24 font, and your name in 24 font (no "by" the author is required).

Here's a tip: the components are continuous; each one does not begin on a separate page. The proposal is written in Times-Roman, and it is not stapled so that copies may be made. All except the Tagline and the description section of the Outline is written double-spaced. The entire proposal will be no more than forty pages. (Except for the headings, the text will be in 12 font.)

Tagline (all headings – 14 font – bold)

"Hook for the book" – 15 words or less – show the literary agent or editor what the book or collection of poetry is about. Single-spaced, 12 font.

Synopsis (fiction/poetry) or Overview (non-fiction)

Synopsis – plot, characters, beginning, middle, and end, 6-10 pages showing the literary agent or editor what the story is about. (Double-spaced, 12 font)

Overview – information provided about the subject, beginning, middle, and end, 6-10 pages showing the literary agent or editor what the book is about.

Author Biography

Provide academic credentials, personal information, and publishing credits, if any, but more important, answer this question: Why are you the one person in the world to write this book? Remember, the literary agent or editor wants to know your credentials, your platform, and your expertise to write the book. (Double-spaced, 12 font)

Key words to begin biography: The author's expertise to write this book stems from _____. (provide experience)

Book Audience

Provide information as to who is the target audience for the book. The broader the audience – the better. Remember, 75% of people who purchase books are women. (Double-spaced, 12 font)

Key words to begin this section: The target audience for (name of book) is _____.

Similar Successful Books

What successful books are similar to yours, and most important, why is yours unique or better? If there are none, why will yours be successful? (Double-spaced, 12 font)

Key words to begin this section: (name of book) is written in the spirit of such bestselling books as _____, _____, and _____, but (name of book) is unique because_____.

Promotion Ideas

Why are you and your book promotable, and what unique ideas, including those connected to viral marketing (website, blog, Facebook, Twitter, etc.) do you have to promote the book? Remember – literary agents and editors love a built-in audience based on your established platform. (Double-spaced, 12 font)

Format/Manuscript Status (Optional)

Provide reader with storytelling sequence and whether manuscript is completed or will be completed within x months of contract. (Double-spaced, 12 font)

Book-To-Film

If you believe your book may be adapted into a film, show why by using examples of successful films that feature your subject matter. (Double-spaced, 12 font)

Book Outline

Provide chapter headings (14 font) and three to four lines describing the subject matter of each chapter (Single-spaced, 12 font))

Sample Text

Provide one to three chapters (usually the Prologue, if any, and Chapter One and Two) depending on length. The writing should be superb; no grammatical or punctuation mistakes permitted. (Double-spaced, 12 font)

Appendix

Include any pertinent information, (media clippings, photographs, etc.) you believe the literary agent or editor should know to assist promotion and marketing of you or the book.

Quotes

Choosing a unique quote or two for the second page of the Book Proposal is advisable.

For the non-fiction book, Forever Flying, the quote chosen read, "Ladies and gentleman, let me introduce you to Bob Hoover, the greatest stick and rudder man alive today . . . No, that's wrong, let me introduce you to Bob Hoover, the greatest stick and rudder man who ever lived."—General James Doolittle. For Melvin Belli: King of the Courtroom, I highlighted this quote from gangster Santo Trafficante to mob lawyer Frank Ragano: "Whatever you do, don't ask Melvin Belli about Jack Ruby. It's none of your business."

If the work is fiction, consider including a clever quote from the text or one describing the gist of the material. For the Vicker Punch Series book, Guilty Conscience, a quote by American novelist Mary McCarthy was selected. It read, "An unrectified case of injustice has a terrible way of lingering, restlessly, in the social atmosphere like an unfinished question."

A clever quote or two piques an agent or editor's interest. They realize the quotes can be used in the marketing campaign for the book.

Overview/Synopsis

Having gained the attention of the agent or editor with the book title and quotes, a non-fiction writer begins drafting the Overview. Akin to a treatment written for a film, the Overview lays out the story so the reader will understand the flow of the book and the story contained therein.

One might believe writing a Synopsis (covers the basic plot, characters, and storyline) for a work of fiction would differ from the non-fiction Overview, but this is not necessarily true since many non-fiction books, especially those written in narrative form, are dramatic. The key is to show the reader a storyline featuring a good beginning, middle, and end.

The Overview or Synopsis is a mini-book, a type of "novella" about the book. This will be normally completed in present tense. Few summaries or conclusions are permitted—just fact, fact, fact. For inspiration, check the inside jacket covers for books similar to yours since the writer has provided a snapshot of the book content akin to an overview or synopsis.

One proven method is to begin the Overview by stating the name of the book and then writing "tells the story of" followed by a few lines regarding the storyline. For example, Miscarriage of Justice tells the story of Jonathan Pollard, the infamous American who spied for Israel in the mid-1980s.

How you describe your story will be a preview of how you will develop your book. The first paragraph or two are the most important. The very strongest material must appear—bang, bang, bang. Author John Boswell states, "Most editors [I would add, agents] read at only two speeds: slow, when editing a manuscript; and scan, when reading everything else." With the latter in mind, your first paragraph or two must be explosive.

Alternative means of gaining attention from the agent or editor include: a shocking statement, strong visual images, "what-if" scenarios, or pointed questions designed to garner curiosity. Select one guaranteed to titillate readers so they must continue to learn more about the book concept.

In Your Novel Proposal, authors Camenson and Cook outlined the elements of a fiction Synopsis. They list, "an opening hook, quick sketches of the main characters, plot high points, the core conflict, and the conclusion." Samples of conflict are presented in the book. Structuring the Synopsis is also discussed.

The length of the Overview or Synopsis will vary. Less is always better, but some stories will stretch to ten pages. Content is most important.

In the Overview for Forever Flying, a strong visual image was chosen. The text read, "The sky is his [Bob Hoover's] playground as he twists and turns the bright yellow P-51 Mustang through majestic maneuvers that make the eagles jealous. On the ground, huge throngs of admirers gasp at his daredevil loops and spins and wonder in awe whether the tall, lanky man with the ready smile and swooping handlebar mustache will survive yet another dangerous encounter with death."

The Overview for Forever Flying swept readers into the aviation world of R. A. "Bob" Hoover, a World War II hero and aviation icon. The writing was visual, not only concerning Bob's flying escapades, but regarding who he was and how he pushed the envelope despite the stare of death at every turn. This type of description convinced readers they wanted to know more: who was Bob Hoover, why he is so important, and why will people purchase a book chronicling his life?

After readers were hooked, the Overview described Hoover's flying genius. The second paragraph read, "Whether he's performing the 'Cuban-Eight,' 'Sixteen Point Hesitation Rolls,' or the 'Dead-Engine Management Maneuver,' Robert A. 'Bob' Hoover and his vintage plane slice through the clouds like a lightning bolt. When the P-51 dances gingerly to Hoover's 'Tennessee Waltz' aerobatics, you can almost hear the melodic music in the background."

I then addressed Hoover's credibility. The third paragraph read, "Called 'the pilot's pilot,' and the 'greatest pilot I ever saw' by famed aviator Chuck Yeager, fun-loving seventy-four-year-old Bob Hoover is the greatest aerobatic pilot who ever lived. A brave World War II POW who escaped to freedom by stealing a German plane, and a test pilot extraordinaire, the bombastic barnstormer is the giant of his profession, a combination of The Red Baron, Waldo Pepper, and Jimmy Doolittle rolled into one."

The text established Bob Hoover's credentials by feeding the reader vital information spiced with the names of famous people such as Chuck Yeager and General Doolittle. In this paragraph, I included the Tagline that would be part of the verbal pitch my agent would use to sell the book. I'm certain he told the editor who purchased the rights, "Bob Hoover is a combination of The Red Baron, Waldo Pepper, and Jimmy Doolittle rolled into one."

After providing additional facts regarding Hoover's remarkable career (winner of the Distinguished Flying Cross, Purple Heart, Lindbergh Medal), describing several life threatening situations (steering a dead-engine P-80 Shooting Star jet to safety, bailing out of a burning F-84 Thunderjet), and utilizing buzzwords to enhance his status ("embodied the very spirit of the American patriot and emerged as a bona fide American hero"), the Overview for Forever Flying backtracked to the early years of Hoover's life. The reader returned to his childhood, flying experiences at age fifteen, his entry into World War II, and his subsequent action as a fighter pilot. The text then described his capture by the Germans when his plane was shot down over the coast of Italy, the torture he endured when he wouldn't reveal Allied secrets and his incarceration in the dreaded Stalag I German prison camp.

As the tale continued, the reader discovered that Hoover stole a German plane and flew to freedom before returning to the United States where he and Chuck Yeager competed to discover who would attempt to break the sound barrier. Hoover's career as a test pilot led to his being crowned the "King of the Air Shows," a tribute to his skill as an aerobatic pilot.

The final paragraph of the Overview provided a frame of reference for Bob Hoover's importance in history. Using modern day sports figures as comparisons, it read, "R.A. 'Bob' Hoover's place in the annals of aviation history is guaranteed. Like Michael Jordan swooping in for a dunk shot from the foul line, Olympic champion Scott Hamilton carving out his gold-medal routine on the ice, or Greg Louganis performing a three-and-a-half double somersault from the pike position, Bob Hoover's incredible artistry with an airplane is an experience never to be forgotten."

The final paragraph is puffy, something normally objectionable. The rest of the Overview is fact, but I needed to provide a standard by which to judge the heroics of Hoover. Comparisons with the sports heroes of that era seemed appropriate.

For those drafting a Synopsis for a work of fiction, similar rules apply. Paragraphs one and two must be sensational because if they are not, the reader may toss the proposal aside. The opening paragraph of a Synopsis written by one of my clients was enticing. It read, "Eight-year-old Jason Twinklebean marched into the kitchen. His mother stood by the stove, the smell of turnips sweeping through the air. 'Mom, I just killed the cat,' Jason reported. 'Now there won't be fur on the couch anymore.' 'That's lovely, Jason,' the mother sighed. 'Now go do your homework.'"

The Synopsis for Moonshine Baby, Anika Weiss' book, reads in part:

> *Rufus Poisson is the Moonshine Baby. He was the boy whose shape the kids outlined in fragments of shell, china and glass on the Bahamian island of Andros in 1972. He is the death row prisoner in Baltimore who, remembering this children's game seventeen years later, decides to drop his appeals and hasten his end.*

> *Ruf's brother Ben, thin-skinned weightlifter, loner, and scholarship student at prestigious Winterbury College in Vermont, stashes his letters from prison away unread for fear that Rufus will drag him down. During orientation Ben meets Lauren Owen, another freshman, who wants to study dance, nothing else. She first fancies him for his provocative value—a black boyfriend, the perfect snub at her family—but will learn that far more than superficial attractions link Ben and her.*

> *Lauren's grandparents still live at Elmshead, the former plantation home where her father Lukas grew up. Unbeknown to the family, Lukas at seventeen produced the illegitimate heir, Rufus, in a tryst with the black maid Eleanor who wouldn't have the abortion Lukas pressed on her. Instead, she changed her name from Ellie to Nora and smuggled her biracial baby, still invisible inside her, into her marriage to Bruneau Poisson, the oyster canner turned fisherman who took her to live on Andros. On the mailboat headed to the out-island Rufus was born, and nine years later, on the island, Ben.*

*After Ellie's disappearance Lukas Owen studied to
become a mining engineer and forgot her. He married
a woman he only half-loved, and they had Lauren who,
due to her mother's migraine attacks, spent many days
of her childhood at Elmshead. On the old mansion's
grounds Lauren's grandmother Viola, haunted by guilt,
grew an unorthodox garden of nightshades, plants of
the same family as the tobacco that made the Owens
rich during slavery. Except she wanted these plants to
have a positive effect. So in the grip of early, unrecog-
nized senility she used a potion of jimsonweed to give
her granddaughter the feeling she could fly—a pesky
delusion in a budding dancer, and one Lauren will beat.*

When you complete a draft of the all-important Overview
or Synopsis, set it aside for a few days. After retrieving it, read the
material out loud, read it to a cat or dog, a lover or spouse, or a tree.
Listen to how it sounds. Then revise, revise, revise with one vital
consideration in mind: clarity—does it get the message across? Will
the literary agent or editor recognize what the book is about? Have
you proven that you can tell the story in a few pages and that you are
a professional writer who should be taken seriously?

Once these questions are answered, revise again and check
grammar and spelling. No material should ever be submitted with
"typos." Such mistakes spell doom for the aspiring writer. If an agent
or editor has to stumble over misspellings or grammatical errors, they
will toss the proposal into the trash. Consult The Elements of Style,
the Chicago Manual of Style, Grammar Report, dictionaries, and a
thesaurus. Work with determination to make your material perfect.

To ensure that the Overview and the Book Proposal are ready
for submission, consider employing a professional line editor. Like
wine, a Book Proposal should never be submitted before its time.

A common error aspiring authors or poets make is to believe
that one, two or ten drafts of the Overview or Synopsis, or for that
matter a manuscript, will suffice. The final draft of the Overview of
Forever Flying was number eighty-one.

This Overview stretched to six-and-one-half pages, double-spaced. The beginning, middle, and end were solid. The Tagline was provided. Strong buzzwords such as "hero" and "patriot," were included. The only thing missing was a guaranteed ride with Bob Hoover in his P-51! I should have added that as a possibility.

Author Biography

To provide readers with a sense of why I was the one person in the world to write a book with Bob Hoover, I provided author credentials in the Author Biography section of the Book Proposal. Included were publishing credits at the time for Down for the Count and Bury Me in a Pot Bunker, as well as USA Today writing experience.

The Author Biography should have featured aviation expertise, but my only experience was having flown in an F-4 fighter jet while investigating a story for ABC's Good Morning America. That day I sped across the sky at Nelles Air Force Base near Las Vegas. Everything was bearable until the pilot inverted the jet. My stomach disagreed with the maneuver and I vomited all over my cockpit. The puke oozed through an opening and doused the pilot in front of me as a camera captured the images. The day the program aired the segment host David Hartman nearly exploded with laughter.

Since I lacked aviation expertise, the Author Biography pointed out that the collaboration would be enhanced by my involvement because the writing would not be so technical as to prohibit non-aviators from enjoying Bob's adventures. By stating this fact, a negative was turned into a positive.

Writers touting works of fiction and poetry should provide information proving their worthiness to write about the selected subject matter. If you have been published, include the names of the publications. Mention any awards you have received, anything to show the literary agent or publisher why you are the one person in the world to write your book.

Credibility is a key. If you have written a mystery based on an unsolved murder in Ireland, mention that you have traveled there to research the facts. Give the literary agent or publisher all the ammunition you can so they realize that you are a writer to be taken seriously.

Book Audience

Publishers considering a Book Proposal will ask one basic question: Who is going to purchase the damn book? Providing a broad reader base is essential to producing hefty sales.

For Into Thin Air, the best-selling tale of brave souls who climbed Mount Everest, the potential audience included those who love mountain climbing and a good adventure story. For five-time Tour de France cycling champion Lance Armstrong's best-selling book, It's Not About The Bike, bicycle road racing fans were a sure bet to read the book. But the publisher also knew Armstrong's inspiring story would captivate those who admired his courageous battle with cancer.

If you have chosen to write fiction, it is essential to identify a broad audience. Harry Potter books attract young readers, but to the publisher's delight, older readers have flocked to the books. Those who write mysteries, children's books, Christian publications, science fiction, sports thrillers, or how-to books will list target audiences so an agent or publisher is certain who the potential reader will be.

Bob Hoover was best known as an aerobatic daredevil, but there was a wide range of potential readership for the book. To specify Forever Flying's audience, the Book Audience section of the Book Proposal read, "Forever Flying will not only be an aviation book, but also a heartwarming, inspirational tale about a great aviator and true American patriot. While the book will accurately depict over fifty years of aviation history and contain numerous aviation terms, the text will be written with the general reader in mind." Providing this information clarified that the text would not be technical and that the average knucklehead who knew nothing about aviation would enjoy the book.

Words of wisdom from Matthew Snyder, a respected book-to-film agent with Creative Artists Agency in Beverly Hills, inspired a line designed to alert an agent or publisher to another aspect of Bob Hoover's story. Matthew said, "Every good story contains a love story." With this in mind, the Book Audience section included the words, "Since Bob and Colleen Hoover have been married almost fifty years, Forever Flying will feature a great love story."

To assist the range of potential readers for the book, the Book Audience stated, "It is estimated that more than 25,000,000 people attend air show and races in North America. At the Experimental Aircraft Association Annual Flying Championships, 800,000 fans attended. Another 100,000-plus watched the National Championship of Air Racing at the Reno Air Show and Races."

Having a large "built-in" audience for a book electrifies publishers. If the book is promoted adequately, they know sales can skyrocket. This causes marketing and sales divisions to become excited about the book whether it is fiction or non-fiction.

Fiction writers may want to note a collective group of readers who will be interested in a particular genre. If the book is a work of fiction about the survival of an ancient tribe of Indians in Costa Rica, include information about clubs, associations, and publications interested in this subject.

Author Weiss provides this information in her Book Proposal for the novel Moonshine Baby. An excerpt reads:

> Moonshine Baby is an operatic, interracial family saga with poignant coincidences and touches of magic.
>
> For readers of a romantic bent, Moonshine Baby also tells two love stories. Happening twenty-six years apart, both are charged with the potency of color but in very different ways since the country has moved from anti-miscegenation laws to the careful hyphenations of political correctness.
>
> For readers who care about social issues, Moonshine Baby strives to lend a human face to people regarded as untouchables. A novel, with its means of empathy, of stepping not just into another person's shoes, but their mind and skin, might do better justice to showing what it means to schedule a man's death than a philosophical or political argument. Tolstoy put it this way: "The

business of art lies just in this,—to make that under-stood and felt which, in the form of an argument, might be incomprehensible and inaccessible..."

For readers of literary fiction, Moonshine Baby counters a currently prevailing simplistic worldview that regards good and evil, black and white as easily distinguishable entities. In vibrant prose this book shows them to be two sides of the same coin.

For readers interested in capital punishment, Moonshine Baby addresses the topic at its most thought provoking by portraying a prisoner who drops his appeals and agrees to his own death. As Governor Ryan's commu-tation of all death sentences in Illinois proves, the death penalty continues to be a controversial subject, eliciting strong feelings (and actions) among supporters as well as opponents. This novel will attract readers on the fence about the issue as well as those on either side of it.

As previously mentioned, if you are attempting to publish your memoir, remember that while the story may be important to you, family and friends, the scope of the story must be broad enough to convince a traditional publisher that it will sell on a national or, at least, regional level. Many aspiring authors and poets become distressed when their life story isn't of interest to a traditional publisher. They must recognize that if publishers released every memoir submitted regardless of sales limitations, their businesses would fail.

Similar Successful Books

Comparing a book to others that have proven successful adds a positive note to the Book Proposal. Publishers relish comparisons that validate the worthiness of a new book. They also favor books that are "the first to tell a story" within a genre that has proven successful.

With Forever Flying, the benchmark for aviation books was Yeager, Chuck Yeager's best-selling autobiography. Others listed in the Similar Successful Books section of the Book Proposal included

Tom Wolfe's The Right Stuff, Loss of Eden, a biography of Charles and Anne Morrow Lindbergh, and Men From Earth by astronaut Buzz Aldren.

Those writing fiction can point to successful books written in a certain genre. For example, if you are a lawyer writing a thriller about the inner workings of a corporate law firm, you will list The Firm as an example of a book that discovered a huge audience.

In Moonshine Baby, author Weiss provided excellent comparisons for her novel while distinguishing its merit. The section reads:

> *Thematically, Moonshine Baby resembles such works as Sister Helen Prejean's Dead Man Walking, Ernest J. Gaines's A Lesson Before Dying and Norman Mailer's The Executioner's Song. It shares their concern with the bleak realities of capital punishment and racism, but places them in a more colorful and fabulous universe.*

> *Stylistically, Moonshine Baby aspires to the vivid imagination and language of such novels as Arundhati Roy's The God of Small Things and Toni Morrison's Tar Baby, another tale of race relations set in the Caribbean. As Roy's book enters the minefield of taboo relationships in India, Moonshine Baby does the same for American and Western culture where interracial relationships still defy the norm and face enormous prejudice.*

When you compare your book with others that have been successful, you must explain why your book is unique and even better. This will stifle any comment that there are too many books being written in a particular genre.

Sources for discovering similar successful books include bookstores, Publisher's Weekly, Forthcoming Books, Books In Print, and Publisher's Trade List Annual.

Promotion Ideas

To illustrate the potential exposure for Forever Flying, a section was added to the Book Proposal titled, "Publications/Associations/

Promotion." It noted that magazines such as Aviation Weekly covered the industry and that multiple aviation groups familiar with Bob Hoover were scattered around the world.

In the Appendix to the Book Proposal, several articles were included featuring Hoover. The text discussed the enormous respect and hero status Bob enjoyed with fellow airmen.

To further stimulate interest, this section explained that Hoover was intent on promoting the book by scheduling personal appearances when requested. He would be an ambassador for the book, appearing at aviation meetings, air shows, and other gatherings of aviation buffs.

If your work is fiction, you may point out various organizations that are candidates to purchase the book. A mystery set on a submarine or affecting the stealth bomber would be a natural choice for those in the military.

In today's fast-paced internet world, social media marketing is a must. Authors must be familiar with promotion and marketing tools including websites, blogs, Facebook, Twitter, Instagram, and Tic Toc. The proposal should include a definite strategy and game plan for implementing these tools. The potential for the author to provide funds for promotion and marketing is also suggested. This may include a book trailer, one similar to that utilized for my Thomas Merton biography. The YouTube link is http://www.youtube.com/watch?v=Fm0Q5r0CnZM.

Additional Voices/Endorsements/Foreword

An important element of the Forever Flying Book Proposal was a section titled "Additional Voices To Be Featured In The Book." Bob was famous among aviation buffs, but not well known outside of it so readers of the proposal needed to know that quotes from several well-known individuals would be included. Listed were Neil Armstrong, Arnold Palmer, F. Lee Bailey, radio commentator Paul Harvey, astronauts Jim McDivitt and Wally Schirra, Barry Goldwater, actor Cliff Robertson, and Chuck Yeager. Providing a list of celebrities enhanced the marketability of the book, since these names could be utilized in any publicity and marketing materials.

If a celebrity, well-known expert, or accredited writer in a particular field related to the book has agreed to write the Foreword or an endorsement, this should be noted whether the venue is fiction or non-fiction. Securing praise from a writer who has been successfully published upgrades the potential to secure a publishing commitment. This provides credibility for the book.

Many times the endorser will ask the author to draft a sample Foreword or endorsement for review. After an interview to determine the viewpoint toward the book, complete the draft in the voice of the endorser and then forward it to him or her. Writing Forewords for Chuck Yeager, Yogi Berra, Greg Norman, and Nancy Lopez has taught me to understand the value of the endorser's busy schedule. Working with endorsers in a professional manner is the key since they do not have time to waste.

Format/Manuscript Status

Because this was a "as told to" collaboration permitting Bob Hoover to tell his life story, my audience for the Book Proposal (agent or editor) needed to know how the book would unfold. Under "Format," I wrote, "Forever Flying will be Bob Hoover's memoir. The book will be written in first person, but occasionally other voices will be introduced to provide stories and anecdotes about Bob Hoover from those who know him best."

This information was essential since Bob's achievements were so outstanding that I was afraid no one would believe they occurred. Like most courageous aviators, he was a very humble man prone to tell a story packed with danger as if it was an everyday occurrence. When I asked Bob about falling to earth in a burning F-84 Thunderjet, he described the event blandly. I forced him to elaborate and also used the voice of a fellow aviator who knew about the incident to describe the life-threatening danger he faced. This permitted the reader to be in the F-84 cockpit with Bob as the aircraft spiraled toward the desert terrain.

To update the status of the manuscript, I wrote, "Book will be completed within six weeks of contract."

Regarding Beneath the Mask of Holiness, the Thomas Merton

biography, I alerted potential editors to my intention to first chronicle Merton's life before he entered the seminary, and then focus on how the "forbidden love affair" affected his mindset. This storytelling sequence was tricky, but it provided readers with a unique perspective of Merton distinguishing it from any of the other biographies written about him.

Book To Film or Television

If your book has motion picture or television potential, provide the essential information. This adds another element for the literary agent or publisher to consider, since an additional form of revenue might exist.

Revenue would occur if your book idea is optioned for a film. The deal will be negotiated either through you as the author, your literary agent or entertainment lawyer, or a theatrical agent. Literary agents will charge 15%, theatrical agents 10%, and entertainment lawyer's hourly fees.

For Moonshine Baby, Weiss' book about a death row inmate, she provided excellent visualization regarding the book's potential to become a film. It reads:

> Picture a prisoner bowled over in the prison yard by a vision of the moon.
>
> Picture a boy drawing the island home he misses with colors from his mother's make-up kit.
>
> Picture young lovers having sex on oriental rugs in search of a flying carpet.
>
> Scenes such as these from Moonshine Baby could translate into striking footage. Moonshine Baby's visual language and rich settings—from Vermont hills to the hidden blue holes of Andros and Baltimore's gothic downtown prison—create the intoxicating atmospherics a movie needs to enchant us.

The book begins by presenting parallel and sharply contrasting worlds, a juxtaposition of the bright (Caribbean island, college town) and the bleak (Ruf's prison cell) that could be very effective in film.

Biting dialogue, the plot's death row metronome and haunting moments of sex and murder propel the story toward a rising action of revelations by domino effect. The tragedy at the core of Moonshine Baby springs from its spirited characters that could inspire powerful screen incarnations. At last, it is these characters' clashing agendas that lead to the inevitable and devastating climax of Rufus's execution. His end is given an unnerving twist: Rufus imagines himself an explorer and the gas chamber a bathysphere used for deep sea exploration. This transformation could be depicted in stunning images.

As highly acclaimed films like Monster's Ball or The Life of David Gale confirm, the death penalty is a topic filmmakers feel compelled to broach.

Book-to-film production for works of fiction and non-fiction are huge now. The book, *The Accidental Billionaires* became the film, *The Social Network*. *Water For Elephants* became a film of the same name. Past book to film examples include Sylvia Nasar's A Beautiful Mind became an Academy Award winning film. *A Civil Action*, Jonathan Harr's work of non-fiction, was an outstanding movie starring John Travolta. Several of John Grisham's novels have been adapted as was John Irving's *Cider House Rules* and *Captain Corelli's Mandolin* starring Nicholas Cage. Films based on Thomas Harris's *Red Dragon*, Robert Ludlum's *The Bourne Identity*, and Janet Fitch's *White Oleander* have excited movie fans. Additional motion picture classics based on books include *High Noon, Cool Hand Luke, The Postman Always Rings Twice, Vertigo, The Thin Red Line, Mutiny on the Bounty, Like Water For Chocolat, Seabiscuit,* and *Catch Me If You Can.*

Film studios and producers often purchase the rights to a book based on the manuscript, but if you believe the book has film potential, you will prepare a "treatment." Akin to the Overview or Synopsis included in the Book Proposal, it sets out in present tense the elements of the story. There is no set length for a treatment. Guidance as to form and substance can be found in many self-help books. A sample book-to-film treatment is included in the Appendix.

A treatment of *Miscarriage of Justice, The Jonathan Pollard Story* titled "Ghost of the Sealed Rooms," a reference to Pollard's nickname in Israel, related his story of spying for the Israelis. Providing a dramatic, visual presentation of the scenario for the film caused Twentieth Century Fox Television to option the rights to the book.

To option the rights, the film producer or studio will pay the author an upfront "advance," or "option money." This will permit them exclusive rights to the material for a designated period of time. Further options to extend the time may be included for additional payments.

The author, or his representative, will also negotiate a "back-end" profit participation based on profits when the film is produced and released. Authors are encouraged to negotiate as much "up-front money" as possible, since "creative" profit participation under Hollywood definitions oftentimes produces little revenue.

Book-to-film advances range from one dollar to millions dependent on the interest in the rights. Authors are encouraged to keep option periods to a minimum so there is flexibility if the producer is unable to produce the film. Any author whose book is considered for film should engage a savvy agent or entertainment lawyer to represent their interests.

If you are interested in writing a screenplay based on your book or other material, consider education regarding the writing mechanics and proper form required. Several courses and seminars exist including Robert McKee's Story Structure. For details regarding the form motion picture professionals expect from a screenwriter, check the website, www.finaldraft.com.

Outline

The Outline included in the Book Proposal for Forever Flying was succinct. Chapter headings included "Flying Lessons," "Escape From Stalag I," "Dogfighting Over Ohio," "Hole In The Sky," "Forty Minutes of Stark Terror," and "Japanese Masseuse Torture."

A fiction writer client provided an outline with creative chapter headings. They read, "Blind Date Prep," "Wolf-Whistle," "You Ever Heard of Rodeo Sex, Darlin?" "Wormwood Wins The Girl," and "Cyber Coitus Interruptus."

Text listed under each chapter heading provides a thumbnail sketch of the anticipated text whether the book is a work of fiction or non-fiction. Clarity is essential, since the reader must garner in a few short lines an understanding of the author's intentions. Sample outlines are included in the Book Proposal section of the Appendix.

Sample Text

The Book Proposal for long-form works of fiction or non-fiction will include at least one, and perhaps two, sample chapters from the book. This text showcases the author's talent and must be extraordinary. The author must revise, revise, and then revise some more until the material is as close to perfection as possible before submission.

For Forever Flying, I chose three chapters detailing critical events in Bob Hoover's life. They chronicled his imprisonment and heroics during World War II, an account of little-known facts regarding his participation in the breaking of the sound barrier, and his ascent to fame as the greatest aerobatic pilot in the world.

Fiction writers will include the first two to three chapters (depending on length) showcasing the uniqueness of their story. Clarity is the key, since the agents and/or publishers will base their initial opinion on an incomplete story. The hope is that they will be so enthused with the writing and your storytelling ability that they will demand a look-see at the prepared manuscript.

Poetry and children's books authors will provide samples of their work in short-form. Essayists and short story writers will do the same. Again, length is less important than quality.

Sample chapter excerpts for fiction, non-fiction, and poetry are included in the Book Proposal section of the Appendix.

Appendix

Selected photographs of Bob Hoover and several celebrities were included in the Book Proposal Appendix for Forever Flying. Among others, there were photographs of Hoover standing with fellow prisoners at the Stalag I German Prison Camp, talking with famed German aircraft designer Willy Messerschmitt, and kneeling with Chuck Yeager and the crew of the X-1 team responsible for breaking the sound barrier.

For the book Stations Along the Way, the life story of a former Hitler Youth leader who discovers self-forgiveness and redemption in the arms of Holocaust survivors, photographs of the woman from birth through adulthood were an important addition to the proposal. This was also true with several other books, including Melvin Belli, King of the Courtroom.

Photographs and illustrations will normally not be included with works of fiction, but they can be appropriate with collections of poetry. They enhance the visual nature of the book.

When listing the photographs available, be sure to discuss ownership. Obtaining the right to publish them can be expensive.

Poetry Book Proposals

There are no set rules, but poetry book publishers expect the following from an aspiring poet: A professionally written Query Letter accompanied by a Book Proposal including a Tagline describing the book in fifteen words or less, a Synopsis of the book of poetry contemplated, information about the poet, details regarding the potential book audience and marketing potential, a list of similar successful books, promotion concepts, an outline, and several sample poems. Attaching a self-addressed, stamped envelope is required. Poet's Market and other publications such as How To Publish Your Poetry by Helene Ciaravino list specific requirements for submission.

Poetry submitted should be typed, not handwritten, on fine quality, 8.5 x 11, bond paper. A paper "weight" of more than 24 is suggested. The accompanying materials will be double-spaced, but the poetry is single-spaced with double spaces between the stanzas. If you are writing non-traditional types of poetry such as free form, the layout will differ.

Proper form includes a cover page listing the title of the work, a subtitle, if any, and the name of the poet. A second page can include a few lines from the poetry to catch the eye of the literary agent or publisher. The third page begins with a Tagline specifying the theme of the poetry followed by the Synopsis, Poet Biography, Book Audience, Similar Successful Books, Promotion Concepts, an Outline if there is one, and the Poetry Excerpts. The various compartments follow one another on the pages to provide a flow to the material. An example of a Poetry Book Proposal is featured in the Appendix. It is general in nature and can be modified for alternative forms of poetry.

Most poetry publications are impressed by poems that are not too lengthy. Do not be afraid to be experimental, since uniqueness is a cherished quality. Each poem should be titled for clarity. The pages of the proposal should not be stapled or bound so copies may be made for multiple readers.

Miriam Sagan, a published poet and UCLA instructor, suggested seven tips for aspiring poets she believes are worthy in *Writer's Digest*. They include: "Line breaks should feel natural, not forced, repetition of lines with a similar number of syllables can add to free verse, the opening word of each line should be compelling: use nouns and verbs whenever possible, and ending lines should strive for maximum reader impact."

To enhance publishing opportunities, photographs or illustrations can be helpful. Many poets forward a self-published book along with the suggested new material. This can be helpful to show agents and editors the worthiness of previous work.

E-mailing of poetry Book Proposals is possible, but discouraged since a hard copy of the proposal is much more impressive. See Poet's Market for details regarding submissions.

Book Proposals for poetry chapbooks (25-50 pages) compare with those for full-length books of poetry. Potential chapbook publishers and guidelines for submission can be found in *Poet's Market*. Additional publishing alternatives are available in *The Directory of Poetry Publishers*, a Dustbooks publication. They also publish *The Directory of Small Press/Magazine Editors and Publishers*.

Regardless of whether you are submitting a Book Proposal for a full-length book or a chapbook, check publisher guidelines. Failure to do so is a death wish. Poetry publishing expert Jim Walker suggests being aware of suggested "reading periods" when publications indicate they will consider submissions. For a university publication, this may be during the school year or the summer month.

Book Proposal Magic

To maximize the opportunity to become published, the aspiring author or poet should submit a Query Letter and Book Proposal. Length of the proposal will vary, but it will seldom be more than 40 pages in length. As stated, a concise proposal of twenty to thirty pages can work to your advantage even when the agency or publisher under consideration requests that only Query Letters be submitted. If the Query Letter is sensational, the concise Book Proposal will gain attention and provide needed information about the book that cannot be specified in a one-page Query Letter.

At a high school seminar on book publishing, I listened as Marie Butler-Knight, former publisher of Alpha Books, an imprint of Penguin Group USA, discussed her interest in the following components of a Book Proposal: Topic (a story that is unique and compelling, information or instruction on a hot topic), Approach (a unique twist on a familiar story, a different way of presenting information), Market Size (how many people want this information), Author Expertise (understanding/knowledge of the subject matter, credentials), and Author Writing Ability (a fluid, coherent, readable style, effectively organized). She also mentioned Author Professionalism (willingness to take editorial suggestions and direction, ability to meet deadlines), Profit Potential (what will book cost to publish, what will it sell for, how many can be sold), and Fit For The Imprint (ability to publish this type of book, ability to promote). These are excellent suggestions any writer should pay attention to regardless of whether they are writing fiction, non-fiction, or poetry.

When your Book Proposal and Query Letter are the best they can be, forward them to a literary agent or editor at a publishing company using priority mail, Federal Express, or UPS. This indicates that you are dedicated and serious about the work and separates you from the thousands of others submitting material. Equally important, it provides you with a tracking number to make certain your package arrived.

Multiple books have been written regarding the preparation of Book Proposals. One is How To Write A Book Proposal by Michael Larsen. A book titled 1,818 Ways To Write Better and Get Published by Scott Edelstein is a competent resource as is Your Novel Proposal.

A final note regarding Book Proposals—it is imperative that each section stand alone. The writer cannot predict if a literary agent or editor will read from cover to cover or leaf through sections that are of particular interest. They may skip ahead to the Sample Chapter section first to decide if the writing has merit, or glance at the Author Biography or the Similar Successful Books material. With this in mind, write each section as if it were being submitted individually for consideration.

When the Query Letter and Book Proposal are submitted to a literary agency, any one of several people may read it. An assistant may peruse it before the intended agent receives the material. Readers are also employed by agencies. Their sole purpose is to scan Book Proposals to judge their worthiness.

The Query Letter and Book Proposal submitted to a publisher enter a hierarchy differing from company to company. At the top sits the publisher who operates as a quarterback dealing with editorial issues, as well as sales and marketing. Reporting to the publisher is the editor-in-chief to whom all of the editors report. Most publishers require that the editor-in-chief and/or the publisher sign off before a deal is finalized.

Reporting to the editor-in-chief, or the production director among larger publishing companies, is the managing editor. He or she deals with deadlines and coordinates information about the book. Reporting to the editors, or senior editors, are editorial assistants, normally young people new to the business. Any one of these people, or all of them, may read the Book Proposal before a final decision is made.

When a traditional publisher agrees to publish a book based on the Query Letter and Book Proposal, the cycle from idea to publication is complete. The accompanying chart at the end of this chapter provides a simplistic view of this process.

Whether the genre is fiction, non-fiction, or poetry, the Book Proposal, and its partner, the Query Letter, reflects the heart and soul of the book contemplated. By preparing ones that are professionally written, you boost your chances toward the ultimate goal—becoming published.

Step # 7 Summary

- Essential Book Proposal components include: Title, Tagline, Author or Poet Biography, Book Audience, Similar Successful Books, Promotion Ideas, Book To Film, Outline, and Sample Chapters or Verses.

- **Search *USA Today, Publisher's Weekly,* or the *New York Times* for best-seller lists for suggested Taglines.**

- Research the correct Book Proposal form.

- Don't boast about your book in the Book Proposal—show readers why it is outstanding and must be published.

Traditional Book Publishing Chart

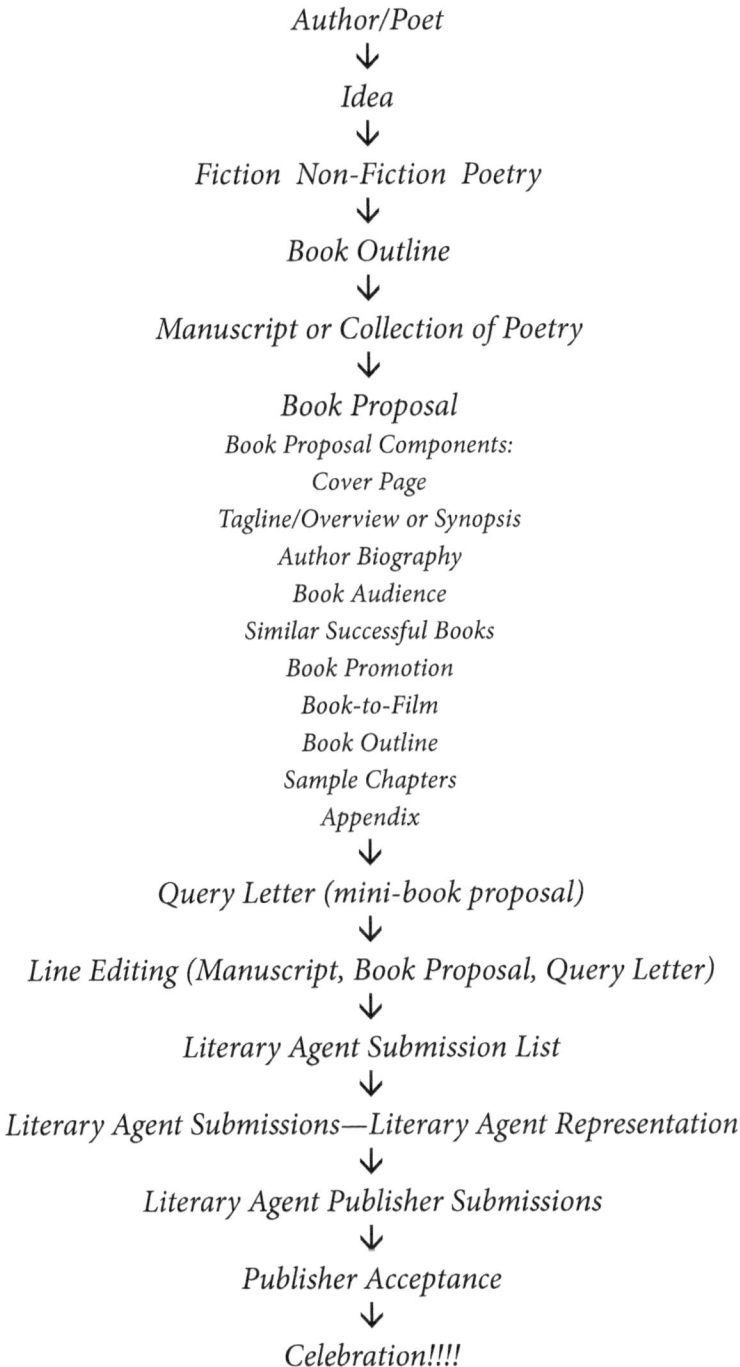

Author/Poet
↓
Idea
↓
Fiction Non-Fiction Poetry
↓
Book Outline
↓
Manuscript or Collection of Poetry
↓
Book Proposal

Book Proposal Components:
Cover Page
Tagline/Overview or Synopsis
Author Biography
Book Audience
Similar Successful Books
Book Promotion
Book-to-Film
Book Outline
Sample Chapters
Appendix
↓
Query Letter (mini-book proposal)
↓
Line Editing (Manuscript, Book Proposal, Query Letter)
↓
Literary Agent Submission List
↓
Literary Agent Submissions—Literary Agent Representation
↓
Literary Agent Publisher Submissions
↓
Publisher Acceptance
↓
Celebration!!!!

I have never known any distress that an hour's reading did not relieve.

BARON DE MONTESQUIEU

Step #8

Write A Query Letter Second To None

Query Letters

To gain the interest of literary agents and publishers, you must implement a well-founded strategy. **Since yearly submission numbers approach seven figures, you need to be creative so your book idea gains the attention of the literary agent or publisher under consideration.** This way it won't be thrown in the dreaded "slush" pile to die a slow death.

As stated, checking literary agent and publisher guidelines is the key. Remember: the material you submit is unsolicited; therefore readers will pay little or no attention unless you follow the guidelines.

Literary agents are more accessible than publishers but regardless, you must learn whether the agent or publishing company will accept only Query Letters for Fiction, Non-fiction or Poetry, Query Letters and a Synopsis or Overview, Query Letters, a Synopsis or Overview and two Sample Chapters, Query Letters accompanied by Book Proposals, or perhaps Query Letters accompanied by exhibits describing important aspects of the book. These may include media clippings describing the material being pitched or background on you.

Using Publishers Lunch is helpful once you find an agent or publisher that fits with your book, you may check their websites to discover exactly what is required and what is not permitted. If you don't follow the guidelines to a T, you risk immediate rejection.

Mastering the art of creating Query Letters is challenging since many writers are not used to this form of writing. Guidance on the proper form and substance is available through many publications such as *Writer's Market.* In addition, many literary agent and some publisher websites provide guidance for writing Query Letters

Brevity is a key—one page is suggested, no more than a page and a half in length. Literary agents or editors have no interest in leafing through an eight-page letter beginning with announcement of the author's birth and ending with a sentence touting the book as the best ever written. Several good examples of Query Letters for fiction may be discovered in Your Novel Proposal by authors Blythe Camenson and Marshall J. Cook.

Journalists Don Prues and Cindy Laufenberg provide excellent advice regarding the substance of Query Letters. In *Writer's Market,* they state, "The tone of the writing is important. Create a catchy Query with confidence but devoid of cockiness."

Remember, the Query Letter is a mini-Book Proposal. In *Your Novel Proposal,* author Cook states, "In Query letters, I look for calm professionalism. I want to know what the book is, who you are—if that's pertinent—the length and that's about it."

Authors Camenson and Cook's description of the essential elements of the Query Letter for fiction include: "The Hook, The Handle (Novel Theme), a Mini-Synopsis, Your Credentials, Your Credits, What You Are Offering, and The Closing." Substitute the word Overview for Synopsis and these elements are applicable to non-fiction or poetry letters as well.

Much of this information can be excerpted from a draft of the Book Proposal. This is why I suggest writing it first and then using information from the draft to build the foundation for the Query Letter.

Writers have informed me that working on Query Letters and Book Proposals assists them with focusing in on their book content and message. Many times, due to the need to be precise with information about the book, they have revised their manuscripts or collection of poetry.

Mention of the book tagline, a "what if" scenario, or a compelling problem requiring a solution work well in the Query Letter's opening paragraph to hook readers. Regarding author or poet credentials, it is important to explain why you are the one person in the world to write this book. Include information about the target audience, a built-in audience due to your expertise, and reference the Book Proposal where the agent and publisher guidelines do not permit you to forward one along. In that case, conclude the letter by writing, "A Book Proposal and the completed manuscript are available upon request."

Most literary agents and publishing company editors require email submissions but if you decide to send your material by snail mail, remember to include a self-addressed, stamped envelope for return correspondence. Literary agents and publishers appreciate saving the cost of the postage necessary to return the Query Letter and/or Book Proposal.

When you check the agent or publisher website, or review the page on Publishers Lunch about one of the other, pay special attention to the "book list" provided. Then you may mention any books that are similar to yours. This lets the agent or publisher know you have done your homework, that you care enough to go the extra mile.

Writing, "I believe *Roots of Evil* will appeal to the same audience as *My Son, The Tyrant*, the book you published last year," will indicate to the publishing company that you have done that homework. A similar line, "Roots of Evil weaves a similar story to that of John, The Mountain Man, the book you represented in 2002," shows the agent you have checked their website or Publishers Lunch listings.

Treat the Query Letter as a prologue to the Book Proposal when they are submitted together. Edit it thoroughly, checking spelling, grammar, and punctuation. Agents and editors will not consider the Book Proposal if the Query Letter contains multiple mistakes. An editor once told me, "The Query Letter is your three minutes to sell the book. Don't screw up."

Laurie Liss, a top agent at New York City's Harvey Klinger Agency who discovered *The Bridges of Madison County,* explains that what she seeks is "a really good, interesting Query Letter . . . What is good to me is if a letter is written really well, is grammatically correct, and lists the agent's name correctly. I need to get the impression that the writer knows what [he or she is] talking about. If you can't write a letter, how are you going to write a book?"

What makes it uninteresting, Liss states, "Is people who write, 'my mother thinks this is the best book she has ever read. I swear my mom is really smart and not biased at all.'" Including photographs apparently doesn't impress Liss. "Selfies make it [Query Letter] really unappealing too. I have never had someone who's given me a picture of themselves who could write."

Liss has other pet peeves as well. "When letters begin, 'You are going to take my book because . . .' I always turn it down. It's almost always subpar. And don't send me a Query Letter saying, 'I am the next Danielle Steel.' My reaction is, no you're not."

The Query Letter form is simple. In an email, insert "Submission for _____" in the Subject Line unless the agent or publisher guidelines suggest otherwise. If you are using snail mail, use letter-sized paper, type the date, the name, and the address of the recipient in twelve font, Times-Roman. After the greeting, (Dear Literary Agent or Editor), begin your letter. Since you only have one page or so to present your book idea, organize it in the following manner:

Fiction/Non-Fiction

- First Paragraph – F/NF – Tagline/Hook for the book
- Second Paragraph – F – Book Description (Plot, Characters, Action, Climax, Ending), NF – (Problem, Solution, other information about book)
- Third Paragraph – F/NF – Author Platform
- Fourth Paragraph –F/NF – Book Target Audience
- Fifth Paragraph – F/NF – Similar Successful Books
- Sixth Paragraph – F/NF – Promotion Ideas including Viral Marketing
- Closing Remarks – May include reference to agent author representation

A sample Query Letter regarding *Melvin Belli, King of the Courtroom*, a biography of the famous lawyer who represented Jack Ruby, provides essential information regarding the hook for the book, (use of catchy, well know phrase instead of the tagline), the gist of the text, the source of material, credibility of the author, anticipated promotion, and target audience. It read:

Dear Literary Agent,

Melvin Belli: King of the Courtroom is the first book to examine the infamous Jack Ruby case and the JFK assassination through the eyes of his attorney.

When William Shakespeare said, "The first thing we do is kill all the lawyers," he must have known that the controversial Belli would drive insurance companies and judges alike batty for more than six decades of the twentieth century.

Armed with the grizzliness of Ernest Hemingway, the wit of Will Rogers, and the legal savvy of Clarence Darrow and Edward Bennett Williams, Belli was a courtroom wizard whose celebrity reached rock star status. Noted attorney Gerry Spence calls Belli, "truly a beacon of light that showed the way."

In *Melvin Belli: King of the Courtroom,* the San Francisco barrister's colorful life renders a slice of history from the 1950s through Belli's controversial death in 1996. The Jack Ruby case, Belli's most famous, provides the spine for the book, one that chronicles famous clients such as Errol Flynn, Mae West, Martha Mitchell, Muhammad Ali, The Rolling Stones, Jim and Tammy Faye Baker, the Zodiac Killer, and mobster Mickey Cohen.

Authorized by his widow, sixth wife Nancy, this biography is written in the tradition of the author's eighteen published works, including *Miscarriage of Justice, The Jonathan Pollard Story, Down for the Count,* an inside look at the Mike Tyson case, and *Testament To Courage,* a Holocaust memoir. More information about the author, a media analyst for the Mike Tyson, O. J. Simpson, and Kobe Bryant cases, can be learned at www.markshawbooks.com.

Melvin Belli: King of the Courtroom will be appreciated by audiences familiar with the "King of Torts," *Life Magazine's* label for him, and those curious about Belli's representation of Ruby, who shot Oswald in the only live broadcast of a murder in television history. Probing the question as to whether the great lawyer may have been hired by the Mafia to discredit, and in effect, silence Oswald's assassin, provides a fresh look at the case.

Numerous promotion opportunities for the book exist through the noted Belli Society, ten thousand strong, and media outlets familiar with the Belli legacy. Promotion will also occur based on several viral marketing opportunities open to the author including website, blog, Facebook, Twitter, newsletter and the potential to fund a book trailer.

Thank you for consideration of the enclosed book proposal. A completed manuscript is available upon request.

Best,
Mark Shaw

For Anika Weiss' winning entry in the fiction category of the $25,000 John T. Lupton "New Voices In Literature" Books for Life Foundation Award, she chose the following tagline to open her Query Letter: "Lauren Owen, only child of a Maryland family of former plantation owners, has always wanted a big brother, if only so he would carry the brunt of that bothersome heritage. As it is, she has one. Her brother is black, and lives on death row."

Michael Boxall, the winner in the non-fiction category, utilized a clever strategy in the first line of his Query Letter. It read, *"Driven by Desire: Sex and the Spread of the New Media* is the first book to trace the rise of the increasingly intimate relationship between sex and the new forms of communications technology."

As stated, the Query Letter for a work of fiction will focus on the plot, the characters, the author's credentials, and the target audience. One written for the novel, Purple Angel, reads as follows:

Dear Literary Agent,

What if Guy Macker, a disgruntled law professor, is forced to defend his pregnant girlfriend for a murder he knows for certain she did not commit?

This scenario sets the stage for Purple Angel, a mystery set on the Harvard University campus. Macker's representation of Roxanne Allworth, the vivacious daughter of a Wall Street powerbroker, vaults him into the real world of the criminal justice system. Prosecutors, suspicious of the professor's involvement, investigate his background discovering a past history of mental illness.

When prosecutors threaten to expose Macker and destroy his career, he must decide whether to save Roxanne, pregnant with his child, or leave campus. Determined to fight, he gains an acquittal for her by acknowledging his participation in the murder.

The author is a former criminal defense attorney whose short stories have been featured in several magazines including Esquire and Gentleman's Quarterly. One of them is the basis for this novel. Promotional opportunities exist due to the author's exposure through the lecture circuit and his appearances on CNN as a legal analyst. To enhance promotion for the book, various viral marketing opportunities will be considered including a book trailer.

The target audience for Purple Angel is anyone who loves a good mystery story. Since you represented Gone Too Far, a bestseller by Harry Reasoner, Purple Angel should be of interest to you.

Thank you for considering the enclosed Book Proposal. I look forward to hearing from you soon.

Best,
Dr. Jerry Bales

Reaction to any Query Letter and accompanying Book Proposal will vary, but remember that it only takes one literary agent or publisher to say "yes." If they do, regardless of a multitude of "no's," your long hours of hard work and perseverance will be worthwhile.

The Poetry Query Letter

Poets attempting to excite literary agents or publishing companies (submitting to publishers is more advisable for poets than fiction or non-fiction writers), regarding their work must write a better-than-best Query Letter. Since there are thousands upon thousands of poetry submissions, poets must write outstanding prose to describe the poetry they have written. Again, the letter should be no more than one page written on 8.5 x 11 inch paper.

Begin the letter with a sentence that will captivate the reader. Use a Tagline (the hook for your book) to pinpoint the theme of the poetry and then provide titillating information designed to make readers say, "I must read the collection of poetry."

Paragraphs two and three of the Query Letter expand upon the theme of the material. Once there is a clear description, offer biographical material that illustrates why, just as with the aspiring author, you are the one best person in the world to write poetry on this theme. Inclusion of publishing credentials is critical as is information on built-in audience for the book. Comparisons to famous poets regarding style and content can be helpful. If you believe your book is similar to one represented by the agency or publisher you are contacting, note the name of the book. This will show the agent or publishing company you have researched their recent books.

As with all writing, clarity, brevity, good word choice, and excellent sentence structure is essential. Any agent or editor questioning the writing ability of a prospective poet will wonder if he or she is a competent wordsmith when writing poetry.

Arrogance must be absent from any competent Query Letter. Lines such as "People say that I am the next Billy Collins or Maya Angelou" will cause instant death to any chances to be published. Be humble while showing the editor that you believe in yourself and possess a fresh voice that must be heard.

Within the letter, provide readers with exact information as to why your poetry is perfect for representation or publication. Once again the goal should be obvious: you want the agent or editor to say, "I must represent or publish this material or someone else will and it will be a huge success and I will be sorry."

In the final paragraph of the Query Letter, explain that besides the poetry submitted, there is additional material to be read upon request. Then thank the editor for their consideration and close with something akin to "Yours truly."

Above all, be certain the person you are writing to is still employed at the agency or publishing company. There is nothing more embarrassing than writing a letter to a former employee.

The Query Letter for a collection of poetry titled, Columbus Was Wrong, reads as follows:

Dear Editor,

Is the world still round, or were the ancient naysayers correct? Answers to that question and more are explored in a new collection of poetry I have written titled, *Columbus Was Wrong.*

Ten poems are included with this letter. Among them are: Flat or Round, Who's To Say, Christopher Was A Baboon, Not An Explorer, The New World or The Old One, and Gold Blinds Us.

The poet's perspective on these issues has been formed from extensive travel throughout the world. During a recent trip to southern Italy, the current collection was created after intensive investigation of Columbus' true mission when he assaulted the new world. The poet believes she is the first to offer through her poetry significant evidence that Columbus' name was actually O'Reilly and that he never set foot on Italian soil.

The audience for *Columbus Was Wrong* includes those fascinated with Christopher Columbus, as well as the historical significance of the discovery of America. Similar works regarding whether men walked on the moon, why Charles Lindbergh did not cross the Atlantic, and how mankind has been hoodwinked into believing global warming threatens our very existence have been published in *Poets Of The Far East, Art Bell's Collection of Serious Poetry, and Dubsdread's Odd Poets of the Twentieth Century.*

Thank you for considering the enclosed book proposal. Further samples of the poetry are available upon request.

Thank you.
Best,
Olathobal Moffit

Query letters are the key to unlocking the door of the publishing industry. Cleverly written with an eye toward exciting the reader, they operate as your invitation to those you hope will share your passion for the subject matter of the book. Strong words and visual images optimize your chances that a literary agent or editor will say, "I must read the book proposal," a second step toward gaining a publishing commitment.

Step #8 Summary

- Literary Agents and Publishers will not read manuscripts or extensive poetry collections from an unpublished author or poet.
- Literary Agents or Publishers expect to receive professionally written Query Letters and/or Book Proposals.
- A Query Letter should be concise and targeted to hook the reader on the book concept.
- The essential elements of the query letter are Tagline, Mini-Synopsis or Mini Overview, Mini-Author Biography, Book Audience, and Promotion Ideas

It is with books as it is with men, a very small number play a great part, the rest are lost in the multitude.

———

VOLTAIRE

Step #9

Book Promotion and Marketing Campaigns

The book has been written. The publishing deal is completed. The champagne celebration has produced a hangover the size of Ted Turner's Montana ranch because the long-awaited book is being released.

So what now? Should you sit back and watch your publisher do all the work to promote the book? Is it time for a vacation to the French Riviera to frolic on the shores of the Mediterranean?

The answer, of course, is "no," since the real work to promote the book has just begun. Regardless of whether the publisher is large, medium-sized or small, or the book is being traditionally self-published, you are expected to do your part concerning promotion, promotion, and more promotion. This means developing a professional book promotion and marketing campaign designed to let the world know about the release of your book.

If a traditional publisher has released the book, there will be author or poet obligations regarding publicity. Book promotion clauses are common in most publishing contracts. They focus on what is expected of the author or poet and what is expected of the publisher when the book is released.

Without sufficient promotion, chances for success are doomed. The extent of the publicity and marketing program will depend on the size of the publisher releasing the book and the perceived importance of the book in the publisher's overall list. Having a major publisher release your book is worthy, but this does not guarantee an extensive promotional campaign. While negotiation is occurring, be certain to learn of the publishing company's commitment to promotion. This factor may be as important as the dollar amount of any advance being provided to you.

If there is a strong commitment to a promotion campaign, the publishing company will assign an expert in this field to coordinate the effort. The campaign may include a nationwide tour featuring television, radio, and print opportunities. Most likely, it will include various social media alternatives including website, blog, Facebook, Twitter and the like. A book trailer may also be provided. The one I provided for *The Reporter Who Knew Too Much* may be watched at https://www.youtube.com/watch?v=_3j496U8ejA.

Medium-sized and smaller publishers' commitment to promotion will vary. They may or may not employ in-house experts to deal with publicity. Yours will depend on what is expected of you in tandem with efforts by the publisher.

Medium-sized and smaller publishers without an in-house promotion or publicity department rely on free-lance book promoters. These experts are hired on a project-by-project basis to expose the book to the media. Campaigns vary in cost depending on whether they involve print, radio, television or a combination of all three.

The publishing contract should contain specific language regarding the extent and length of the campaign and who is responsible for the cost. You may be required to expend funds to promote the book. If so, a clause should be included in the contract providing for this likelihood.

If you are willing to fund publicity or a promotion campaign for your book, consider noting this in the Query Letter and Book Proposal. Doing so may make a difference between a "yes" and a "no."

Regarding the specifics of the promotion and marketing campaign, various tools are available to assist the effort. These include your website, use of Facebook, Twitter, Linked In, Tik Tok, Instagram, a blog, and perhaps a video of you speaking about your book. All of this may be featured on what has been dubbed a "landing page" where potential readers of the book can learn more about all aspects of the book. The landing page may also contain positive reviews of the book, an outline with chapter headings and a short description of the text, biographical information about the book, and a link to the publisher website as well as Amazon.com, Barnes&Noble.com. and other sales outlets. An example of a landing page for *The Poison Patriarch* is at www.markshawbooks.com.

Use of the landing page, your marketing foundation for your book, will be linked to the various promotion tools available to you. One is book signings.

Book Signings

In recent years, the occurrence of book signings has dwindled with the disappearance of many independent bookstores. Also, some stores decline author's request to appear unless he, or she, can guarantee a certain number of attendees. There are even stores that now charge a fee for people to attend a book signing.

Regardless, when possible, book signings provide an opportunity for authors to meet the public and sell books. Major publishers will coordinate the appearances. Medium-sized and smaller publishers may assist, but the author or poet will assume an active role with scheduling.

The publishing contract should clarify respective roles and provide guidelines for book signing promotion, since it is essential to success. At least three months before the event, a coordinated campaign involving the author, the bookstore, and the publisher should be planned. Storefront signs and signs in the store are critical as is the announcement of the book signing in print publications and on radio and television.

Book signings must be strategically planned. Competition from other local events can impede success. Research newspaper and magazine calendar sections to discover competing events that may draw potential customers away. Discussing the best day and time for your book signing with the bookstore owner is essential. Some stores are "dead" on the weeknights; others flourish. Weather may play a part regarding scheduling. During the winter, few customers flock to book stores when there is five feet of snow on the ground. Summer months can be terrific weather-wise, but when the weather is too good, customers will stay away from their favorite bookstores.

Book signings during seasonal holidays can be advantageous.

Books are great gifts for Christmas, Mother's Day, Father's Day, and Valentine's Day.

Mall bookstore signings can be terrific since there is normally a steady stream of customers walking about. Coordinating a book signing during peak hours is advisable.

For *Larry Legend*, my biography of NBA superstar Larry Bird, the publishing company arranged appearances at an unlikely venue: grocery stores. On one occasion I chuckled after being seated next to the frozen food section across from a sign reading, "Frozen Flounder, $1.99 a pound, Larry Legend $24.95."

No matter where the book signing is held, you should feel proud when your book is purchased. Thank buyers and take the time to sign the book with a personal greeting they will appreciate.

When *Testament To Courage* was purchased, I wrote, "May Cecelia's Words Inspire You," a reference to Cecelia Rexin's undying courage during the Holocaust. For youngsters whose parents bought *Larry Legend*, I wrote a message conveying how hard work and dedication helped Bird achieve success. With *The Perfect Yankee*, I wrote, "Don Larsen's achievement proves miracles do occur." For *Miscarriage of Justice*, I quoted Martin Luther King. The message read, "Injustice anywhere is a threat to justice everywhere."

Self-publishing guru Dan Poynter suggested authors and poets consider holding mini-seminars instead of book signings. In a Writer's Digest article, he quotes Teri Lonier, author of *Working Solo*. She stated, "An autograph party says, 'Come and appreciate me and buy a book;' a seminar says, 'Come on down, and I will give you something for free that will improve your life.'" Poynter and Lonier agree that it is important to think of "the potential benefit to the customer. How can you lure them out of the house and down to the store?"

Author Beth Crawford, a working mother, has been successful with sales of her novel through a unique approach. After she wrote *Silent Storm* and decided to self-publish it, Beth discovered the high cost of printing. Determined to continue, she and her husband purchased an inexpensive printing machine to print the book. When she became proficient at the process, Beth began promoting her novel in connection with seminars about the printing procedure. She presents a fifteen-minute speech about printing and then reads from her book. Beth also traveled throughout her home state before the release date of her book to meet people at bookstores and libraries. The result has been numerous appearances and successful sales of *Silent Storm*.

When you appear at the book signing or seminar, remember people love stories. They may be interested in the ones featured in the book, how you decided to write it, or the research tools employed. The more entertaining you are, the greater the chances you will sell your books.

Promotion Ideas

If the publishing company funds the promotional campaign, you will gain needed exposure. If the publishing company cannot fund the campaign, or if you are self-published, consider expending funds to cover promotional costs. Outstanding public relations companies exist, but make certain they specialize in book promotion. Ask for references and copies of public relations campaigns they have designed for other authors or poets.

Regardless of who is funding the promotional campaign, you must be clever to promote the book through any means possible. The saying, "The Lord helps those who help themselves," is most appropriate. Once again, this includes social media, the key to book promotion and marketing in the 21st century.

One author who splashed onto the national scene through self-promotion was Terry McMillan. When *Mama*, her first novel was published in 1987, she handled the marketing and promotion for her book. She forwarded hundreds of letters to African-American organizations requesting them to promote the book.

McMillan contacted bookstores with requests for book signings. Her efforts resulted in appearances and readings across the country. Mama was a moderate success, but when *Disappearing Acts*, her second book, was released, additional recognition occurred. In 1992, *Waiting To Exhale* became a bestseller. Four years later, *How Stella Got Her Groove Back* proved McMillan, the self-promoter, was a literary star.

To circulate interest about your book, keep an "address book" in your Word documents listing every friend and acquaintance since childhood. When book signings or other promotional appearances are scheduled, mail invitations to everyone in the area you know. You will form a group of loyal readers who will purchase future books.

Free publicity is the author or poet's best friend. Convince magazines or newspaper editors to print an excerpt from the book. To gain exposure, telephone radio shows, contact libraries to schedule readings, and work through local writer's centers. Public speaking also provides the opportunity to promote the book.

Author or poet Internet websites are a must in the twenty-first century. Designing them has become an art form, and there are multiple companies available to assist the writer. How fancy the site is depends on your pocketbook, but you can promote your book online to enhance sales opportunities.

Publicizing a traditionally self-published book not yet in the bookstores on online is the kiss of death. If buyers interested in the book based on media exposure visit the store or a website and the book is unavailable, chances are they will not buy it later one. Make certain the publisher and the bookstores coordinate stocking the book at least a month before the promotional campaign begins. If you decide to self-publish, consider handling the matter yourself.

Double-checking everything about your book signing is essential until the day it occurs. Make sure media exposure is secure and check the store a week or two before your book signing to see if posters are on the front window and displayed throughout the store. Most bookstores employ "community relations" managers to handle book signings, but they have many other duties. Good communication is a key to assurance that your book signing will be a success.

Regardless of how many books you sell at the book signing, request the opportunity, if it is not offered, to sign multiple books to be stocked in the store. Most stores do this as a courtesy, but publishers relish this opportunity since a signed book cannot be returned to them. This also applies to self-published authors or poets guaranteeing that you will be paid for the books left at the store.

If you are self-published, negotiate your share of the cover price with the bookstore. Splitting the revenue is fair, but many stores will permit you to keep as much as 70 percent.

If you appear for a book signing at a library or not-for-profit organization, consider donating a portion of the cover price. This promotes goodwill.

Book Promotion References

Several worthy publications will help you better understand book promotion. One is the updated *The Complete Guide To Book Publicity,* written by Jodee Blanco, a seasoned professional who is also an expert on self-publishing. Using the tips she includes in her book can be very worthwhile. One discourages authors from mentioning their book more than once or twice during an interview. Another discusses what to wear for television appearances.

Blanco suggests that authors or poets write a book with promotion in mind. She believes that to successfully expose the book to the reading public, there must be a "promotional" tone, one signaling to the media that the book is timely and important. Integrating an issue or cause into the story permits a built-in promotional package. This permits a hook for the author or poet, the publisher, and the public relations firm representing the book.

Blanco's advice is questioned by those who believe a writer must write true to their heart and not with commercialism in mind. This "one or the other" stance fails to recognize that one can do both. Many authors or poets believing in an issue or cause convey their feelings while keeping an eye open toward promotion. As long as they don't sacrifice their beliefs, they are being true to themselves, as well as being practical.

Promotional ideas must be considered in light of expense and coverage. Make certain you are targeting the right audience for your book. Spend money wisely to reach the largest group of people who will be interested in the type of book you have written. Be creative and you will be amazed at the amount of publicity you can generate for your book.

Learning From Others

Masters of book promotion include the *Chicken Soup* authors Jack Canfield and Mark Victor Hansen. Millions of their books have been sold worldwide and Canfield believes he knows the reason why.

The co-author attributes his success to good, old-fashioned research. He told *Writer's Digest*, "I read every book I could on how to market books. It's something you have to study. It's something you have to make as important as the craft of writing."

Canfield's interview revealed other jewels of information that can assist an author or poet. He said, "Spend 90 percent of your time after your book comes out selling, marketing, and self-promoting."

Canfield suggested creative methods involving marketing and self-promotion. He gave away free books to potential reviewers and the public at large while creating a web site where excerpts from the books could be downloaded at no cost. He promised to give a percentage of the retail price of the book to a charitable organization. Doing so, he said, "Created a buzz about the books."

Lessons learned from authors like Jack Canfield are essential to the continual learning process. They provide inspiration, as well as a proven game plan for success.

One strategy successful authors and poets employ is to provide free readings at libraries, high schools, colleges, and universities. Invite the media to such events as well as those who will be interested in the book topic. Canfield and others realize those attending may tell others about the book, creating an interest. Encouraging supporters to contact bookstores about the book may assist efforts to place the book there.

An avenue open to authors or poets self-publishing their book is the Internet bookstore. As stated, Amazon.com provides an "Advantage" program. It permits the author or poet, under guidelines posted on the website, to sell their book to the public. This permits wide exposure for the book especially if readers post positive reviews of the book. Asking friends and family or others who praise the book to post their review is proper. This builds credentials for the book to those who check the website.

Building A Career

Book promotion is an important component to building a professional writing career. The goal is to create interest in both the current book and the next one. To this end, remember to act like a professional when dealing with those who take the time to visit a bookstore, chat about the book, and purchase one. Keep a mailing list in your Word documents so you can advise them of the next book being released.

Continued contact with the bookstores is important as well. Many authors and poets send "thank you" notes to the manager after an appearance. When the author or poet is ready for another appearance, the manager will recall the good manners with a smile.

Another means of promoting your book is to issue a newsletter every month or so beginning about three months before the book is published. That has proven very successful regarding all of my books with my having accumulated more than 4000 email addresses. Each time a book is published, we use these addresses to provide news about the new book.

Publishers take note of how their authors and poets handle public appearances. The writer may or may not be interested in securing the same publisher for the next book, but don't gain a reputation as someone who is difficult. The book publishing industry is small and a bad reputation with regard to promotion can impede chances regarding the next book and the next.

Above all, be proud of your book. From nothing but an idea, you have produced a bound book presenting your message to the world. Shout "hooray" and enjoy the experience.

Step #9 Summary

- Authors are expected to cooperate with a traditional publisher regarding the promotion and marketing program for their book

- Authors should consider all aspects of the program including use of a website, blog, Facebook, Twitter, Linked In and other social media promotion tools. Also consider sending out a newsletter to promote new books, etc.

- Creating a "landing page" where prospective readers can learn more about the book should be considered. This will be the home base for the book promotion and marketing campaign

- Authors should research all aspects of promotion and marketing campaigns to educate themselves about the various means of exposing their book to the reading public.

People say life is the thing, but I prefer reading.

LOGAN PEARSHELL SMITH

Step #10

Book Contracts
Protecting Your Literary Legal Rights

Book Contract Terms – Literary Agencies

When a literary agent offers you a contract, seriously consider having an entertainment attorney review it. This will ensure that you are protected even though most agency agreements feature standard clauses.

These include authorizing the agent to act in your behalf regarding worldwide rights to the book, permitting them to solicit offers for the rights to the book from various publishers, and the right to represent you with your next book. In return for their services, the contract will specify their retention of 15% of your earnings from the book based on any advance offered by the publisher and royalties from domestic sales (20% for foreign).

If possible, be certain to restrict the agent's representation to no more than your current book and the next one. Tying yourself to the agent for an extended period of time may prohibit your switching agents in the future. Also watch the expenses section of the agreement to make certain that you are only being charged for incidental costs (copying, mailings, etc.) for promotion of the book to publishers. If possible, put a cap on the amount that may be spent without your written authority.

As stated before, under no circumstances will you pay the agent for reading fees or to represent you. If he or she demands same, say thank you and move on.

An example of a literary agent agreement is featured in the Appendix. Your agreement may differ, but the sample will permit you to understand a basic contract.

Book Contract Terms – Publishers

The literary rights transferred (the Copyright Act requires any and all transfers to be in writing) from the author or poet to a publisher will vary with each book. A sample publishing agreement with tips is featured in the Appendix.

Most publishing contracts contain standard language. Terms are negotiated, but publishers are less likely to be flexible when a first-time author or poet is involved. Remember that the most important thing is to be published, and if there is no advance and the royalties are minimal, so be it. You can look forward to earning revenue on a future book.

Rights extended to a publishing company can include the English speaking countries, specific territories, or the world. If possible, transfer as few rights as possible depending on the advance offered by the publisher. Domestic rights and foreign rights can be separated or negotiated together. If you do not have an agent, seek advice from an entertainment attorney.

Publishers will normally access literary rights to the hardcover (cloth) edition of the book, paperback rights, eBook rights, audio rights and so forth. Reserve the motion picture and television rights if possible. Owning them, as mentioned earlier, can be worth substantial revenue at a later date, provided the work is appropriate for being adapted to the big or small screen. If a film or television producer expresses interest in those rights, contact an entertainment attorney.

Revisions

Special attention must be paid to the "Revisions" clause of any publishing contract. Working with an editor at the publishing company, you will revise the manuscript in preparation for release.

Each draft will be reviewed, but at some point, the publisher will okay the revisions. If you then decide to revise once again, the "Revisions" clause may dictate that you pay for costs incurred by the publisher to make the changes. To avoid this cost, attempt to negotiate an agreement absent this provision.

For certain types of non-fiction books, the word "revision" may mean something totally different, namely the preparation of a new, revised edition of the book. This would occur after a period of time, assuming that the book contains information that needs to be updated periodically. Including a clause in the contract that guarantees you will be hired to provide updates or make revisions is suggested.

Photographs/ Quotes

Obtaining the rights to book photographs may be expensive. *The AP (Associated Press), Reuters,* and other outlets such as stock photograph houses charge expensive fees. Many publishers assume the cost, but you should check the "Photographs" provision to make certain you are not responsible.

If photographs are an essential part of the text of the book, you are generally held responsible for securing permissions to use the photographs. The cost of obtaining permission may be included with the advance paid by the publisher. Publishers normally always pay for cover or jacket photographs.

Fees charged for photographs utilized in an "insert" section of the book are not as expensive as those proposed for the front or back jacket covers. If possible you, your agent, or your attorney should attempt to gain the rights to use the photographs for both the hardcover and anticipated paperback editions of the book.

A publishing agreement should specify the party responsible for costs if you are requested to take photographs. Camera and film expense can escalate.

If you self-publish, make certain you have the right to use photographs. A simple "release agreement" can be drafted to protect your interests.

Approval to use quotes from other printed material can be garnered through similar agreements. If you use quotes sparingly, provide the source of the quote and a mention in the bibliography. If you intend to use more than a few sentences of text at a time, a release from the author, poet, and their publisher may be required.

Free Books/Purchased Books

Publishers provide the author or poet with free books. The number will vary. They may be sold or given to friends and family.

You may purchase books from the publisher at a discount. It ranges from 40 to 55 percent. Many companies will invoice you; others require a credit card at the time of purchase.

Self-published authors and poets are free to distribute free books as they wish. Keep track of the number given away for tax purposes.

Next Book

Most publishers will include a "Next Book" clause in the publishing contract. Having invested their resources in your book, they expect you to be loyal. To guarantee this occurs, language is drafted requiring you to submit any material for a new book to the publisher. They then have a set amount of time to consider the book idea. If they decide to commit, a new agreement is negotiated in good faith. If they pass, you are free to submit the material to other publishers.

Demand that language inserted provides the publisher with "a right of first refusal based on fair negotiation." It requires the publisher to commit or pass within a short period of time.

If you self-publish and decide to employ an independent distributor to handle release of your book, be certain to restrict the representation to one book. This will permit you to seek other outlets if you are not satisfied with distributor performance.

Final Approvals

Attempt to gain final approval of title, subtitle, size and placement of cover print, front and back cover photograph or illustration, book text, author jacket biography and photograph, the photograph insert, font size and print style, and appendix materials. This may be difficult to gain, but discuss these details with the publisher or have your agent or attorney do so.

A clause ensuring no revisions will be made to any aspect of the book after you have "signed-off" is advisable. This guarantees that no editor at the publishing company will alter the text prior to the book being forwarded to the printer.

When possible, require the publisher to designate the release date for the book. Many publishers include a clause providing their right to publish the book within eighteen months of the time a final manuscript is approved. Shorten the time if you can. This is especially important if the book is tied to an anniversary or event that will provide free publicity for the book.

If you self-publish, provide enough time from the date you receive your completed book from the printer to the release date. Allow sufficient time for delivery of the book to outlets before your publicity campaign begins. Proper planning will guarantee that your book is released with a professional tone.

Important Book Contract Factors

In addition to the issues discussed above, the book publishing agreement should address the following issues:

- » The agreed-upon length of the manuscript (flexibility is important)
- » Manuscript or poetry collection delivery deadlines
- » Royalty amounts (attempt to gain a "gross" definition)
- » Royalty statement dates (quarterly basis)
- » "Reserve account" amounts (publishers retain a certain percentage of revenue to cover cost of returns)
- » The agency commission clause (normally 15 percent, 10 percent for television/film agents)
- » Author or poet's right to audit (every six months)
- » Out-of-print provisions (rights revert to author if the book is out of print for a specified period of time)
- » Dispute resolution clause (arbitration alternatives may be advisable)
- » Literary agents and/or entertainment attorneys can advise you regarding these matters.

References

Several reference books exist regarding protection of author's or poet's rights. Among them is Kirsch's Guide to the Book Contract: For Authors, Publishers, Editors, and Agents.

Jonathan Kirsch's book is helpful, but you are encouraged to seek advice from competent literary agents or entertainment attorneys. This guarantees that you will abide by Mark's Step #10. When Considering A Book Contract, Watch Your Backside.

Step #10 Summary

- Remember the essential elements of a publishing contract— length of manuscript or collection of poetry, revisions, photographs, free books, purchased books, next book, final approvals, and delivery date.

- Obtain professional advice through a literary agent or entertainment attorney regarding agency or publishing contracts.

- **Consult** *Kirsch's Guide to the Book Contract.*

Epilogue

How to Become a Published Author: "Idea to Publication" has presented one author's perception regarding the art of writing, the state of the publishing industry, and the opportunities for aspiring authors and poets to be published. I trust the ideas presented have caused you to recall the promise you repeated at the beginning of the book—**I Will Be Published!**

Dedication to this goal is critical for any aspiring author who dreams of being published. I know this from experience. Besides several photographs of Ernest Hemingway and ones of Jack Kerouac and Thomas Merton, my writing studio is speckled with a collection of work-in-progress manuscripts. Whether they will ever be read by anyone other than me and my wife remains to be seen.

These millions of words represent countless hours of writing and rewriting. There is no substitute for experience. This is especially true of the wordsmith's craft.

Once you have honed your skills and polished your text to a level of professionalism, test the marketplace. As noted, this requires submitting Query Letters and/or Book Proposals to selected literary agents and publishers.

Many writers are reticent to try traditional publishing. An aspiring author on the West Coast studied the craft for eight years. He attended several writers' conferences and workshops. For two years, he worked with a writing group. During that time, he wrote several unfinished manuscripts, one totaling more than 1,500 pages. Despite this accomplishment and the fact that he was a gifted storyteller, he was reluctant to test his material with literary agents or publishers.

The writer suffered from a dreaded disease I call "Rejectionitis." A common illness of many who are afraid to have someone say "no" to their idea or concept, it runs rampant within the world of the writer. Symptoms include long faces, slightly damaged keyboards, and stacks of yellowed paper.

To combat Rejectionitis, writers must develop skin as thick as an armadillo's and remember one single fact – Rejection Is Not Part Of A Writer's Vocabulary.

Irwin Shaw (*The Young Lions*) was immune to rejection. He wrote, "Failure is inevitable for the writer. Any writer. I don't care who he or she is, or how great he or she is, or what he or she has written. Sooner or later, they are going to flop and everybody who admired them will try to write them off as a bum." Albert Einstein wrote, "Great spirits have always encountered violent opposition from mediocre minds." This does not mean criticism may be ignored. Don't forget that Ernest Hemingway said of writers, "We are all apprentices in a craft where no one ever becomes a master."

You can avoid criticism and rejection by never submitting work for publication. Your life will be filled with smiles, pretty days, and walks in the park. Nothing you have written will ever be read by the outside world, nothing you have written will produce a laugh or a tear from a reader, and nothing you write will ever make a difference by causing people to stop and think. But you will keep your sanity and the satisfaction of never having been stung by rejection or a bad review.

If you choose to take a risk, know that you will encounter rejection at one time or another. In the publishing industry, it is a way of life. Pearl Buck, author of the classic, The Good Earth and seventy other novels, received a rejection letter regarding submission of a short story to a magazine the very week in 1935 when she was awarded the Nobel Prize for Literature.

As mentioned, those who don't try, never succeed. Actor/producer/director/writer Woody Allen believes rejection is an essential part of the human existence. He wrote, "If you're not failing now and again, it means you are playing it safe." An old Japanese proverb states, "Fall seven times, stand up eight."

Believing in yourself and in the Good Lord's plan for you is essential. Lessons learned from Noah can be helpful since he symbolizes what it means to have faith. When God asked him to build the ark to withstand a flood, Noah did not hesitate even though he had never seen rain, lived hundreds of miles from the nearest ocean, and had no way to transport it to the nearest ocean. Regardless, he had faith and trusted God's word. You must do the same if you believe strongly in your book idea, one that is morally right.

Attempts to persuade agents and publishers that my first book, Down for the Count, was worthy produced an excess of emotions. Utilizing a "help book," I compiled a list of prospective agents and publishers. I then forwarded the manuscript (I did not know about Book Proposals) to several agents and publishers.

Each day at noon, after completing the writing assignment for the day, I packed my dogs in "Big Blue" (an old Ford truck), and headed to downtown Nashville, Indiana. With a spirited walk, I stepped into the post office and walked to P.O. Box 787. When I noticed a long yellow card requiring a trip to the postal counter, I knew one or more of the manuscripts had been returned. Since there had been no telephone call offering me agent representation or a publishing commitment, I concluded that the material had been rejected.

After retrieving the manuscript from its packing, I glanced at the accompanying letter. To counter disappointment, I immediately placed the manuscript in a new package pre-addressed to another literary agent or publisher. Inside was a fresh Query Letter describing the book. I then mailed the same material to a new source in search of a "yes" instead of a "no."

Maintaining a positive attitude is critical to moving forward. There is nothing we can do about past experiences but learn from them. As I used to tell listeners of my radio program, "Keep the faith, you never know when there is a miracle right around the corner."

For me, taking a pre-addressed package to the post office worked the same way. Instead of dwelling on the negative response to the manuscript, I forwarded it to another source in search of success. Same goes with emailed material; get a rejection, move ahead with more submissions. This attitude is symbolic of an essential characteristic for writers: never giving up, preserver for those who do are the ones that become published.

If you choose to explore the world of traditional publishing, focus on securing a literary agent. From the "usual suspects" list compiled from your research, choose those most likely to have interest. Forward the Query Letter and/or Book Proposal to them.

If you do not receive a response in three-four weeks, telephone the agency for an update. Be inquisitive, but not intrusive. Explain the reason for the contact and request an update. Five in circulation at a time maximizes the potential for results.

If no literary agent responds positively, consider contacting publishers while realizing that many do not permit un-agented submissions. A better idea may be to pursue a new book idea and decide that the previous one may be the second book you publish.

If you decide to contact publishers, peruse the list you have compiled through your research. Forward five submissions to selected editors. Wait three-four weeks and telephone for an update.

Be persistent, but not pushy. Patience is the byword.

A sample Agency-Publisher Submission Record is provided in the Appendix. Keeping good records allows you to track submissions. The listings may also be helpful with future books. Note agents or editors who have rejected material, but requested a look-see at future works.

It is not necessary to do so, but after receiving a rejection letter, consider responding with a note of appreciation for the consideration shown by the agent or editor at the publishing company. When a future submission is made, the agent or editor will remember the common courtesy.

When submitted material is not returned, many writers want to scream, "That's not fair." Instead, remember that the agent or publisher did not request submission of the Book Proposal and/or manuscript and have no duty to return it. Many Book Proposals and/or manuscripts fall into a black hole and never surface. Since you will have protected the material by having it copyrighted, accept your fate and continue the process of securing agency representation or a publisher commitment.

Rejection is a badge of courage. John Grisham contacted many publishers who rejected his first book idea. Most thought he was some hayseed from Mississippi who should be ignored.

Jack Canfield and Mark Victor Hansen, the Chicken Soup authors, provide inspiration. Thirty-three publishers in New York and another hundred attending the American Book Publishers Association convention decided the first book possessed no merit. Canfield and Hansen licked their wounds, and never gave up. Health Communications, a small Florida-based publisher, believed in the authors and together they have published bestseller after bestseller.

Another author of note who never gave up was John Steinbeck. Born in Salinas, California, he attended Stanford. In 1925, Steinbeck traveled to New York to seek work as a free-lance writer. No one took him seriously, and he returned to California a failure. Undeterred, he began to write short stories. Ten years later, after several attempts to achieve recognition, he published a series of humorous stories about the Monterey *paisanos* titled *Tortilla Flats*. In the next four years, Steinbeck produced the classics *Of Mice* and *Men and The Grapes of Wrath,* among others.

Remember that Babe Ruth held the record for the most home runs during a baseball season until Mark McGuire broke it. The Babe also held the record for most strikeouts. Businessmen all over the globe have founded companies, made millions, hit hard times, filed for bankruptcy, then started again and made millions. As my father used to say, "Nothing good comes easy."

To expand your horizons, explore publishing industry alternatives, connect with fellow authors and poets, and find encouragement when rejection has occurred, consider attending writers' conferences. Information about such conferences can be found in Writer's Digest, Poets and Writers Magazine, and other publications.

Networking with industry heavyweights at the conference is of great benefit. Various social functions permit writers to interact with literary notables, including those from the literary field, film, and television. Attendees can sign up for meetings with literary agents and editors from publishing companies and "pitch" a book idea. If author Sylvia Nasar had attended a conference, she would have told the agent or editor, "The idea I have is to write a book about John Nash, the mathematical genius who suffered from schizophrenia and eventually won the Nobel Prize." The literary agent or editor in all likelihood would have requested to see any text she had written since her "pitch" or "Tagline" was superb and indicative of the book that became A Beautiful Mind.

Realize that agents and editors are constantly searching for new "stars." They need writers with bestseller potential as much as those writers need them.

When attending a writers' conference, arrive with a definite game plan, since first impressions are critical. Never tell anyone in the publishing world, "Well, I'm not sure what I want to write."

Be focused, listen, learn, ask questions, and be attentive. If you have chosen a book idea, be prepared with the fifteen words or less Tagline so you can describe your book. Many people met at conferences will be valued resources as your writing career progresses. Impress them with your ability to answer the question, "What are you working on?" with "I'm currently completing a biography of Albert Einstein," or "I'm writing a novel about the daughter of a famous politician who learns her father was a Nazi sympathizer."

If you have completed a Query Letter or Book Proposal regarding your book idea, be ready to present it to any literary agents or publishers you meet. Be certain it is ready for submission after having been thoroughly reviewed and edited. You only have one shot with agents and publishers so be certain your material is the best it can be.

Attending writers' conferences permits you to soak up the flavor of the publishing industry. The conference provides a crash course in the practical aspects of how you can realize the dream of being published.

If you promise to forward material to a literary agent or editor, follow through. Building a reputation for being accountable is essential. Literary agents and editors are looking for responsible, professional writers who can be counted upon. They are not interested in working with disorganized writers who don't keep their word.

Similar accountability will be imperative when you sign a publishing contract. Meeting deadlines is critical for any successful author or poet, since publishers will dictate a timetable for completion of the book. They will set a publishing date and then work backwards. You will be expected to submit material on time. Doing so will create a reputation for dependability imperative in the publishing industry. One of the selling points my literary agent uses while discussing a book idea with an editor is that I have never missed a deadline. This separates me from countless others who have never met one.

Many aspiring authors have formed writer's groups. Some have a few members; others more than twenty. They meet once or twice a month to discuss projects of interest, exchange ideas, and provide critique. Encouragement is also a plus since rejection is the aspiring author or poet's middle name.

Members of writer's groups form an enviable bond. Whether the writer is a beginner or a published author, the sharing of thoughts about the writing process and the literary industry is refreshing and quite beneficial.

Beginning a writer's group is easy. Posting signs on university and library bulletin boards or in newsletters will stir interest. Everyone has a story to tell or a book in them, and there are many who welcome the chance to work with others to improve their craft.

Many writers have joined writer's centers. This provides the opportunity to congregate with aspiring authors and poets of all genres. These centers offer classes and seminars helpful in writing fiction, non-fiction, poetry, short stories, and magazine articles.

Many writer's centers and poet's groups offer "open microphone" nights when reading of works is possible. Take advantage of these opportunities to expose your writings to others. Feedback is beneficial and you never know if someone with a valuable contact in the publishing world might be listening.

Bookstore cafes and local coffeehouses are gathering places for writers. Mingle with others who share your passion for books and the publishing process. They may have fresh ideas regarding your book. Learning from others is a great tool for any writer who dreams of saying, "Yes, my new book will be released next month."

As a professional writer, you need to make things happen. Sitting on your duff won't work. Take advantage of opportunities and never be afraid to ask questions of those who have a working knowledge of the publishing industry. Mentoring by experienced writers is a given and your inquiries will be welcomed. Across the world, there are organizations ready to assist your efforts to become published. Be proud that you are a writer with publishing aspirations. Most important, never let anyone tell you that you can't succeed.

I trust my words and those of other experts quoted have both educated and inspired. I hope you have read this book and said to yourself, "Hey, if Mark Shaw, based on his background, can be published, so can I," since no one has greater respect for the world of the writer than I do. Above all, I trust you will disregard the temptation subsidy presses provide, and attempt to be traditionally published. If you are unsuccessful securing a publisher, then consider self-publishing. Either way, you are building a writing career as a professional.

Those who become published authors or poets experience a satisfaction difficult to describe. The first time I was asked "What are you doing these days, Mark?" and I was able to say, "I just had my first book published," I grinned from ear to ear. Being able to tell someone I am an author is most satisfying since being a published author or poet means I am a member of a select group.

The task from idea to publication is formidable, but the reward is significant. Besides having conveyed an important message to the world, you will discover a definite respect for those who are published. The written word is a special communication between the author or poet and readers, and to hold your book in your hand provides a special moment to remember.

To be self-published or published by traditional means arms you with a credential leading to your next book. Remember that those who have attained celebrity status as bestselling authors began by writing one book. It led to the next and the next.

With proper training, education, and a will to never give up, you can look forward to the moment when someone writes an email to you or says, "Hey, I just read your book and I loved it." Say "thank you," and know that all of the hard work paid off.

William Saroyan, a gifted playwright awarded the Pulitzer Prize, sums up my belief regarding the mindset you must possess to achieve your goal of being published. In *The Writer's Handbook*, he wrote, "First, forget that you are an unpublished writer. Regard yourself, so far as you are concerned, as the only writer in the world. This is very important: it is not pride, not egotism; it is simply a necessary viewpoint for the serious writer. You must believe that you alone of all the writers in the world are writing the story of the living."

Saroyan added, "I want you to write in a way that no one else in the world has written. Any writer who is a writer can do it . . . The way not to write like anybody else is to go to the world itself, to life itself, to the senses of the living body, and translate in your own way what you see there, and hear, and smell, and taste, and feel, and imagine, and dream, and do: translate the thing or the act or the thought or the mood into your own language."

Tom Clancy's comment to *Writer's Digest* completes the thoughts of Sayoran. It sums up what I believe is the most important characteristic an aspiring writer must possess in order to realize the dream of being the author or poet of a published book.

Clancy said, "Keep at it. The one talent that's indispensable to a writer is persistence. You must write the book, else there is no book. It will not finish itself. Do not try to commit art. Just tell the damned story. If it is entertaining, people will read it, and the objective of writing is to be read."

Thanks, Tom, you've said it all.
Mark Shaw

Appendix

Sample Non-Fiction Book Proposal
With Comments

Cover Page
(ten spaces)

(Book Title) Beneath the Mask of Holiness
(normally 36 Font, Bold)

(three spaces)

(Sub-title)
Thomas Merton and the Forbidden Love Affair That Set Him Free
(24 Font, Bold)

(four spaces)

(Author name) Mark Shaw
(24 Font, Bold)

(No copyright information)

> *(Tip—It is recommended that titles be six words or less. Titles should be symbolic of the story being told. They must be strong—unforgettable—titles sell the book.)*

Page 2 – quotes
"The man who loves for the sake of love only –
he is completely free."

> *(Tip—Short, snappy quotes are best to pique agent/publisher interest. They can be about the subject of the book (#1, 2, and 3), by the subject (#4), or drawn from the book text.)*

Page 3 – additional quote – optional

> *(Tip—A lengthy quote from the book generates excitement and visualization. Remember—your book is like a conversation with the reader. Choose quotes that will cause an agent or editor to snap to attention.)*

Page 4 – Contents (Optional)

Contents
(18 Font, Bold)

Page 5 – Tagline/Overview

(Book title) Beneath the Mask of Holiness
(24 Font, Bold)

Book Tagline
(14 Font, Bold)

True love experienced through an inspiring relationship with a student nurse half his age transforms famous monk and spiritual guru Thomas Merton from a tormented loner to an enlightened disciple of God free of sinful demons haunting his past. *(12 Font, Single--Spaced)*

> *(Tip—The Book Tagline is the "hook to sell the book." In fifteen words or less, preferably less, the book should be described so readers instantly understand its content. The Tagline will be used to promote the book. Examples of superb Taglines can be discovered on the Book Page of the Thursday edition of USA Today in the bestseller list and in the Sunday New York Times Book Review. If you cannot describe your book in fifteen words or less, consider another book concept.)*

Overview
(14 Font, Bold)

(Summary of book—six to ten pages— double spaced)

> *(Tip—Utilize text from book with description or just description. Write in present tense. Use strongest material possible to hook the reader. 12 Font—Not Bold. Double-Spaced.)*

For famous Catholic monk Thomas Merton, described by revered Dutch priest Henri Nouwen, as "the most important spiritual writer of the twentieth century," his untold story is simple: Despite appearances to the contrary, in 1966 he was a troubled, lonely monk; he met the woman of his dreams (and thereby a part of himself that had been denied) and learned the true meaning of loving, and being loved; he struggled with the challenge of whether to choose her over his God; and when he chose God, he emerged with a pure heart and a reformed soul. Because of his struggles, Merton's spiritual self became stronger and surer than it would have been without the temptation God presented.

This surprising scenario sets the stage for *Beneath the Mask of Holiness: Thomas Merton and the Forbidden Love Affair that Set Him Free*. It is the first book to expose the struggling, scarred Merton, an orphan at age sixteen with no moral compass whose youthful conduct included an addiction to alcohol, womanizing, and an obsession with eroticism. Lost, confused, and in pain like a forsaken Jesus, he actually staged his own "crucifixion" brandishing a false stigmata on his hands in 1933, the same year the Vatican agreed to the infamous Reichskonkordat with Germany's Adolph Hitler, recently appointed Chancellor.

When Merton fathers an illegitimate child in 1934, a rich relative saves the privileged youngster from scandal but insists he leave the hallowed halls of Clare College at Cambridge, and England, for New York. Days at Columbia nourish an academic thirst, but despite Merton's progression as a writer, a dark side continues to disturb him as he relishes the seedy side of life embodied by sex and pornography. As his twentieth birthday dawns a year later, Merton, roaming the streets of Greenwich Village, finally becomes disgusted with the "extremely unpleasant sort of a person – vain, self-centered, dissolute, weak, irresolute, undisciplined, sensual, obscene, and proud" he has become. Dubbing himself a "mess," he notes that "even the sight of my own face in a mirror was enough to disgust me."

Suddenly enlightened through the words of such spiritual writers as William Blake, Etienne Gilson, and Gerald Manley Hopkins, Merton seeks transformation through the Catholic Church where he wishes to "tear out the roots of sin." But even after being baptized as a "converted Christian" during the cold, snowy month of November 1938 at the Church of Corpus Christi, he cannot resist the temptation of lust admitting to an adulterous affair with a barfly at one of New York City's watering holes. Suddenly, Merton realizes his only chance for salvation is through monastic living, and after being rejected by the Franciscans, he turns inward by seeking solitude and peace as a monk/priest at Gethsemani, the oldest Trappist monastery in America in late 1941. For several years, the monk enjoys reflection and prayer as he commences a spiritual journey where, like the seasons changing before his eyes, the traits of love and compassion replace arrogance and self-centeredness.

The solitude Merton seeks is interrupted when Abbot Dom Frederic Dunne encourages him to write his autobiography, *The Seven Storey Mountain*. Despite the book's international bestselling success in 1949, the same year his favorite writer, William Faulkner, wins the Nobel Prize for Literature, old wounds are opened when Merton re-visits his spent youth, one pockmarked with immoral decisions hurting those around him. Worse, Catholic censors demand he tell only "part of the truth" regarding his bad-boy days and sexual indiscretions. Since, among other things, no mention of the illegitimate child or the stigmata is revealed, readers are led to believe Merton's soul has been cleansed through monastic living. But the guilt-ridden Merton knows better, having written earlier about "this shadow, this double, this [sinful] writer who had followed me into the cloister." Of him, Merton notes, "He is still on my track. He rides my shoulders, sometimes like the old man of the sea. I cannot lose him. He still wears the name of Thomas Merton. Is it the name of an enemy?" The dilemma: "He stands and bars my way to liberty. Nobody seems to understand that one of us has got to die."

Merton's true self, the flawed one beneath the mask of holiness, lies dormant during the next decade-plus. While acting as the poster boy for the Church, Merton, alone with his typewriter in a monastery spare room, writes numerous bestsellers embellishing the contemplative life even though he realizes he is not the contented monk he appears to be. This condition is exacerbated through the domination of the new Abbot, Dom James, who uses Merton the author as a "cash cow" to increase monastery coffers while refusing his requests to quit writing or leave the monastery. By 1960, Merton, despite his fame, has become the abused spouse in a marriage to the Catholic Church and Gethsemani, a restless dreamer who feels imprisoned and psychologically battered by the abbot he calls "dangerous."

Merton's disjointed mindset triggers depression and an evaluation by noted psychiatrist Gregory Zilboorg. He depicts the tormented monk as "somewhat in bad shape and . . . neurotic," telling him, "You like to be famous, you want to be a big shot, you keep pushing your way out – to publicity – Megalomania and narcissism are your big trends."

Despite Merton's struggles with fame replacing solitude, he continues to project the "holier than thou" image promoted by the Church while seeking insight into the one subject he yearns to know more about: true love. Haunted by memories of a mother who never loved him, a father who all but abandoned him, a near step-mother he hated, and failed relationships with nearly every women he met, he suggests on "a beautiful frosty morning": "The first thing to do is to admit I do not know the meaning of love in any context – ancient or new."

Realizing this character flaw prevents him from becoming the "whole man" he desires to be, Merton, alone with his thoughts in the snowy monastery woods, dedicates his days to learning about love. Influences such as the Desert Fathers, St. John of the Cross, and St. Theresa of Avila pound his brain with compassionate ideas about sharing, equality, sacrifice, and mutual respect, loving emotions appearing in such books as New Seeds of Contemplation, No Man Is An Island, and Thoughts in Solitude. Progress is slow, but steady, since while Merton longs to shed the "old man of sin" of his pre-monastic days, he is haunted by memories of the lustful Merton. Simply put, he is more human than the plastic saint projected through more than fifty inspirational books where he tells others how to lead their lives despite being unable to savor his own. Never one to share his inner feelings, he is a lonely wanderer suffering as an emotional time bomb ticks within him.

Having learned the keys to what true love is all about, Merton yearns for a female companion while lamenting old relationship "guilt" and experiencing sexual dream fantasies featuring everyone from his literary agent to "two lovely women in white" he meets near

Gethsemani. After a playful flirtation with one of his brother monk's sister near a monastery pond, he prays for resurrection but instead is confused and neurotic while admitting in 1965, at age fifty, "The depressions are deeper, more frequent . . . . People think I am happy." Such feelings are apparent since Merton, despite being permitted to live in a cozy woods hermitage where his best friends are red deer, squirrels, and chipmunks, realizes that while he now knows what true love means, he will never be able to put into practice what he has learned since any female relationship is forbidden according to monastic rules. Since he believes "true freedom [equals] true love," Merton, a short, balding man with bushy eyebrows who sometimes wears black horned rimmed glasses, is left to live a hermit's existence without ever experiencing true freedom permitting him to achieve his ultimate goal, being with "God alone."

As 1966, a year when Vietnam War protests steal the headlines, dawns, Merton is literally chained to the monastery both physically and mentally, the former by the abbot who refuses to free him, and the latter by knowledge that any sense of sharing love with a woman is impossible. Then, as if the skies have opened just for him, a gift from above appears when Merton, while recovering from a back operation at St. Joseph's Hospital in Louisville in March 1966, is visited by Margie Smith, a beautiful young nurse with a gleam in her eye. After some chitchat about their mutual interest in the Peanuts cartoon character, she comforts Merton with a sponge body bath. With gentle touches, Margie electrifies Merton's senses as her fingers wander through his nakedness.

Upon return to the hermitage, Merton, realizing the symbolism of a spiritual baptism, notes, "I do feel a deep emotional need for feminine companionship and love. [That] I must irrevocably live without it ended up tearing me up more than the operation itself." Regardless, smitten with Margie's youth and beauty, the famous monk begins a relationship through letters and telephone calls. When they meet again, the affair intensifies with each passing day as one kiss becomes two and Merton presses his body against hers during a clandestine meeting at his psychiatrist's Louisville office. Recalling the passion, he describes her as "small, shy, almost defiant, with her long black hair, her grey eyes, her white trench coat. (She kept saying she was scared).”

Despite realizing God has blessed him with a special angel, Merton initially backslides to his former self by becoming obsessed with Margie's physical being: “When we become very erotic I do not feel guilt because I love her so much and we are both totally committed to each other.” Summing up the initial stages of the relationship after walking the monastery trails as the hot sun splashes through sycamore trees, Merton notes, “Margie and I are so much, in so many ways, Eve and Adam.”

Still stuck in the mud mindset of the “old Merton, scandal for the Catholic Church looms when the priest secretly plots to marry Margie, live in sin in violation of monastic vows, or have Margie as his “mistress.” Such emotions escalate during a secret May 1966 picnic on Gethsemani grounds where the couple “ate herring and ham (not very much eating!) and drank our wine and read poems and talked of ourselves and mostly made love and love and love for five hours.” The result: “We now love with our whole bodies anyway and I have the complete feel of her being (except her sex) as completely me.” Connecting past and present, with an indication that for the first time in his life, Merton has fallen “in love,” he mentions “deep capacities for love, especially for her. I have never seen so much simple, spontaneous, total love.”

Violating monastic rules, Merton telephones Margie from the Abbey's cellarer's office. When the scheme is revealed to Dom James, he chastises Merton for his irreverent conduct. After one lecture in the abbot's messy office forbidding him to see Margie, Merton teases him, “When the baby is born you can be its godfather!” According to Merton, the reaction is immediate: “A slight shadow crossed his face and he laughed with less enthusiasm. Was I really kidding? We are a pair of damn cats.”

Despite the order barring him from seeing Margie, Merton continues the romance with a woman he calls “the miracle in my life.” While reflecting as a candle burns bright beside his hermitage bed, Merton admits being “flooded by peace . . . . Instead of feeling impure I feel purified . . . my sexuality has been made real and decent again after years of rather frantic suppression . . . I feel less sick. I feel human.”

This mindset transcends Merton as he contemplates his love for Margie. Tears flood his eyes as he thinks of the woman he may trust with innermost feelings: "The fact that I love her with my whole being is simply to be accepted and coped with: and she loves me as I love her. It is beautiful and difficult, full of pain and joy, and it is real love; it is rewarding and irreplaceable."

Discovering, for the first time, by experience, the true meaning of loving, and being loved, Merton, having endured the suffering of so many years, is able to remove his false mask and discover his true identity: "Whatever may be right or wrong about my love for M. [Margie], this is what is being shown me; the true relationship is not between her and my ideal self, but between her and my real, actual self . . . . " To prove his love, Merton shares more than forty journal pages of "A Midsummer Diary for Margie," exposing heartfelt feelings of dedication to their oneness.

Such feelings permit Merton to enjoy the beauty of a pure, sweet love as the months pass. But new maturity causes him to realize he must think of Margie more than himself. Torn between continuing the relationship to the extent of marrying her and leaving Gethsemani, and being true to his God, Merton agonizes as he attempts to consider what is best for Margie. Sleepless nights and long walks in the desolate woods trigger the realization that while he loves her dearly, any long term relationship is impossible, and more important, his devotion to God is stronger. Finally, on a crisp September 1966 morning, after hours of prayer, Merton commits to hermit existence, "to live in solitude for the rest of my life in so far as health may permit." This decision triggers another, "[This is] a final day of rather tormented struggle and inner letting go of my selfish hold on [Margie] or wrong need (I hope) . . . I love her but no longer crave her."

Displaying courage as never before by deciding to give up the love of a woman he has prayed for, Merton slowly removes himself from Margie's life as the year 1967 appears. Though he suffers while doing so realizing her heart is broken, his knowledge that he is choosing God over the flesh warms his heart with the understanding that the "old Merton" is dead; the new Merton, the true, complete Merton, lives on. He is the one who has proclaimed, " . . . for the first time really since going to the hospital, I have real inner freedom and solitude – I love [Margie] but in a different way, peacefully, and without disturbances or inner tension. I feel that once again I am all here." Her feelings are reciprocal, with a friend telling Merton, "Margie loves you and will always love you." Merton's response: "Margie's love . . . is actually part of a great insurmountable way of liberation that goes far beyond our affection and its expression."

This exuberance of personal liberty, of freedom, is extended when Dom James retires and is replaced by a more understanding abbot. With his permission, Merton travels to the Far East in the latter days of 1968. There, in Bangkok, after having met the Dalai Lama, he will die from an accidental electrocution but not before attaining a state of grace he mentions in a novice lecture in 1965. Speaking about his favorite topics, love and freedom, Merton tells his students, "[One who is truly free] is one who is always living at the point where with one step he can walk over the line [die] and there is no unfinished business to deal with."

This mindset is symbolic of Merton's prophetic words: "We imprison ourselves in falsity by our love for the feeble flickering light of illusion and desire. We cannot find the true light unless this false light be darkened. We cannot find true happiness unless we deprive ourselves of the . . . happiness of empty diversion. Peace, true peace, is only to be found through suffering and we must seek light in darkness."

(Tip—Remember—the first few sentences of the Overview must be superb to hook the reader. Be creative, visual, brief, and clear. Ask yourself—If I were an editor or publisher reading this material, what would I want to know about the book so as to decide whether to read further?)

(Note: subsequent text in the Overview details Belli's representation of Jack Ruby.)

(Comment: This latter section of the Overview presents an example of descriptive narrative detailing the intended story you want to tell. Make certain to provide a good beginning, middle, and end so the agent or editor realizes you are a

competent storyteller. Include the highlights of the book to entice the reader to say, "This is a book I must represent or publish.")

(Tip—Be careful not to exaggerate or attempt to boost the material. Facts, facts, facts—are the key. They should speak for themselves. Agents and editors are turned off by those who promote instead of tell the story and let it stand on its own.)

Author Biography
(14 Font, Bold, 4-6 paragraphs at most)

The author's expertise to write **Beneath the Mask of Holiness** stems from his experience as the author of fifteen books, extensive research about Merton, and his expertise regarding the subject of conversion garnered while earning a May 2008 Master's degree in theological studies at San Francisco Theological Seminary. After first encountering Merton during a spiritual direction course, the author read New Seeds of Contemplation triggering his becoming a true contemplative, and a dedicated "Mertonist." This has led to further study of Merton's teachings about the contemplative life and his belief in the inclusive nature of all religions and spiritualities.

Participation in the "Bridges to Contemplative Living" retreat series offered at Bethany House near Gethsemani by the Merton Institute for Contemplative Living enhances the author's credential. He has visited The Thomas Merton Center in Louisville on research missions, and also traveled to Rome where he was able to locate the pensione where Merton stayed when he experiences what many believe was a conversion moment, the spiritual vision of his dead father in 1933. No one had previously discovered this location, leading The Merton Seasonal, a quarterly publication of the International Thomas Merton Society, to include the author's article in the June 2008 publication. This increases the author's exposure within the Merton "community" since the Seasonal is forwarded to "Mertonists" around the world.

More about the author, currently living in Burlingame, California with his wife Wen-ying Lu, head of cataloguing at the library at Santa

Clara University, may be learned at www.markshawbooks.net. The author's books, all written prior to his seminary experience, include biographies of Jonathan Pollard, Mike Tyson, Melvin Belli, New York Yankees "perfect game" pitcher Don Larsen, and famed aviator R. A. "Bob" Hoover. A former defense attorney and columnist for the Aspen Daily News, he has been a television legal analyst for ABC, CBS, and ESPN.

> *(Tip—Above text provides author "credentials" or "platform" to write the book.)*

Book Audience
(14 Bold, 2-3 paragraphs)

This unique, controversial perspective of Merton is targeted for a broad, curious audience including not only those of the Catholic faith familiar with the famous monk, but people of all spiritualities since it captures the true essence of the human side of Merton. Readers will associate with Merton's quest – the basic human need to discover the true meaning of loving, and being loved – so as to be free. It will certainly strike a nerve with Merton loyalists surprised by his forbidden affair but then inspired by his selfless conduct toward Margie Smith and dedication to God.

Books presenting the "other side of the story" about legends in various genre, Hemingway or Shakespeare (literature), Bach or Mozart (music), Einstein (science), Michelangelo or Rodin (art), and the Dalai Lama or Mother Teresa (spirituality) provide a psychographic measure for those interested in such books. Motivation to learn about the "rest of the story," or a potential "dark side" of a famous personality like Merton, is a compelling factor regarding purchase of the book. Since so little is known about Merton's struggle to overcome suppressed feelings about love, this book is a natural selection for this demographic. Comparable books include *Mother Teresa: Come Be My Light* by Mother Teresa and Brian Kolodiejchuk, and *The Open Road: The Global Journey of the Fourteenth Dalai Lama,* by Pico Iyer, *Hemingway: A Biography* by Kenneth Lynn, *Will in the World* by Stephen Greenblatt, Einstein: His Life and Universe, by Walter Isaacson, and The Life You Save May Be Your Own, by Paul

Elie, an excellent book chronicling Merton's journey as a true pilgrim in context with the lives of Dorothy Day, Walker Percy, and Flannery O'Conner.

Affinity groups interested in *Beneath the Mask of Holiness* include the millions of people who have struggled with loving, and being loved, in various relationships. In many ways, Merton's struggle parallels our own as many search for love "in all the wrong places." Merton's experience with Margie, and the beautiful prose he writes about his feelings will be an inspiration to anyone but especially those facing the end of a relationship and what lies beyond. Church groups may discover this book as a teaching tool to educate anyone thirsting for practical knowledge about loving, and being loved.

Since this is the first, complete perspective of Merton, warts and all, this book will have academic relevance as a course selection for studies of the life and times of one of the most famous spiritual writers in history. It may also be applicable to courses focusing on conversion since this subject is considered in the book regarding Merton's true quest for freedom.

Additional potential audience members for this book include: Merton Center "Reflection" Email Subscribers, (5000 at last count), Bridges of Contemplative Living attendees, International Thomas Merton Society members, Catholic Study Groups, Seminarians and Priests, and those familiar with Merton as a beacon of light for peace.

Publication of *Beneath the Mask of Holiness* is suggested in late 2009, the 60th anniversary of *The Seven Storey Mountain's* bestselling status. It is also the year when the semi-annual meeting of the International Thomas Merton Society in Rochester, New York, will be held. The author, a member, will be attending this conference.

(Tips – Sets out broad book audience. Be concise but include all possible audiences).

Unique Storytelling Method/Similar Successful Books
(14 Font, Bold, 2-3 paragraphs)

Just as *The Seven Storey Mountain* tells the story of Merton's ascension from sinner to solitude, this historical biography relates his true conversion/transformation from tormented loner to a free and loving monk more in tune with the essence of writings inspiring millions of people around the world. This portrayal of a monumental season in Merton's life is presented with a provocative, yet inspiring tone, while inspecting Merton's legacy and the relevance of his encouraging message to a whole new generation of potential "Mertonists" confused with the world's current state of affairs.

In essence, two stories provide the main theme for the book. The "outer story" is Merton's frustration with Gethsemani's pressure-cooker atmosphere where instead of being permitted to live in solitude and anonymity, he is thrust into the limelight when his autobiography becomes a bestseller. Over the years, his restlessness and dissatisfaction with Abbot Dom James reaches the boiling point, especially when Merton's request to leave the monastery for another one is rejected not only by the abbot, but also by the hierarchy of the Vatican. When this occurs, Merton feels trapped within the monastic walls as one denied the freedom to roam the world in search of his true identity.

Connected to this main "outer story" is the drama unfolding as to exposure of Merton's forbidden love affair with Margie Smith and the question as to whether he will leave Gethsemani to marry, or live, with her. Even when he is ordered never to see Margie, Merton plunges ahead in violation of Dom James' order as if it does not exist in violation of the Rule of St. Benedict, the standard of behavior for Trappist monks. Scandal looms large since Merton, by his own admission, is "this close" to turning his back on God by marrying his lover.

The "inner story" of *Beneath of the Mask of Holiness* focuses on the battle raging within Merton regarding the true meaning of loving and being loved. Just when he believes there is no hope for anyone to love, Margie Smith arrives and becomes the vehicle through which he may debate emotions buried, but never dead, concerning relationships with women, including his "distant" mother. Once he has learned to understand what love may be all about in theory, it is logical to believe Merton prays for someone to love. If so, God presents Margie so that the lonely monk, during an admitted mid-life crisis, might see if he may put into practice the lessons learned about loving, and being loved, he suggests in his books, in real life. In the end, Merton receives what he asks for causing him to re-evaluate the man he has become and to decide whether he truly wants a companion in life, or to be with "God alone." This conflicting drama bonds with everyone who has ever loved, or wanted to be loved, and must choose whether to stay the course or abandon what they wanted, even prayed for.

By revealing the "human side" of Merton, the one beneath the mask of holiness, his story is even more compelling than ones written by those attempting to protect the "holier than thou" image projected by Catholic Church superiors. To the contrary, as evidenced by a May 1967 journal entry, Merton wants his story, warts and all, to be told: "I have no intention of keeping the M. [Margie] business out of sight. I have always wanted to be completely open both about my mistakes and about my effort to make sense of my life. The affair with [Margie] is an important part of me . . . . "

A third perspective of this book is the unfolding potential scandal for the Catholic Church caused by Merton's irreverent conduct. But perhaps more important is the book chronicling a wondrous, magical love affair, a great love story between two people starving for affection caught in a web of deception and intrigue against the backdrop of the Catholic Church since the love they seek is forbidden. Learning how Merton decides between the passions of a caring, young woman who longs to be his wife, and a God who demands his obedience, provides a dramatic tone as passions escalate towards Merton breaking his vow of chastity.

This book may captivate readers with explosive, little-known facts about Merton's forbidden love affair with Margie Smith, but ultimately the book presents a balanced portrait of the famous monk including his inspiring messages about the life of contemplation and love. It traces his complete spiritual journey from orphan to youthful roustabout to Columbia activist to religious zealot joining the Catholic Church to bestselling author and spiritual guru who appears to be content but is restless and searching to his core.

By including many direct quotes from his writings and audio taped lectures, Merton's strong voice rings true. No other book has presented the "complete, unvarnished Merton." No other book has examined his goal of achieving true freedom in his life in the context of the love affair with Margie Smith and the backdrop of scandal for the Catholic Church. The love affair, profoundly and ironically, is the key to understanding who Merton really is, and why he suffered in silence for so many years until God presented him with the gift/ temptation of the sensual student nurse.

> *(Tips: Points out uniqueness of storytelling method and why important. Agents and publishers relish comparing a book under consideration with a successful one. List as many as possible, but be certain to explain why yours is better. Terminology such as "This is the first book to . . . is suggested.)*

> *(Sources to discover similar successful books include: Bookstores, Publisher's Weekly, Books In Print, Publisher's Trade List Annual, and Forthcoming Books. Similar books may have a bibliography that will list other similar books.*

Endorsements

The author intends to provide several endorsements for *Beneath the Mask of Holiness*. Currently, they include:

- Novelist Ron Carlson (*Five Skies*): "[This book] can only deepen and add weight to our respect for this scrupulous and devoted and tormented man."

- Merton's fellow Gethsemani monk Dr. Rudy Bernard: "An accurate portrayal of Thomas Merton. He had a great need for love."

- Novelist Patrick Hasburgh (*Aspen Pulp*): "This book permits us to find what is inspirational about Merton – his strength and determination to overcome, and at times accept, his human frailness and vulnerability all while battling for self-discovery and solace."

- Noted Conversion expert, and author Dr. Lewis Rambo: "This book will provide people with a new view of the deeply human, but transcendent, love story of Thomas Merton – loving God and loving a woman. [It will be] a great contribution to the spiritual journey of thousands of people."

(Tips – important for publisher's re marketing efforts).

Promotional Ideas

Although Thomas Merton is the author of more than sixty books, most still in print, and well-known within Catholic circles, it will be important to promote Beneath the Mask of Holiness to those unfamiliar with him by focusing on the untold love story gripping Merton affair's with Margie Smith and his willpower to overcome temptation by choosing God over the woman he loves. Presenting Merton as a flawed monk/priest who yearns to discover love against the backdrop of a Catholic Church facing scandal provides the spark of interest for readers curious about the spiritual guru. The book will also serve as a companion piece to Merton's significant oeuvre by shining new light and understanding on this deep-thinking believer.

Regarding those familiar with Merton, the author, as a member of the ITMS, has extensive relationships with leadership at The Merton Center and The Merton Institute for Contemplative Living. These relationships will enhance promotion of the book through all of the resources available including The Merton Center's website at www.merton.org. Recently, the author has met the president of the Canadian chapter of the International Thomas Merton Society providing another avenue to promote the book.

Personal promotion will be available through the author's Weblogs and his extensive email list of Mertonists responding to blog postings. Excerpts from the book may be presented as well as listings of promotional events and book signings.

Upon publication, the author will benefit from The Merton Center's 5000-plus email address list. Speaking engagements regarding the book will also be available through the center.

Aiding the promotion effort will be bullet points focused on little-known facts about Thomas Merton. They include:

- Orphaned at age sixteen
- Obsessed with writing at early age
- Recalls "spiritual vision" of dead father while in Rome at age eighteen
- Experiences several failed love affairs as a young adult
- Frolics with prostitutes
- Is a womanizer and philanderer
- Is obsessed with "erotic" sex acts
- Fathers an illegitimate son
- "Mock" Crucifixion stigmata appears on his hands
- Draws pornographic figures at Columbia University publication
- Is a near alcoholic, admits depression, and potential for "nervous breakdown"
- Commits post-baptism/confession acts of adultery
- Rejected by Franciscans Order
- Evades military draft by entering Gethsemani
- After success of The Seven Storey Mountain, is forced to write additional books
- Writes more than fifty inspirational books
- "Holier-than-Thou" Image is protected by Catholic Church propaganda
- Is dubbed "hair-brained" and "neurotic" by Gethsemani Abbot
- Is under psychiatric care for depression
- Is refused permission to leave abbey by Catholic Superiors in Rome
- Falls madly in love with Margie Smith
- Violates monastic vows through forbidden love affair
- Is never disciplined for violations of monastic vows

- Is permitted special treatment by Gethsemani in violation of Rule of St. Benedict
- Considers having Margie Smith as "mistress"
- Realizes he is deeply in love with Margie
- Matures by understanding he must think more of her than himself
- Gives up the woman he loves for the God he loves
- Attains freedom from past sinful demons
- Accidentally dies by electrocution in 1968
- The Seven Storey Mountain acclaimed as one of "Best 100" books of Twentieth Century

(Tip—Publishers seek authors who have the ability to gain media attention for the book. Be certain to provide creative examples of how the book can be promoted.)

Format/Manuscript Status
(14 Font, Bold, 2-3 paragraphs)

The manuscript will be completed within one month of contract.

(Tip—Manuscript status—Provide information concerning what material is presented with the proposal and when you contemplate completing the book. This permits the agent or publisher to monitor your progress and request that more material be presented for review.)

Outline
(14 Font, Bold)

(Tip—Agents and publishers need to know that the writer is organized and has completed a book outline. Headings are provided along with "snippets" of text topics. Brevity is key, but clarity is essential.)

Chapter 1: Perfect Freedom Equals Perfect Love

As novice master, the famous monk lectures Gethsemani students about the writings of 12ᵗʰ century abbot, Saint Bernard of Clairvaux. The message: "the man who loves out of desire – then love is dominated by desire. The man who loves for the sake of love only – is completely free."

Chapter 2: Margie

After meeting sensual student nurse Margie Smith, a woman half his age, at a Louisville hospital where Merton undergoes a back operation, he is captivated with her charm. He admits, "I do feel a deep emotional need for feminine companionship and love" before beginning a clandestine, forbidden relationship with her.

Chapter 3: We Are Terribly In Love

Madly in love with Margie, Merton considers marriage after a letter from her telling him "I want to love you, to walk hand in hand with you straight to God." But danger lurks when the affair is exposed and Merton is threatened with punishment by the abbot. Regardless, a picnic with Margie causes him to note: "We . . . drank our wine and read poems and talked of ourselves and mostly made love and love and love for five hours (not physical love)."

Sample Text
(14 Font, Bold)

(12 Font, double-spaced, suggested length 10-20 pages)

(Most writers choose the Prologue, if there is one, and the first two or three chapters of the book. Some choose the first two and the final one, but continuity and clarity can be a problem. Make certain that this material is the best of the best you have written. Edit it so many times that you have the material memorized. The text can be single-spaced.)

Chapter One - Perfect Freedom Equals Perfect Love

A light rain shower on April 20, 1963 cleared the skies over Gethsemani, the oldest Trappist monastery in America. The abbey "common room" had a humid, sticky feel to it as the short, balding monk sat before young, wide-eyed novices gathered to hear him speak.

There were few distinguishing marks about the forty-seven-year-old priest's appearance. He had a round face, bushy eyebrows, and delicate ears fitting the mix. At times, he wore black horn-rimmed glasses. Perhaps his probing, blue eyes had a bit more sparkle to them, but they were not revealing eyes. Instead, they appeared to be reflective, darting here and there as his distinctive voice spouted out inspiring words often peppered with humor to curious minds thirsting for wisdom. When this gifted storyteller relaxed, a soft, gentle appearance filled his face as he smiled, or laughed, his best characteristic. For to see Thomas Merton laugh was to know the image he wished to project, the congenial, learned, happy, revered, humble Catholic monk whose celebrity was widespread.

Fourteen years had passed since his autobiography, *The Seven Storey Mountain*, became an international bestseller catapulting him to instant fame. Since then, he had written numerous books including *New Seeds of Contemplation, The Wisdom of the Desert,* and *No Man Is An Island.* These books, and more than fifty others, would stand the test of time and continue to educate and inspire millions of people searching for Merton's view of the detached, contemplative life, and how all religions and spiritualities were inclusive in nature. He would also speak out on social issues important to him including race, religion, war, and nuclear arms. After his untimely death in Bangkok by accidental electrocution five years later, acclaimed Dutch priest and spiritualist Henri Nouwen called Merton "the most important spiritual writer of the twentieth century."

On this hot, dry morning just south of Louisville, Kentucky, as the novices' hungry minds anticipated in silence Merton's inspiring message, he shuffled a pile of papers while monastery bells clanged in the background. An avid reader, he was currently completing Etienne Gilson's *The Unity of Philosophical Experience,* a book he found "very lively and articulate." Teaching was something Merton loved, and these lectures were important to him since they focused on two of his favorite topics – love, and freedom. Today he would speak for an hour-plus, but in the end, there would be three or four phrases among the rest more memorable than the others.

Despite outward appearances, Merton was "teaching from experience" in a stiff manner, one dogmatic and judgmental in tone. This was consistent with inner frustrations for both his monastic existence and with personal difficulties causing him to be restless and confused about his station in life.

Such would only be clear three years later, in 1966, when the words he spoke were positioned in the proper context after Merton fell in love with Margie Smith, a young, sensual student nurse half his age. This surprising romance would cause him to vacillate between whether to choose the God to whom he swore obedience, or succumb to human desires and marry Margie. If he chose the latter, and compromised his monastic vows, scandal within the Catholic Church was a certainty. All this would occur as he battled church officials who denied his requests to leave Gethsemani, and thus handcuffed him to the monastery as, in his mind, a prisoner, unable to step into the outside world. This predicament, and a continuing war of words with Abbot Dom James, whom Merton labeled as "dangerous," had, in contrast with his public image, caused grief and depression for the celebrated author who was a cash cow for the monastery through revenues from his many books.

This morning, Merton did not know God would tempt him with forbidden love in future years, and thus he spoke with no knowledge of being put to the test regarding the exact subject he was about to discuss. His heartfelt message, one focused around a letter of Charity and Love written by Saint Bernard of Clairvaux, the 12th century French abbot, and a letter Merton had received from a depressed Catholic layperson seeking his guidance, rang through the crowded room as the novices leaned forward to hear every word. Unless they had read *The Seven Storey Mountain*, none of the students realized that much of what Merton related about the unhappy man applied directly to Merton's pre-monastic state of mind when he had been a selfish, sinful wanderer in search of his true identity.

As the novices attempted to warm up in the chilly, musty room,

Merton, his voice crisp and lively, first called the depressed man who had written the letter "a baby who never grew up, immature" since he was self-centered. After noting the man's "great desire to be loved," Merton told the novices that the "only thing that may change your heart is love," and that "the man who loves out of desire – that love is [then] dominated by desire. The man who loves for the sake of love only – he is completely free."

Continuing, Merton, sitting erect in the wooden chair, and gesturing gently as he spoke, explained that St. Bernard wrote of three forces in a person, "fear, desire and pure love." Merton then professed his belief that "a man's life is governed by the way he loves, you see. The problem with this man [the letter writer] is that he loves himself."

Checking his notes, Merton told the novices that when love occurs, people must "let themselves go," and that "if you just simply take, and don't give anything, you are buffaloed." He explained that St. Bernard was seeking what was going to "convert [change] the soul, and that while fear and mercenary desire won't work, real charity [love] will."

Addressing what "converting the soul" meant, Merton, after coughing, informed the novices that it was a "change of one's whole self . . . one's whole life, you see. What St. Bernard is talking about is a revolution." Fear and desire may change one's direction, Merton added, "but when there is partial love, there is partial hate . . . [there] must be total love . . . . "

Merton, his voice now bursting with enthusiasm, laughter apparent when he made light of himself, next suggested "what is required for [true conversion] is a complete change in the depths of the soul. What is necessary for us is to become completely free." Quoting St. Bernard, he added, "[One] can't arrive at freedom without real conversion and then real conversion is only operated by love."

Affirming the idea that neither fear nor desire substituted for love, Merton related "perfect freedom [is to] do the will of God and be free from the desire of anything contrary to the will of God. You don't desire anything but the will of God." Summing up, he added, "The most perfect freedom is to not be capable of desiring anything but the will of God."

Interrupting Merton's thought pattern, a novice to the rear

of the room raised his hand with the question. "Does this mean perfect freedom equals perfect love." Without hesitation, the gifted wordsmith and teacher agreed before releasing the novices to their manual labor for the day.

To Merton's brother monks, academic colleagues, close friends, and the legion of admirers in the outside world familiar with his writings and teachings, these words about conversion, love, and freedom were no surprise. But beneath the mask of holiness, there was a different face of Thomas Merton, unknown to any of these people who believed he was a contented, loving monk appearing to be at peace in the solitude of the monastery. This myth had been perpetuated by Merton, and a Catholic Church protecting a holier than thou image by projecting him as the poster boy for monastic living. They had concealed information about his past through censorship of his autobiography, controlled his every move, refused to let him leave, and forced him to continue writing even though he was hesitant to do so.

Through these actions, and his own continuing battle with inner demons leftover from a sinful pre-monastic life, Merton was at times a depressed, unhappy, lonely man. He suffered, not outwardly so anyone would know, but inwardly, for he was aware of a deep, dark secret haunting his body and soul blocking any chance of attaining his true goal in life – freedom. Only when God challenged him through temptation of the flesh, in the person of Margie Smith, would Merton know whether he was truly a man who was one with "God alone," or simply a selfish hypocrite who spoke and wrote one thing, but lived his life in direct contradiction to everything he stood for. In the final analysis, Thomas Merton would experience the "revolution" in his life St. Bernard mentioned, and while doing so, finally understand what nearly every human being yearns to know, the true meaning of loving, and being loved. Then, and only then, would Thomas Merton be free.

Appendix

Unique Photographs, If Any
(14 Font, Bold)

Provides agent or publisher with relevant photographs that may be included in the photograph insert. Beware—book photographs are expensive so be certain to indicate whether you have the rights to them. Less is better since many agents and publishers shy away from books that will require too many photographs.)

Author Publicity Material

If appropriate, include newspaper and/or magazine articles about you or the subject matter of the book. You may also include brief articles written by you to provide further writing samples.

Sample Fiction Book Proposal
With Comments

Cover Page
(Ten spaces)

(Book Title) Courtroom Calamities
(36 Font, Bold)

(four spaces)

(Sub-Title) A Vicker Punch Mystery
(24 Font, Bold)

(four spaces)

(author) Mark Shaw
(24 Font, Bold)

(no copyright information)

> *(Tips—It is recommended that titles be six words or less. Titles should be symbolic of the story being told. They must be strong—unforgettable—titles must sell the book.)*

Page 2 – Quotes
Injustice anywhere is injustice everywhere.

(14 Font, Bold, Single-spaced)

Unknown (12 Font, Bold)

> *(Tip—Short, snappy quotes are best to pique agent/publisher interest. They should be symbolic of the book theme.)*

Page 3 – Contents (Optional)

Contents
(18 Font, Bold)

Page 4 – Tagline/Synopsis

(Book title) Courtroom Calamities
(24 Font, Bold)

Book Tagline
(14 Font, Bold)

A lawyer facing disbarment seeks redemption for two mentally retarded men imprisoned for a murder they did not commit.
(12 Font, Not Bold, Single-spaced)

> *(Tip—The Book Tagline is the "hook to sell the book." In fifteen words or less, preferably less, the book should be described so readers instantly understand its content. The Tagline will be used to promote the book. Examples of superb Taglines can be discovered on the Book Page of the Thursday edition of USA Today in the bestseller list and in the Sunday New York Times Book Review. If you cannot describe your book in fifteen words or less, strongly consider another book concept.)*

Synopsis
(14 Font, Bold) (Summary of book—five to ten pages)

> *(Tip—Use text from book plus description or just description. Written in first person. Use strongest material possible to hook the reader. 12 Font—not bold. Double-spaced.)*

Lawyer Vicker Punch sits in his black Audi in 101 degree Arizona heat deciding whether to dive into demon drink or resist the temptation and continue his life on the run. His sojourn from Lakeville, Kentucky, a bedroom suburb of Louisville, left behind a $350,000 judgment destined to plunge him into bankruptcy, a wife poised to divorce a drunk, and a past filled with memories of a client gone mad who beheaded a DEA agent and then killed three teenagers.

Just as Vicker decides Jim Beam is the answer to all his problems, longtime friend Reggie Robinson, the leader of an erstwhile band of do-gooders called the Wild Bunch, calls. It seems two borderline mentally retarded men convicted of a murder they did not commit have been released from prison. Reggie's plea—return and serve a good dose of justice to those responsible for the injustice.

After a Jeff Gordon fan reminds Vicker that it is the downtrodden who need his services more than anyone, he returns to Kentucky and agrees to represent Art Meadows, who suffers from Elephant Man disease, and Matt Morrison, a slow learner who was putty in police officers' hands. Vicker's motive is simple – the large amount of money he believes can be retrieved from city, county, and state coffers for the acts of retribution committed against his clients.

Reconciliation with wife Alex occurs as both agree that Vicker will cease his drinking. Together with Reggie, and the Wild Bunch, Vicker begins his investigation, one focusing on detective Jake Jamison, a maniacal, out-of-control officer who controls law enforcement in Lakeville. This investigation broadens to include other police officers, the county prosecutor, and a county judge. In the clear appears to be Simon Pelfrey, Ike Fellows' public defender, the son of Senator Amos Pelfrey, a Presidential aspirant.

When Vicker, a former legal analyst for national trials, sues for fifty million dollars, the media, including The New York Times and CNN, spotlight the case while referencing the potential connection to Amos Pelfrey. As the case progresses, Luther overcomes several obstacles while continuing to battle his drinking problem. His maturation is seen as he fends off a cover-up designed to protect the powers-that-be in Lakeville.

A month before trial, Vicker decides to settle the case in the best interest of Art Meadows, whose severe psychological problems stem from being raped while in prison. Just before a settlement is reached, Ike decides he wants those who persecuted him punished and Vicker resumes his crusade not only for the legal fees he will earn but to clear the names of Meadows and Morrison.

As the trial date nears, tragedy occurs when Vicker's enemies kills Reggie. Armed with new determination and with revealing evidence provided by a former CIA operative who has electronically reproduced the illegally obtained confessions of Fellows, Vicker decides he will not only prove his client's innocence but finger the true killer of the drug dealer Art and Matt were supposed to have killed.

During testimony from detective Jamison, Luther sets him up for the playing of the incriminating audiotape. Confronted with having killed the drug dealer, Jamison turns on Simon Pelfrey and accuses him of the murder. Pelfrey is taken into custody and both he and his President-to-be father, implicated in providing hush money, are indicted.

When the jury returns with their verdict, Art and Matt are awarded twenty-five million dollars. Vicker and Alex celebrate with two men whose story proves that there is no peace for the wicked.

(This sets up the story – descriptive text to provide the beginning, middle, and end of the story along with character descriptions, plot points, etc.)

The Author
(14 Font, Bold, 4-6 paragraphs at most)

(Tips—Details mini-biography of author. Key elements include expertise to write the book (knowledge of subject matter, etc.), publishing credits, and brief personal information about the author. Question you want to answer is: Why am I the one person in the world to write this book?)

The author's expertise to write this book stems from his experience as a defense lawyer turned television legal analyst and author of eighteen published books. Three are legal in nature – *Down for the Count* chronicling the Mike Tyson trial, *Miscarriage of Justice, The Jonathan Pollard Story,* and *Melvin Belli, King of the Courtroom.*

A veteran of more than 70 jury trials, most of them murder cases, the author has drawn upon his experiences in the courtroom to write Courtroom Calamities. Inspired by a true story, the book presents a fresh look at how the legal system treats those too weak to defend themselves.

The author's media credits and continuing media exposure include his current coverage of the Kobe Bryant case for ESPN and *USAToday.com.* He has also analyzed the Mike Tyson, O. J. Simpson, and Claudine Longet trials.

The author's publications include *From Birdies To Bunkers,* to be released by HarperCollins, Down for the Count, chronicling the Mike Tyson case, Forever Flying, the autobiography of famed aviator R. A. "Bob" Hoover, and Larry Legend, a biography of NBA legend Larry Bird. More about the author can be learned at <u>www.markshawbooks.com.</u>

Book Audience
(12 Font, Bold, 4-5 paragraphs)

> *(Tip—Presents potential readers for the book. Also suggests that there is a built-in audience for the book based on the author's previous work. Tip—If warranted, sales figures from the previous books could be mentioned.)*

The target audience for Courtroom Calamities is those people who have concerns about the hundreds of men and women who have been released from prison based on the discovery of new evidence proving their innocence. In the spirit of this theme, the book will appeal to readers interested in a disturbing, yet inspiring story of one lawyer's crusade to right a terrible wrong. Readers will also be intrigued with the love story between the lawyer and his wife as she deals with his alcohol tendency; ones that threaten to destroy their marriage and his career.

The inside look at the legal system through the eyes of a former trial lawyer will appeal to readers fascinated with how the system can be manipulated by powerful individuals with no concern for the less fortunate. A realistic reaction from those reading the book may very well be, "But for the grace of God go I," based on the realization that what occurred to Ike and Homer could easily happen to them.

Similar Successful Books

> *(Tip—Compares the book to others that have been successful. Also details why this book is even better.)*

Courtroom Calamities is written in the spirit of mystery legal thrillers such as Presumed Innocent and The Verdict. The unique aspect of the book deals with its raw inside look at a legal system manipulated by a chosen few who have no hesitation to destroy the lives of two innocent men. Unlike other books in the same genre, Courtroom Calamities grabs the throat of the criminal justice system and won't let go until redemption occurs.

Format/Manuscript Status
(14 Font, Bold, 2-3 paragraphs)

> *(Tip—Provides agent or publisher with suggested format for book. Permits them to realize that you are organized.)*

Courtroom Calamities chronicles a flawed lawyer's attempt to secure redemption for the wrongful arrest, conviction, and imprisonment of two mentally retarded men for a murder they could not possibly have committed. It details their story from beginning to end while documenting the escapades of the trial lawyer, one threatened with disbarment. The culmination of the book features a scintillating trial where the men's reputations are restored while the true killer is revealed.

A 395-page manuscript is available upon request.

> *(Tip—Details progress with book. Permits agent or publisher to monitor status of book and potential completion date. Remember that publishers are not interested in "works in progress" books that will need nurturing. They want as close to the finished product as possible.)*

Book To Film
(14 Font, Bold, one to two paragraphs)

Courtroom Calamities translates easily to film or television since it features strong drama (Ike and Homer, two innocent men imprisoned for a murder they did not commit), a lead character with a dubious past (lawyer Luther Parsons), and his feisty wife (Jessie), who attempts to keep him from drinking himself to death. The courtroom ending provides a thrilling climax when the true murderer is revealed. Similar films of interest are A Civil Action, The Verdict, and The Firm.

> *(Tip—Presents agent or publisher with concept that additional revenue from book may be possible. Remember the tagline for the book will be used to promote the book.)*

Outline

(Chapter Headings 14 Font, Bold, Text 12 Font, Not-bold))

> *(Tip—Provides the agent or publisher with a snapshot of the chapter titles and potential text. Tip—Titles must be provocative and snippets of text exciting and descriptive.)*

Prologue

Art Meadows' release from jail. He is hounded by an out-of-control cop determined to send him back to prison. Art slithers through the streets intent on making it home safely.

Book I

Chapter One – Call For Help

Lawyer Vicker Punch reaches a crossroads while on sabbatical in Arizona. Confronted by demons intent on destroying his life through alcohol, he must decide whether to return to Ohio to help two border-line mentally retarded men imprisoned for a murder they did not commit.

Chapter Two – Help Me

Art Meadows visits Vicker and discusses background of case and potential representation.

Chapter Three – Call For Help

Art visits Vicker's office again and pours out his story—one depicting his having been persecuted for a crime he did not commit.

Chapter Four – Art's Journey

Background re Art—disclosure of Elephant Man's disease, absence of education, family history, trouble with the law.

Chapter Five – The Lawyer

Background re Vicker Punch, family, law school, rise to prominence as a defense lawyer. Hint of trouble with a case that may lead to disbarment proceedings.

> *(Note—Remainder of chapters will provide similar text to disclose snippets of information to be relayed to the reader. See Outline in Non-fiction Proposal for more examples.)*

Note—Books II, III, and Epilogue would follow.

Sample Text
(14 Font, Bold)

(12 Font, Not-bold, double-spaced, suggested length 10-15 pages)

> *(Tip—Most writers choose the Prologue, if there is one, and the first two or three chapters of the book. Some choose the first two, and the final one, but continuity and clarity can be a problem. Make certain that this material is the best of the best you have written. Edit it so many times that you have the material memorized).*

> *Note: This material will be double-spaced in the proposal.*

Chapter One Call For Help

To drink or not to drink, this is the question.

The world may be threatened by terrorism at every turn, and global warming is a distinct menace causing icebergs to disappear daily in the Arctic, but I, Vicker Punch, a practicing attorney and part time television legal analyst, have a life-changing decision to make. Watching what's left of a burnt-orange ball of sun settle behind the western-most peak of the Maricopa Mountains in central Arizona, I'm clutching the neck of a full bottle of Jim Beam in my right hand. Staring at me is a multi-colored, wooden Jesus hanging from the rear-view mirror. Am I about to be crucified like Him, or might redemption occur if I resist the temptation to become a drunk again?

For nearly a half hour, I've been plastered against the reclining leather seat of my beloved Jeep Cherokee debating with myself, sizing up the devil. One sip of whiskey, I know, will lead to a second, and a third, and within thirty minutes, the bottle will be empty. By morning, I'll be lying in bed soaked in my own vomit, my body infiltrated by the same poison that has demonized me many times before.

I headed for the Arizona desert in a rage lasting from the Kentucky border until I crossed the muddy Mississippi. Ignoring two preliminary hearings, the sentencing of a rapist who is the worst human being on the face of the earth, and an oral argument in front of the State Supreme Court regarding a change of judge motion appealed on a whim, I marched out of the courthouse in Lakeville, Kentucky, climbed into the Cherokee, and headed for Interstate 70 and points west. My excuses for leaving were a town full of hypocrites who think I'm a dimwit, a law practice that has been shrinking in size ever since an unbalanced client of mine named Dr. Afeld Whitaker went on a rampage and killed innocents including children, a civil judgment awarded to an angry client against me for $350,000 that will more than likely trigger bankruptcy, and another dragged-out fight with my wife, Alex, a bombastic wisp of a woman who edges my temper into the red zone.

During what seemed like the fiftieth fight of the month, this one over accusations that yours truly was a bit too friendly with the sexy, brunette bailiff in Superior Court 4, she airmailed a bedroom lamp in my direction. It crashed into the wall, barely missing me. When morning arrived, a road trip appeared to be the logical remedy. Arizona was my old stomping ground, a comforting place where I could raise hell without someone hurling light fixtures at me.

The moment my Cherokee crossed the Arizona state line and a towering saguaro came into view, my blood pressure dropped fifty points. Passing by cacti, roadrunners, jackrabbits, and coiling rattlesnakes hissing in the 100-degree heat, I opened the sunroof and gulped new life into my lungs.

Continued on .

Appendix

Unique Photographs, if any

Publicity Materials

(Include newspaper and magazine articles about the subject matter, author, etc., and other pertinent material)

Sample Poetry Book Proposal
With Comments

Cover Page
(Ten spaces)

(Title) Parade of Ladies
(36 Font, Bold)

(three spaces)

(Poet) Diana Meadows
(24 Font, Bold)

(No copyright information)

> *(Tip—It is recommended that titles be six words or less. Titles should be symbolic of the story being told. They must be strong—unforgettable—titles sell the book.)*

Page Two

(Title) Parade of Ladies
(18 Font, Bold)

Tagline (14 Font, Bold, Single-spaced)

A Parade of Ladies is a collection of poems that depict a time gone by when respect for the fair sex was the call of the day.

> *(Tip—clarity is a key. If someone asked you what your book is about, what would you say?)*

Synopsis
(14 Font, Bold, Text Double-Spaced)

"Where have all the ladies gone?" I ask in a tone familiar to that of a professor addressing his students. Have males forgotten that the fair sex is to be pampered with love and affection and not demeaned for standing up for their rights? Whose to say that those women that choose to stand up for what they believe in still aren't as feminine as the ones that stay at home, keep their mouths shut, and raise children?

Twenty-five years ago, women were respected for their opinions and not chastised as "feminists" on the prowl. But all that changed when men, threatened by the strength shown by their wives, girlfriends, and sisters, decided enough was enough. Soon women were being looked down upon and laughed at for speaking their minds. Too often they were threatened with reprisal, sexual or otherwise, unless they promised to shut up.

In A Parade of Ladies, this poet tells stories of those women, unknown though they are, who stood their ground and said "Take me as I am or leave." Woven through the collection is a theme of pride and believing in oneself despite the odds. In "John Waterford's Wife Carol," the woman of the house tells her husband that she is applying for college since their four children have left the nest. In "Rex Walter's Girlfriend," Olivia decides to join the NAACP despite warnings from her spouse that she will be pigeonholed as a "communist sympathizer." In "Ralph Johnson's Sister," Sidney Anne Johnson is a mother of eight that intends to leave her abusive husband in spite of threats that he will kill her.

Twenty-four poems are presented featuring twenty-four women with stories to tell, each essential to *A Parade of Ladies.*

(Tip—Outlining the theme of the poetry collection is imperative. Catch the interest of the agent or publisher with an exciting overview of the stories to be told by the poems.)

Poet Biography
(Text Double-Spaced, 12 font)

The author's expertise to write this book stems from her being a single parent to six children, ages four to eighteen. After being abandoned by her husband, she worked sixteen-hour days while studying for her bachelor's degree in education on the weekends.

Diana began writing poetry to suppress spousal abuse. After her husband left, she began to write in earnest. One poem from her self-published first collection, *A Family of Flowers,* was printed in Poets and *Writers Magazine.* Other poems have appeared in the Village Voice and various newspapers. In September of 2002, she received first prize in the poetry and prose competition conducted by the Alpha Foundation.

Ms. Meadows, a first grade teacher at Northwest School in Louisville, Kentucky, resides with two of her children, four dogs, and five cats, in the woods near Lexington, Kentucky.

(Tip—Presenting the poet's credentials, her platform for speaking through her poetry is essential. Any agent or publisher will realize this lady knows about the subject matter being featured.)

Book Audience
(Text Double-spaced)

Women interested in overcoming any self-doubt will be readers of *A Parade of Ladies.* Inspirational in nature, the material is hard-boiled but right on point. Through the women featured, readers will understand that the poet is expressing her thoughts regarding the state of womanhood today. The Louisville-Courier Journal properly dubbed the poet's first collection of poetry, A Family of Flowers, "the hard knocks of family life." *A Parade of Ladies* promises a similar hard-edged style while making women stop and think about whom they really are.

(Tip—Publishers seek the largest audience possible for a book. Attempt to show that there may be multiple readers that will be interested in the poetry.)

Similar Successful Books
(Text Double-Spaced)

A Parade of Ladies is written in the spirit of *Ollie's Fables,* a series of poetry books emphasizing the rights of women. This collection is unique because it examines the subject matter in an objective manner based on the poet's personal experiences.

Another similar collection is *Peace On Earth,* by Elouise Johnson. A *Parade of Ladies* compares favorably with this book, but extends the subject matter.

Promotion Ideas
(Text Double-spaced)

Through her exposure as a leading advocate of women's rights, and a monthly newsletter sent throughout the country to battered women, the poet has a built-in audience for her collections of poetry. *A Family of Flowers* was promoted through the poet's web site at <u>www.standonyourown.com</u> and more than three thousand copies were sold. A ***Parade of Ladies*** will be promoted through the newsletter and the website and at the poet's speaking appearances.

(Tip—Attempt to validate that the poet has readers interested in the book either through previous works or media exposure. Agents and publishers know sales are dependent on promotion, promotion, and promotion.)

Collection Status
(Text Double-spaced)

The poet has written sixteen of the poems for the collection. The remaining eight will be completed within two weeks of contract.

(Tip—Provide the agent or publisher with the status of writing. This shows professionalism and good organizational skills.)

Outline

(Partial List of Poems)

John Waterford's Wife Carol
Peggy First, A Woman Alone
Rex Walter's Girlfriend
Pink Dye's Older Sister
Wilma Pam's Dead Lover
Ralph Johnson's Sister
Olivias Creek's Missing Husband
Bart Black's Dead
Have You Seen Christina Applebaum?
Poor Little Red Chambers

(Tip—Provides agent or publisher with thumbnail sketch of poetry. Titles are catchy, easy to remember.)

Sample Poems

(Tip—Sample poems will be typed one to a page. If a Cover page is not used, then type in upper left hand corner name, address, telephone number, and e-mail address. Space down six lines or so, center, and print the title of the poem in 18 Font, Bold. The poems will be single-spaced, double-spaced between stanzas. If the poem stretches beyond one page, continue to the next by indicating your name, a keyword from the title of the poem, and the page number at the upper top left-hand corner of the page.)

John Waterford's Wife Carol

(18 Font, Bold)

She was a lovely thing, you see,
When John Waterford spied her in the bar.
He was smitten like never before,
Carol was his dream come true.

The wedding was a day to recall,
Special feelings all around,
Four children soon filled the household,
John and Carol, the perfect couple.

But Carol wasn't certain who she was,
A high-school graduate but nothing more,
She wanted to find herself,
When the children left the nest.

An ad for a college caught her eye,
But John laughed at the idea.
Carol raised her voice,
John raised his fist.

Months went by,
Carol afraid to try,
John the roadblock,
To self-respect, a chance to change.

Then God paved the way,
When John was hit by a truck.
She was sad to see him go,
But not that sad.

And then the day arrived,
College student Carol,
How proud she was to be in class,
Her dream instead of his fulfilled.

Six years hence,
And Carol found her way,
She loves life,
Most of all herself.

(Tip—Use strong words, words that improve pacing of the poem. Remember that all good stories are love stories.)

(Note: Between five and ten poems would follow this one.)

Appendix
(Includes photographs, illustrations, media coverage for the poet, etc.)

Sample Agent Agreement
With Legal Tips

(Tips—If you are offered a literary agent agreement, hire a competent entertainment lawyer. He or she can best represent your interests. Regardless, familiarizing yourself with the basic outline of an agent agreement can be helpful.)

Representation Agreement

This letter of agreement will confirm the arrangement between us by which you have appointed Scarborough Literary Agency as your exclusive agent in the sale, lease, license, and/or other disposition of literary and related rights to any and all works penned by you during the term of this agreement.

(Standard language detailing the representation during a defined period.)

You understand such appointment to cover the active marketing throughout the world of all your literary rights, including but not limited to, publishing, motion pictures, electronic, stage, radio, television, recording rights, and generally to advise you professionally.

(Details specifics of representation. Tip—Keep language as specific as possible to avoid confusion. The clause, "Generally to advise you professionally"—should be left out if possible.)

Scarborough Literary Agency will actively market and represent your best interests to the best of its ability utilizing its contacts throughout the entertainment industry. The agency will not enter into an agreement on your behalf without your written consent.

(Provides language requiring agency to act in your best interest, but restricts their ability to enter into agreements without your having final approval. Tip—This latter language is essential to protecting you against acts by agent that are adverse to your interests.)

You agree that Scarborough Agency will collect for you revenues due from the marketing of any and all works covered by this agreement. Said revenues will be forwarded to you within fifteen days of receipt by the agency.

(This language authorizes your agent to act as your depository for monies earned. Tip—Learn when the reporting periods are for your publishers and be certain to check as to whether revenues are due.)

In consideration of Scarborough Agency's representation, it will retain a fifteen percent commission of all revenues collected in the United States of America and twenty percent of all revenues collected from foreign sources.

(Standard fees for literary representation. Tip—Attempt to include the word "gross" as in gross revenues so there is no doubt of the amount being commissioned. Tip—When dealing with theatrical agencies, the commission will be ten percent.)

When marketing your literary work, Scarborough Agency will incur certain out-of-pocket expenses including photocopying, postage, messengers, and overnight courier services. You agree to reimburse the agency for said expenses within ten days of billing. Any other expenses must be approved by you in advance. Scarborough Agency agrees to keep all expenses to a minimum.

(Specifies your responsibility to pay for out-of-pocket expenses. Tip—Insert "under one hundred dollars" after the word "expenses" in line four. This protects you against excessive overruns.)

This agreement is effective as of the date both parties have signed below. It will continue to be valid for a period of one year unless cancelled by either party with sixty days written notice.

(Details term of agreement. Tip—Stay away from any agreement longer than one year. Also—watch for language that continues agreement indefinitely subject to one party or the other canceling.)

Regardless of the cancellation by either party to this agreement, Scarborough Agency will continue its representation and collection of revenues for all works initiated or completed during the term of representation.

> *(Standard language protecting agency after cancellation of agreement. Tip—If possible, limit collection of revenue to five years.)*

This agreement is binding under the laws of the State of _____.
All parties agree that in the event of dispute, the matter shall be subject to arbitration under the auspices of the American Arbitration Association.

> *(Specifies mechanism for legal matters. Tip—Attempt to designate your state as venue.)*

Agreed to by all parties designated below this ___ day of ____, ____.

_____

Maude Bonderbast, President Scarborough Literary Agency

_____

Author

Sample Publisher Agreement
With Legal Tips

(Tips—If you are offered a publishing agreement, hire an entertainment lawyer or utilize the services of a literary agent to represent you. They can best protect your interests. Regardless, familiarizing yourself with a publishing agreement can be helpful.)

Publishing Agreement:

This is an agreement between Author (hereafter referred to as "author") and Afterlife Publishing Company (hereafter referred to as "publisher") regarding the publication of the book titled, Guardians of the Heavens.

(Sets out parties to the agreement and subject matter.)

Author and Publisher agree:

The author will write for publication a book tentatively titled Guardians of the Heavens. To the publisher, the author grants all rights including but not limited to the exclusive right to publish, sell, create derivative works and distribute the book during the full term of the copyright and renewals thereof throughout the world and in all languages. The author reserves the electronic rights and the motion picture and television rights.

(Details the issuance of rights to book from author to publisher. Tip—Delete the words, "including but not limited to" if possible. This will prevent confusion. Also—If all rights are not being transferred, specify exact countries where publisher can market book. Also—It is important to reserve motion picture and television rights for later sale.)

The publisher shall have the right to copyright the book in the name of the author.

(Important that copyright remains in the name of the author. Tip—Never give up that right.)

The author will complete and submit to the publisher a manuscript of not more than 250 pages by _____. After the manuscript is accepted by publisher, it shall be published at the publisher's own expense within eighteen months. The publisher reserves the right to prevent publication due to circumstances beyond its control. If they do not publish the book within eighteen months, all rights revert to the author.

(Details the conditions for publication including length of manuscript and due date. Also specifies period of time within which publisher can publish book. Tip—Attempt to shorten period of time for publication to one year or less. If possible, pin down publication date. Also—be certain that the reversion clause is included to protect your interests.)

Publisher will pay to the author an advance against royalties in the amount of $10,000. Half will be paid upon acceptance of the manuscript and half will be paid on the date the book is published.

(Sets terms for the advance to be paid to author. Tip— Attempt to obtain as much of advance as possible up front. Also—if possible, add clause specifying that no portion of the advance will be returned to the publisher if they do not publish book.)

Publisher will pay to the author royalties based on retail price of the book. The breakdown for such payments shall be: 10 percent of revenues produced by sale of 10,000 books, 12½ percent of revenues produced by the next 5,000 books, and 15 percent of revenues thereafter.

(Details standard revenue-sharing terms for most books. Tip—Attempt to negotiate "retail price" or "invoice price" as standard for measuring royalties. "Net revenues" will provide less money due to discounts.)

No royalties shall be paid to author on copies given to or purchased by the author, sample copies, damaged copies, returned copies, or copies given away for publicizing the work or to promote sales. Royalties on non-trade special sales may be independently negotiated without the mutual consent of the author and the publisher.

(Specifies books that will not be subject to royalties. Tip—Limit this category as much as possible.)

The publisher shall have the right to reserve a percentage of royalty payments, not to exceed 20 percent, in anticipation of copies of the works being returned by its customers. If the author has previously submitted to the publisher a work that was subsequently published by the publisher, then publisher has the right to combine royalty statements for multiple works written by the author for the publisher. If the author has purchased books from the publisher and has not paid the publisher's invoice, the publisher may deduct the amount due on the invoice from the amount of the royalty due the author during any royalty payment period.

(Protection language for the publisher. Tip—Restrict the reservation amount as much as possible. Attempt to bring all revenues owed current after two years.)

Net proceeds derived from the disposition of "subsidiary rights" shall be divided equally between publisher and author. They include: digest, abridgment, condensation or selection, book club first and second serialization, reprint edition through another publisher, syndication, translation and foreign language book publication, publication in the English language outside the United States, the right to public display, the right to grant reprints and other uses to third parties, and all other rights and uses now known or hereinafter to become known.

(Sets out other potential sources for sale of book. Tip—Restrict this clause as much as possible. Delete general languages such as final phrase above concerning "all other rights.")

The publisher will report on the sale of the work by providing royalty statements on a quarterly basis. All balances due author shall be paid at that time.

(Denotes publisher obligation regarding earnings statements. Tip—Even though most publishers report twice a year, attempt to secure quarterly reporting.)

The author is responsible for submitting the manuscript (electronically/floppy disk, and hard copy) including a Table of Contents, Foreword, Epilogue, Appendix materials, and Bibliography. The author shall also submit suggested photographs applicable to the book. Publisher shall be responsible for all costs of printing the book, including the inclusion of photographs.

(Details materials to be submitted by author. Tip— Photographs can be expensive so make certain the cost is the responsibility of the publisher.)

The author warrants that he or she is the owner of the work and has full power and authority to copyright it and make this arrangement. He or she asserts further that the work does not infringe any copyright, trademark, trade secret, or other intellectual property, violate any property rights, or right of privacy, or contain any scandalous, libelous, or unlawful matter. The author agrees to defend, indemnify, and hold harmless the publisher against all claims, suits, costs, damages, and expenses that the publisher may sustain by reason of any scandalous, libelous, or unlawful matter contained or alleged to be contained in the work, or any infringement or violation by the work of any copyright or property right; and until such claim or lawsuit has been settled or withdrawn, the publisher may withhold any sums due to the author under this agreement.

(Asserts publisher's rights if publication is challenged. Tip— publishers will insist on this clause. It will be a deal breaker.)

The publisher shall have the right to edit the work for publication, but the author shall have final approval of the text prior to release of the book. The author shall also have final right of approval over the cover art and text, back, front, inside front, and inside back, and the photographic insert, if any.

(Language re approvals. Tip—Many publisher agreements do not provide author with final approvals. Seek to gain this right.)

The publisher shall provide twenty-five copies of the book free to the author.

(Author free copies. Tip—Attempt to induce publisher to provide as many free copies as possible for give-aways as well as personal use.)

If the work is not in print for a period of six months or the publisher declares that the work is no longer worthy of print for continued sale, all rights revert to the author. He or she may purchase all remaining copies of the book at publisher's cost. He or she may also obtain from publisher all plates, books, sheets, and photographs.

(Out of print circumstances. Tip—Require publisher to relinquish rights to book if it does not sell a certain amount of copies per year.)

The author agrees that during the term of this agreement he or she will not agree to publish a work on the same subject that will conflict with the sale of this book.

(Key terminology is "conflict with the sale of this book." Tip— Make certain language is definitive regarding this point.)

The author agrees to submit his or her next work first to publisher for their evaluation. Publisher shall have thirty days to either agree to negotiate in good faith a publishing agreement or decline to do so.

("Next book" language. Tip—Avoid if possible.)

The author agrees to provide publisher with an eight-by-ten snapshot. He or she also agrees to promote the book as requested by the publisher. This includes interviews for newspaper, radio, television, book signings, and other promotional events. Publisher shall be responsible for all expenses incurred by author to promote the book. Publisher agrees to expend $____ to promote and market the book.

(Sets out author obligation. Tip—Keep language as broad as possible. Attempt to bind publisher to expend x dollars to promote book.)

The author designates Sleepy Time Literary Agency as his or her author representative. All revenues due author and other correspondence with the agency shall be forwarded through its address at 345 Park Avenue, New York, New York 20002.

(Designates author's literary representative.)

This agreement constitutes the entire agreement between the parties. It supersedes any oral or written proposals, negotiations and discussions. The agreement may not be altered in any form without the express, written consent of all parties to the agreement.

(Standard language)

This agreement is binding and shall inure to the benefit of the heirs, executors, administrators, or designees of the author and to the assigns of the publisher. The author may assign their rights under this agreement as they wish. The publisher cannot do so without the written consent of the author.

(Specifies future rights. Tip—If possible, do not permit the publisher to assign the rights to the book with your consent.)

This agreement shall be binding under the laws of the state of Massachusetts. Any and all conflict shall be first submitted to the American Arbitration Association.

(Provides guidelines re conflict resolution. Tip—Attempt to include languages providing your state as governing body for law.)

Signed this _____ day of ___, _____.

_____
Scarborough Publishing Company

_____
Author

Agent/Publisher Submission Record

Document: Book Proposal—*Las Vegas, A Novel*

(Tip—Prepare one sheet for each submission. Print and collect in loose-leave notebook marked "Submissions.")

Submission Date	
Agent/Publisher	Rosalie Thompkins Agency
email	RThompkinsAgency@aol.com
website	
Address	56 West 57th Street New York, NY 20002 212-789-7890
Contact at Agent/ Publisher	Jeanette Furber, Agent
Four – Six Week Reaction	No response, telephoned agency. Spoke with Furber's assistant. Proposal in stack to be read. Estimated time—two weeks.
Follow- up	6/17—Furber's assistant telephoned. Requested full manuscript. Forwarded by Fed Ex.
Revisions, if any	
Decision	Hooray! Jeanette has agreed to represent book. Suggested revisions being forwarded.
Outcome	Revisions completed. Submitted to Jeanette. She submitted it to four publishers. Riverhead books' offer accepted. Hooray again!

(Tip—First submit material to four or five literary agents. Follow-up, keep four to five in play at a time. If no positive response, then repeat process to selected editors at publishing companies. Continue process until successful, but keep good records for future use.)

Sample Collaboration Agreement
With Comments

(Tips—If you are asked to collaborate on a book, or wish to work with a collaborator on your book, hire an entertainment lawyer or utilize the services of a literary agent. Regardless, familiarizing yourself with a collaboration agreement can be helpful.)

Agreement

Eugene Fixbaker ("Fixbaker") and Anne Spellbinder ("Spellbinder") hereby agree to collaborate on a book with the working title, Around The World In Twenty-Six Days ("work") under the following terms and conditions:

(Sets out the parties and the book covered by the agreement.)

Fixbaker will provide research for the work and his writing expertise and Spellbinder her writing expertise and use of her literary agent to solicit interest in the work. The parties agree to collaborate on the text for the work with Fixbaker having final approval.

(Details the respective responsibilities of the parties and the contribution of each party. Tip—Be as specific as possible to avoid conflict.)

The work will be written in first person detailing travel tips for completing a trip around the world in twenty-six days. The length of the completed manuscript will approximate 250 pages. Spellbinder agrees to provide photographs from a recent trip abroad for the work.

(Specifies the theme of the book, the length, and one author's responsibility to provide photographs. Tip—Book description essential. Make certain the parties understand clearly the book that is being written.)

The parties agree that an acceptable draft of the manuscript, subject to Fixbaker's final approval, will be completed on or before

September 1, _____. At that time, the manuscript will be submitted to Afterburner Literary Agency for evaluation by Spellbinder's agent. Revisions shall be performed by the parties forthwith so that the manuscript and accompanying query letter can be submitted by the agent to selected publishers by October 1, ___.

> *(Details the completion date for the manuscript, one party's right to approval, and a timetable for submission to the agent and potential publishers. Tip—Be realistic as to deadlines so that there is no rush to forward material before its time. You only get one shot with agents and publishers— make certain the material is the best of the best.)*

The parties agree that they shall be fifty-fifty partners in the work. To that end, all expenses and any and all revenues from all sources for the work shall be shared. The parties designate Afterburner Literary Agent as their sole literary representative.

> *(Sets up financial arrangement between the parties. Tip— Essential to any agreement so there is no question of who gets what. Most collaborations are fifty-fifty but others may be tilted toward one party.)*

Credits for the work shall read, "Around The World In Twenty Six Days" by Eugene Fixbaker and Anne Spellbinder. The parties agree to perform all services, including promotion and marketing of the book, under the auspices of any contract with a publisher. Fixbaker shall have final approval over the selection of the said publisher.

> *(Specifies credits for the respective authors and the right of one author to have final approval. Tip—Detailing credits is as important as the financial arrangements. Be clear so there are no misunderstandings and hard feelings. Also— providing one party with final approval provides solution when disputes arise.)*

If the work is not acquired by a publisher, the parties agree to consider alternative means of publishing, including self-publishing. The parties agree to negotiate in good faith the particulars of such an endeavor. If no publisher is selected and self-publishing is not attempted, the parties agree to shelve the project for a one-year period of time. When that has expired, the parties agree that new submissions may be made, but if none are, the work becomes the property of Fixbaker.

(Provides out-clause in event manuscript is not publishable.)

The parties agree that all decisions made regarding the work shall be with the consent of the other subject to the approvals mentioned above. This agreement shall not be revised without the written consent of the parties. The parties agree that in the event of any disputes the law of Ohio shall govern and that said dispute shall initially be submitted to the American Arbitration Association for resolution.

(Covers boilerplate details regarding essential elements of the agreement.)

Signed this _____ day of ___, _____.

_____
Eugene Fixbaker

_____
Anne Spellbinder

Work for Hire Agreement
(Ghostwriting)

This is an Agreement between Ben Bookman, hereinafter "Bookman," normally doing business at _____, and Freddy Famous, hereinafter "Famous" normally doing business at _____.

This Agreement covers the preparation of a book project with the working title of Famous Freddy, an autobiography by Famous being written for hire by Bookman. Bookman will receive a total fee of $100,000 ($50,000 upon signing of this agreement; $50,000 upon satisfactory completion of an approved manuscript of no less than 80,000 words). Bookman will deliver to Famous the said manuscript on or before _____, 20__.

Bookman is an independent contractor. This work is considered work-for-hire under the United States Copyright Act of 1976 and the book copyright shall remain in Famous' name. All concepts, ideas, copy, sketches, art-work, electronic files and other materials related to it remain the property of Famous. Bookman acknowledges that project title or description is being created by Bookman for the exclusive use of Famous and shall remain in his ownership.

At Famous' sole and absolute discretion, he may make any changes in, deletions from, or additions to project title or description. Famous is not under any obligation to use project title or description or derivative materials. Regarding credits, the book shall be by Famous with no mention in the book of Bookman's having been hired to write the book.

Bookman acknowledges that project title or description is being created by Bookman for use by Famous and that project title or description is a work made for hire under the United States Copyright Act of 1976. At all stages of development, the project title or description shall be and remain the sole and exclusive property of Famous. If for any reason the results and proceeds of Bookman's services hereunder are determined at any time not to be a work made for hire, Bookman hereby assigns to Famous all right, title and interest therein.

Bookman represents and warrants to Famous that to the best of his knowledge the text, concepts, ideas, copy sketches, artwork, electronic files and other materials produced do not infringe on any copyright or personal or proprietary rights of others, and that he has the unencumbered right to enter into this Agreement.

Bookman will indemnify Famous from any damage or loss, including attorney's fees, rising out of any breach of this warranty.

Any proprietary information, trade secrets and working relationships between Bookman and Famous and its clients must be considered strictly confidential, and may not be disclosed to any third party, either directly or indirectly.

With reasonable cause, either party reserves the right to cancel this Agreement without obligation by giving 30 days written notice to the other party of the intent to terminate. In the event that either party shall be in default of its material obligations under this Agreement and shall fail to remedy such default within 60 days after receipt of written notice thereof, this Agreement shall terminate upon expiration of the 60 day period. Should Bookman's work-for-hire be cancelled or postponed for any reason before the final stage, Famous agrees to pay a cancellation fee based on work completed.

Any disputes between the parties shall be governed by California law. The Parties agree that any and all disputes shall be submitted to arbitration.

Please indicate acceptance of the terms set forth above by signing this Agreement.

_____

Freddy Famous

_____

Ben Bookman

_____

Date

Writing Samples

There is no doubt that your writing will improve each time you write but if and only if, you continue to learn. Reading good writing is essential to achieve this goal since we can learn much from those who have become successful authors and poets. By reading their selected works, you will see that they have mastered the art of storytelling through the use of strong, visual words providing excellent pacing and a sense of drama.

As you read the text and lines of poetry included, note the tone of the writing, the voice, and most important, the excellent use of grammar and punctuation. I often suggest in our How to Become a Published Author seminars that writers read good writing before they begin to write. Through osmosis, the good writing creeps into the writer's brain and provides inspiration and ideas that improve the text whether it is fiction, non-fiction, or poetry.

By presenting a wide variety of writing, I trust you will discover authors and poets who write in the genre you have chosen for your work. There is also a reading list provided after the excerpts to guide you to additional books that are excellent resources.

When you read the following text, you will note that many of the published writers have broken rules suggested in this book. Many times their having done so is based on the style of the writer, but be careful not to emulate the mistakes made. Style is one thing, but persistent use of bad grammar and punctuation is a death knell for aspiring authors and poets. Learn from the good writing and avoid the bad.

Fiction

Anthony Burgess

A Clockwork Orange

The chelloveck sitting next to me, there being this long big plushy seat that ran round three walls, was well away with his glazzies glazed and sort of burbling slovos like 'Aristotle wishy washy works outing cyclamen get forfiulate smartish.' He was in the land all right, well away, in orbit, and I knew what it was like, having tried it like everybody else had done, but at this time I'd got to thinking it was a cowardly sort of a veshch, O my brothers. You'd lay there after you'd drunk the old moloko and then you got the messel that everything all round you was sort of in the past. You could viddy it all right, all of it, very clear – tables, the stereo, the lights, the sharps and the malchicks – but it was like some veshch that used to be there but was not there not no more. And you were sort of hypnotized by your boot or shoe or a finger-nail as it might be, and at the same time you were sort of picked up by the old scruff and shook like it might be a cat. You got shook and shook till there was nothing left.

Note: This example has a completely new language integrated into the text with English. Nadsat is a Russian-based language Burgess created for the text and replaces words like "man" with "chelloveck" and so forth. This is a great example of Burgess's mastery of the English language and his ability to manipulate it.

Mary Higgins Clark

Daddy's Little Girl

"Have you had any response to that sign you carried outside Sing Sing?"

"As a matter of fact, I have," I said, giving him what Peter Lawlor calls my mysterious self-satisfied smile.

He frowned. I had piqued his curiosity, which is exactly what I wanted to do.

"It's all over town that you had some pretty nasty things to say to Rob Westerfield at the Parkinson Inn today."

"There's no law against being honest and there's certainly not one that says you have to make nice with murderers."

The Second Time Around

"When I met Dr. Kendall last week, I had thought of her as not being particularly attractive, but now when she looked directly at me, I realized that there was a compelling, almost smoldering fire that had not then been apparent to me. I had noticed her determined chin, but her dark blunt-cut hair had been tucked between her ears, and I had not taken in the curious shade of her grayish green eyes."

Note: Clark's books feature terrific dialogue through character interaction. We learn about them through what they say instead of excessive description.

Sue Grafton

M Is For Malice

"The run itself was unsatisfactory. The dawn was overcast, the sky a brooding gray unrelieved by any visible sunrise. Gradually, daylight overtook the lowering dark, but the whole lot of it had the bleached look of an old black-and-white photograph."

Note: Word usage sets the mood, gives readers a sense of what the scene looks like.

John Grisham

The Firm

"They left Chickasaw Gardens and drove west with the traffic toward downtown, into the fading sun. They held hands, but said little. Mitch opened the sun roof and rolled down the windows. Abby picked through a box of old cassettes and found Springsteen. The stereo worked fine. 'Hungry Heart' blew from the windows as the little shiny roadster made its way toward the river."

"The warm sticky, humid Memphis summer air settled in with the dark. Softball fields came to life as teams of fat men with tight polyester pants and lime-green and fluorescent –shirts laid chalk lines and prepared to do battle. Cars full of teenagers crowded into fast food joints to drink beer and gossip and check out the opposite sex."

Note: Grisham's writing style provides the essentials to push the story Forward. He is criticized for not providing detail and depth, but this bestselling author knows modern-day readers don't want to be bogged down with needless facts.

Graham Greene

The Ministry of Fear

"There are dreams which belong only partly to the unconscious; these are the dreams we remember on waking so vividly that we deliberately continue them, and so fall asleep again and wake and sleep and then dream goes on without interruption, with a thread of logic the pure dream doesn't possess.

Rowe was exhausted and frightened; he had made tracks half across London while the nightly raid got under way. It was an empty London with only occasional bursts of noise and activity. An umbrella shop was burning at the corner of Oxford Street; in Wardour Street he walked through a cloud of grit: a man with a grey dusty face leant against a wall and laughed and a warden said sharply, 'That's enough now. It's nothing to laugh about.' None of these things mattered. They were like something written; they didn't belong to his own life and he paid them no attention. But he had to find a bed, and so somewhere south of the river he obeyed Hilfe's advice and at last went underground."

Note: Watch the pacing, how Greene moves the story along with nary a word wasted.

Ernest Hemingway

The Old Man and the Sea

"He could not see the green of the shore now but only the tops of the blue hills that showed white as though they were snow-capped and the clouds that looked like high snow mountains above them. The sea was very dark and the light made prisms in the water. The myriad flecks of the plankton were annulled now by the high sun and it was only the great deep prisms in the blue water that the old man saw now with his lines going straight down into the water that was a mile deep."

Note: good example of visual writing – notice how Hemingway makes readers feel like they are right in the boat with the fisherman.

A Moveable Feast

"Sylvia had a lively, sharply sculptured face, brown eyes that were as alive as small animals and as gay as a young girl's, and wavy brown hair that was brushed back from her fine forehead and cut thick below her ears and at the line of the collar of the brown velvet jacket she wore. She had pretty legs and she was kind, cheerful and interested, and loved to make jokes and gossip. No one that I ever knew was nicer to me."

Note: Hemingway breaks the rules with a run-on sentence, but his description is powerful. Use of "that" in the final sentence could be avoided.

Greg Isles

Sleep No More

"Looking up, he saw Eve Sumner standing at the top of the stairs. Gone were the navy skirt suit and heels. She wore a bright yellow sundress that looked like something a St. Croix islander might wear. Her feet were bare, and her hair was tied back with a ruby scarf, exposing her fine neck."

"His arms and legs felt shaky, as thought he couldn't trust them. Memories of his last hour with Eve flashed through his mind like flares in the darkness, blanking out his thoughts. She came to him, like quick cuts in a film."

Note: Good use of metaphor in the final sentence provides clear picture of action. Notice correct punctuation usage with dialogue, especially positioning of period inside quotation marks.

James Joyce

The Portrait of an Artist As A Young Man

"O how cold and strange it was to think of that! All the dark was cold and strange. There were pale strange faces there, great eyes like carriage lamps. They were the ghosts of murderers, the figures of marshals who had received their death wounds on battlefields far away over the sea. What did they wish to say that their faces were so strange?"

The Dead from The Dubliners

"An old man was dozing in a great hooded chair in the hall. He lit a candle in the office and went before them to the stairs. They followed him in silence, their feet falling in soft thuds on the thickly carpeted stairs. She mounted the stairs behind the porter, her head bowed in the ascent, her frail shoulders curved with a burden, her skirt girt tightly about her."

Note: Joyce was the master of description. Note the use of adjectives has a nice balance to it. The phrase "her frail shoulders curved with a burden" nails the appearance of the character.

Jack Kerouac

On the Road

"Everybody was rocking and roaring. Galatea and Marie with beers in their hands were standing on their chairs, shaking and jumping. Groups of colored guys stumbled in from the street, falling over one another to get there. 'Stay with it, man!' roared a man with a foghorn voice, and he let out a big groan that must have been heard clear out in Sacramento, ah'haa!"

"We drove on. Across the immense plain of night lay the first Texas town, Dalhart, which I'd crossed in 1947. It lay glimmering on the dark floor of the earth, fifty miles away. The land by moonlight was all mesquite and wastes. On the horizon was the moon. She fattened, she grew huge and rusty, she mellowed and rolled, till the morning star contended and dews began to blow in our winds – and we rolled."

Note: Kerouac's writing makes readers feel like they are in the car with him as he travels across America. Note the terrific description of the moon.

Harper Lee

To Kill A Mockingbird

"Scout," said Atticus, "nigger-lover is just one of those terms that don't mean anything – like snot-nose. It's hard to explain – ignorant, trashy people use it when they think somebody's favoring Negroes over and above themselves. It's slipped into usage with some people like ourselves, when they want a common, ugly term to label somebody."

Note: Lee's vivid language is powerful and drives his story. Clarity is apparent, Lee never minced words.

Jack London

Call of the Wild

"It was only an old and battered harmonica, tenderly treasured and patiently repaired; but it was the best that money could buy, and out of its silver reeds he drew weird, vagrant airs which men had never heard before. Then the dog, dumb of throat, with teeth tight-clenched, would back away, inch by inch, to the farthest cabin corner."

Note: London's writing makes the reader almost hear the tone of the harmonica being played. And see the dog retreat to a corner in protest.

Terry McMillan

How Stella Got Her Groove Back

"I try my damnedest to wipe the smirk off my face and say, 'Nothing. And your check's on the kitchen counter. Go get it.'"

"You didn't go down there and fall in love with a twenty-one-year old, did you Stella?"

"Are you crazy?"

"No. I'm not crazy. Are you? And she is staring at me like she hasn't seen me in twenty years or like I've just cut off all my hair or dyed it some outrageous color and she is giving me a serious make-over. "Something is different about you Stella, and Ima tell you something. You look better now than I've seen you look in a long time. I'm not kidding, you actually have like a twinkle or something in your damn eye."

Note: Excitement prevails through word usage and the tone of the writing. The story being conveyed is topped off with the descriptive words "you actually have a twinkle or something in your damn eye."

Larry McMurtry
Dead Man's Walk

"We could run for them hills – shoot our way through," he said. "I doubt that five or six of us would make it. We'd give the man scrap, at least, if we did that."

"Not a one of us would make it," Bigfoot said. "Of course, they might spare Matilda."

"I don't want to be spared if Shad ain't," Matilda said.

"You're a big target, Matty," Bigfoot observed in a kindly tone. "They might shoot you before they even realized you were female."

Note: Good example of exciting dialogue between characters. Crisp language brings the story alive.

Herman Melville
Moby Dick

"In the midst of the consternation, Queerqueg dropped deftly to his knees and crawling under the path of the boom, whipped hold of a rope, secured one end to the bulwarks, and then flinging the other like a lasso, caught it round the boom as it swept over his head, and at the next jerk, the spar was that way trapped, and all was safe. The schooner was run into the wind, and while the hands were clearing away the stern boat, Queequeg, stripped to the waist, darted from side to side with a long living arc of a leap."

Note: Melville's text produces a film-like image for readers as to what is occurring on the ship. We can almost hear the waves splashing, threatening the ship's very being.

Jacquelyn Mitchard
The Deep End of the Ocean

"But Candy knew, as everyone knew, as Beth knew, that the whole legal process would turn out to be mostly theater, an elaborate pantomime intended for no purpose but competition, like binding up the newspaper corner to corner, with twine and setting them at the curb. All the hearing would accomplish, Candy predicted, would be to provide a public witnessing of tying that knot, securing it, snipping the cord."

Note: Use of the metaphor is effective, but not overdone. Readers understand the message, the clear meaning of the author's words.

Margaret Mitchell
Gone With The Wind

"Scarlett, Melanie, and Ms. Pittypat sat in front of the Daily Examiner office in the carriage with the top back, sheltered beneath their parasols. Scarlett's hands shook so that her parasol wobbled above her head. Pitty was so excited her nose quivered in her round face like a rabbits, but Melanie sat as though carved of stone, her dark eyes growing darker and darker as time went by."

Note: The use of the metaphor describing the nose quivering is effective. Great example of "showing" readers what is occurring instead of "telling" them.

James A. Michener
Centennial

"They form a strange pair, this short, stocky Frenchman and this slim red-bearded Scot. Each taciturn when on the prairie, neither pried into the affairs of the other. Without commenting on the fact, McKeag had now heard Pasquinel tell others that his wife was in Montreal, Detroit, and New Orleans, and he began to suspect there was none."

Note: The writing provides good character description and a sense of drama. This paragraph has a complete beginning, middle, and end.

Joyce Carol Oates
We Were The Mulvaneys

"There was the Mulvaney cork bulletin board on the wall. Festooned with color snapshots, clippings, blue and red ribbons, Dad's Chamber of Commerce 'medal,' dried wallflowers, gorgeous seed-catalog pictures of tomatoes, snapdragons, columbine. Beneath what were visible were more items, and beneath those probably more. Like archeological strata. A recent history of the Mulvaneys."

Note: visual words are used to set a scene. The bulletin board comes alive. Use of the verb "Festooned" is original and clever.

George Orwell
Down and Out in Paris and London

"My hotel was called the Hotel des Trois Moineaux. It was a dark, rickety warren of five stories, cut up by wooden partitions into forty rooms. The rooms were small and inveterately dirty, for there was no maid, and Madame F., the patronne, had no time to do any sweeping. The walls were as thin as matchwood, and to hide the cracks they had been covered with layer after layer of pink paper, which had come loose and housed innumerable bugs. Near the ceiling long lines of bugs marched all day like columns of soldiers . . ."

"Charlie was a youth of family and education, who had run away from home and lived on occasional remittances. Picture him very pink and young, with the fresh cheeks and soft brown hair of a nice little boy, and lips excessively red and wet, like cherries. His feet are tiny, his arms abnormally short, his hands dimpled like a baby's. He has a way of dancing and capering while he talks, as though he were too happy and too full of life to keep still for an instant."

"The room had a dirty, mixed smell of food and sweat. Everywhere in the cupboards, behind the piles of crockery, were squalid stores of food that the waiters had stolen. There were only two sinks, and no washing basin, and it was nothing unusual for a waiter to wash his face in the water in which clean crockery was rinsing. But the customers saw nothing of this. There were a coco-nut mat and a mirror outside the dining room door, and the waiters used to preen themselves up and go in looking the picture of cleanliness."

Note: Orwell uses visual words to captivate readers into the story. Notice how he uses the five senses to bring the characters alive. Readers find themselves drawn in with the story, thinking "I'm glad I never ate at this restaurant."

James Patterson
Suzanne's Diary for Nicholas

"They went to bed for the first time on that rainy night, and he made her notice the music of the raindrops as they fell on her street, the rooftop, and even the trees outside her apartment. It was beautiful, it was music, but soon they had forgotten the patter of the rain, and everything else, except for the urgent touch of each other."

Note: A simple, touching use of words to describe passion. Instead of flinging body parts around and providing heavy breathing, the author presents us with a touching portrayal of two people who are in love.

Anna Quindlen
Blessings

"Mount Mason had seemed dusty, too dusty, and out of date, aging the way that the cheap houses around the industrial park did, peeling, cracked, disintegrating, instead of mellowing. So many of her landmarks had gone, the old limestone bank building chopped up into a travel agency, a beauty parlor, a used bookstore, the boxy brick hardware store refaced with some horrid imitation stone and made into a place that sold records."

Note: The author uses effective, visual words to describe a slice of history. The use of "some horrid imitation stone" is the perfect way for the author to make a point.

Ayn Rand
Atlas Shrugged

"She glanced at him with the faint suggestion of a smile, thinking of how often she had said these words to him and of the desperate bravery with which he was now trying to tell her: Don't worry. He caught her glance, he understood, and the answering hint of his smile had a touch of embarrassing apology."

Note: The author uses a minimum of words to describe the emotion present between the characters. Other authors might need several paragraphs to give us the tone of the moment, but Rand ties it up with key words that leave no doubt as to what is occurring.

Anne Rice
Interview With The Vampire

"I held fast to Claudia, ready in an instant to shove her behind me, to step forward to meet him. But then I saw with astonishment that his eyes did not see me as I saw him and he was trudging under the weight of the body he carried toward the monastery door. The moon fell now on his bowed head, on a mass of black wavy hair that touched his bent shoulder, on the full black sleeve of his coat."

Note: Terrific description provides exactly what readers need to know about what the character feels while approaching the man. "The moon fell now on his bowed head" provides an effective description.

Tom Robbins

Villa Incognito

"Sure, as catalogued earlier, he had his charm and wiles, attractions that survived the metamorphosis from beast to man, and there were high-bred city women for whom his backwards manners were actually a kind of turn-on, a thrilling intrusion of the rustic over the overly refined."

"Let me pour you some bubbly, baby. I want to hear your news on America. Obviously, the ol' homeland is still hiding behind its mask of lipstick democracy and mascara faith, but what bouncy enterprising weirdness is leaking out around the edges of its disguises? That's the real America. That's what defines its existence."

Note: Robbins' language is rich with meaning. Notice how he makes his point regarding feelings about America.

Salman Rushdie

Haroun and the Sea of Stories

"As Haroun passed through the huge doors of P2C2E House, his heart sank. He stood in the vast, echoing entrance hall as white-coated Eggheads walked rapidly past him in every direction. Haroun fancied that they all eyed him with a mixture of anger, contempt, and pity. He had to ask three Eggheads the way to the Walrus's office before he finally found it, after many mazy wanderings around P2C2E House that reminded him of following Blabbermouth around the palace. At last, however, he was standing in front of a golden door on which were written the words: GRAND COMPTROLLER OF PROCESSES TOO COMPLICATED TO EXPLAIN. I.M.D. WALRUS, ESQUIRE. KNOCK AND WAIT."

Note: Terrific description; great name selection. Readers can imagine themselves right into the thick of this story.

J. D. Salinger

The Catcher In The Rye

"It wasn't snowing out any more, but every once in a while you could hear a car somewhere not being able to get started. You could also hear old Ackley snoring. Right through the goddam shower curtains you could hear him. He had sinus trouble and he couldn't breathe too hot when he was asleep. That guy had just about everything – sinus trouble, pimples, lousy teeth, halitosis, crummy fingernails. You have to feel a little sorry for the crazy sunuvabitch"

Note: Salinger sets the stage for our sense of hearing with perfect language. The descriptions of Ackley make readers feel like they know him.

Dai Sijie

Balzac and the Little Chinese Seamstress

"The branches whistled through the air as they swung, one after another. The blows left livid weals on Luo's flesh but my friend underwent the flogging impassively. Although he was conscious, it was as though he were in a dream where it was all happening to someone else. I couldn't tell what he was thinking, but I was very anxious, and the remark he had made in the mine shaft a few weeks before came back to me, reverberating in the cruel whoosh of the branches; 'I've had this idea stuck in my head; that I'm going to die in this mine.'"

"The room served as shop, workplace and dining room all at once. The floorboards were grimy and streaked with yellow-and-black gobs of dried spittle left by clients. You could tell they were not washed down daily. There were hangers with finished garments suspended on a string across the middle of the room. The corners were piled high with bolts of material and folded clothes, which were under siege from an army of ants."

Note: Sijie's locations come alive through strong images. Readers are transported into the room where the seamstress works. Use of "under siege from an army of ants" is superb word usage.

John Steinbeck

In Dubious Battle

"Look, Jim, I want to give you a picture of what it's like to be a Party member. You'll get a chance to vote on every decision, but once the vote's in, you'll have to obey. When we have money we try to give field workers twenty dollars a month to eat on. I don't remember a time when we ever had the money. Now listen to the work: In the field you'll have to work alongside the men, and you'll have to do the Party work after that, sometimes sixteen, eighteen hours a day. You'll have to get your food where you can. Do you think you could do that?"

"Yes."

Nilson touched the desk here and there with his fingertips. "Even the people you're trying to help will hate you most of the time. Do you know that?"

"Yes."

"Well, why do you want to join, then?"

Jim's grey eyes half closed in perplexity. At last he said, "In the jail there were some Party men. They talked to me. Everything's been a mess, all my life. Their lives weren't messes. They were working toward something. I want to work toward something. I feel dead. I thought I might get alive again."

Of Mice and Men

"It was Sunday afternoon. The resting horses nibbled the remaining wisps of hay, and they stamped their feet and they bit the wood of the mangers and rattled the halter chains. The afternoon sun sliced in through the cracks of the barn walls and lay in bright lines on the hay. There was the buzz of flies in the air, the lazy afternoon humming."

Tortilla Flat

"When the beans are ripe, the little bushes are pulled and gathered into piles, to dry crisp for the threshers. Then is the time to pray that the rain may hold off. When the little piles of beans lie in lines, yellow against the dark fields, you will see the farmers watching the sky, scowling with dread at every cloud that sails over; for if a rain comes, the bean piles must be turned over to dry again."

Note: Steinbeck is the master of storytelling. Watch the pacing of the writing, the drama, how the author provides visual images certain to keep the reader's attention. Use of verbs such as "nibbled," "stamped," and "rattled" bring the text alive.

Hunter S. Thompson

Kingdom of Fear

"So the following night I took the little auto that I'd bought with me to Rio, a cheap automatic. I carried it all over South America, usually loaded. Why carry one that's not? I tied it around my neck with a string it was too hot to carry anywhere else."

"A shudder ran through me, but I gripped the wheel and stared straight ahead, ignoring this sudden horrible freak show in my car. I lit a cigarette, but I was not calm. Sounds of sobbing and the ripping of cloth came from the backseat. The man they called Judge had straightened himself out and was now resting easily in the front seat, letting out long breaths of air . . ."

Note: Thompson's flair for the dramatic is his trademark, but his word usage is captivating. The use of "sudden horrible freak show in my car" provides exactly the image he seeks.

Scott Turow

Presumed Innocent

"Carolyn, for her part, was chilling in her command. The weekend after our initial night together, I spent hours – dazed, unrooted hours – pondering our next encounter. I had no idea what was to follow. At the door to her apartment, she had kissed my hand and said simply, 'See you.' For me, there was no thought of resistance. I would take whatever was allowed."

"Around the office, Tommy Molto was nicknamed the Mad Monk. He is a former seminarian; five feet six inches if he is lucky, forty or fifty pounds overweight, badly pockmarked, nails bitten to the quick. A driven personality. The kind to stay up all night working on a brief, to take three months without taking off a weekend. A capable attorney, but he is burdened by a zealot's poverty of judgment."

Note: Turow is quite apt at naming characters, and describing them so readers can visualize their look, characteristics, and outlook on life. Use of "burdened by a zealot's poverty of judgment" provides a character portrayal essential to the story being told.

Virginia Woolf

Mrs. Dalloway

"You served with great distinction in the War?"

The patient repeated the word "war" interrogatively.

He was attaching meanings to words of a symbolical kind. A serious symptom, to be noted on the card.

"The War?" the patient asked. The European War—that little shindy of schoolboys and gunpowder? Had he served with distinction? He really forgot. In the War itself he had failed.

"Yes, he served with the greatest distinction," Rezia assured the doctor; "he was promoted."

"And they have the very highest opinion of you at your office?" Sir William murmured, glancing at Mr. Brewer's very generously worded letter. "So that you have nothing to worry you, no financial anxiety, nothing?"

He had committed an appalling crime and been condemned to death by human nature.

"I have-I have," he began, "committed a crime-"

"He has done nothing wrong whatever," Rezia assured the doctor. If Mr. Smith would wait, said Sir William, he would speak to Mrs. Smith in the next room. Her husband was very seriously ill, Sir William said. Did he threaten to kill himself?

Note: Compelling dialogue, terrific word usage. Note the correct use of punctuation with the dialogue.

Non-Fiction

H. W. Brands

The First American –
The Life and Times of Benjamin Franklin

"[Franklin] made numerous observations of the finned fish of the Atlantic. Most striking were the flying fish and the dolphins (the gilled kind, not the mammals). The reason the flying fish took to the air was to escape the dolphins, which raced beneath them, ready to gobble them up as soon as they touched down. Franklin confirmed this by noting that whenever dolphins were caught by persons on the ship – they invariably had flying fish in their bellies."

Note: Good sentence structure. Notice that this paragraph is complete – good beginning, middle, and end.

Richard Ben Cramer

Joe DiMaggio

"It would not be a happy summer for either of the Yankees' big stories. Mantle got to the grand Bronx ball yard, took a look at the towering tiers of seats, the monuments to Huggins, Gehrig, Ruth, in the vastness of center field, the pennants and World Series flags fluttering in rows atop the scalloped balustrade . . . and he stopped hitting atomic home runs. In fact, he was trying so hard to crush the ball, to be the miracle advertised, to hit as he believed a New York Yankee must hit (harder, surely, than he'd ever hit) . . . he couldn't hit a thing."

Note: Good description of Yankee Stadium – readers feel like they are right there with DiMaggio and experiencing his emotions.

Laura Hillenbrand

Seabiscuit

"Even the jaded horsemen would take a respite from their labors to see [Seabiscuit], eating their breakfasts outdoors on the benches near the siding. To joyful applause and popping flashbulbs, the horse would draw up in his railcar. He would step from his three-foot deep bed of straw, give Smith an affectionate bump with his nose and leave the train bucking."

"Spectators murmured among themselves at Smith's homemade bell. They watched quizzically as Smith lined up his horse, stepped behind him, and hit the bell, sending Seabiscuit into a rock start. Woolf hustled him deftly; having begun his career booting horses through walk-up match races in Indian country, he knew how to hit the gas on a horse."

Note: The author uses terrific language to show what is occurring instead of telling us what is happening. Show and don't tell to make your writing more effective.

Barbara Kingsolver

Seeing Scarlet

"Then a bend in the road revealed a tiny adobe school, its bare dirt yard buzzing with activity. The Escuela del Sol Feliz took us by surprise in such a remote place, though in Costa Rica, where children matter more than the army, the sturdiest shoes are made in small sizes, and every tiny hamlet has at least a one-room school. This one had turned its charges outdoors for the day in their white and navy uniforms so the schoolyard seemed to wave with nautical flags."

Note: Good word usage provides excellent descriptions. Note the strong adjectives used to add zest to the story.

Jon Meacham

Franklin and Winston

"To meet Roosevelt the president, 'with all his buoyant sparkle, his iridescence,' Churchill once said, was like 'opening a bottle of champagne.'"

Note: terrific use of the language to pinpoint a strong characterization of President Roosevelt.

"Roosevelt was about to say something else when suddenly, in the flick of an eye, he turned green and great drops of sweat began to bead off his face; he put a shaky hand to his forehead," Bohlen recalled. "We were all caught by surprise."

Note: The pacing of the writing is terrific. Action – "Roosevelt is about to speak," drama – "suddenly, in the flick of an eye," more action – "he turned green and great drops of sweat began to bead off his face," more action – "he put a shaky hand to his forehead," and finally reaction "We were all caught by surprise."

Sylvia Nastar

A Beautiful Mind

"When Eleanor irritated him with her complaints, Nash would needle her. He called her stupid and ignorant. He made fun of her pronunciation. He reminded her that she was five years older. Mostly, however, he made fun of her desire to marry him. An MIT professor, he would say, needed a woman who was his intellectual equal. 'He was always putting me down,' she recalled. 'He was always making me feel inferior.'"

Note: Use of words like "irritated," and "needle" provide fresh meaning for the text. Also notice the correct punctuation regarding the quote used with the quotation marks outside the comma and period.

Marina Picasso

Picasso, My Grandfather

"I feel the sting of the banderilleros' barbs. I wish the film could be run backwards, so the bull would recover all his glory; the bloody lances soiling his coat would disappear as well as the barbs planted on his neck. I wish the barrera and the steps would vanish into thin air, and that a strong gust of wind would blow away the toreros and their idolatrous public. I wish the bull could be back in his field with his herd. I wish this bullfight had never been."

Note: Good example of first person writing. Also the paragraph builds with drama as the writer creates the mood and the message intended.

"Two inseparable creatures, like birds who can only live in couples, Pablito and I bound to each other, hand in hand, forehead against forehead. We refuse to take pare in the ignominy of men."

"We hear 'ole' and strident whistling. We are paralyzed with anguish as if brimstone were about to descend from the sky. 'Do you think he will suffer?' whispers Pablito."

Note: Good use of simile regarding the closeness of the two characters.

Reverend Rick Warren

The Purpose Driven Life

"It's not about you.

The purpose of your life is far greater than your own personal fulfillment, your peace of mind, or even your happiness. It's far greater than your family, your career, or even your wildest dreams and ambitions. If you want to know why you were placed on this planet, you must begin with God. You were born by his purpose and for his purpose."

Note: Excellent beginning for book. Immediately hooks the reader.

Emile Zola

The Dreyfus Affair

"In Paris, the all-conquering truth was on the march, and we know how the predictable storm eventually burst. M. Matthew Dreyfus denounced Major Esterhazy as the real author of the bordereau just as M. Scheurer-Kestner was about to place in the hands of the Minister of Justice a request for a revision of the Dreyfus trial. And this is where Major Esterhazy appears. Witnesses state that first he panicked; he was on the verge of suicide or about to flee. Then suddenly he became boldness itself and grew so violent that all Paris was astonished."

Note: The dramatics presented set the tone for the paragraph. The last sentence is very powerful, providing the sense of history.

Grammar Grabbers

Imagine you are a literary agent or an editor at a publishing company. Upon returning from one of those famous New York three-hour lunches at a fancy restaurant, you sit behind a desk and stare at the three-foot-tall stack of query letters and book proposals your assistant has delivered. Before she did so, any manuscripts received from unpublished authors or poets have been thrown in the trash bin since you do not have time to read a four-hundred-page novel or a fifty-page collection of poetry.

Armed with a full tummy of sushi and hot sake, you begin to scan the query letters and book proposals. You are impressed that these aspiring authors and poets have done their homework by checking the guidelines presented in this book and other credible self-help books that are a writer's best friends.

Selecting one book proposal with the title, The Day the Earth Moved, you begin to read the accompanying query letter. Per your guidelines and industry standards, it is one page in length, single-spaced. Immediately, the first line grabs your attention since it presents a "what-if" scenario. Your emotions stir as you think, "Hey, maybe this is just the novel I have been looking for," but then your face reddens as you notice several glaring grammatical errors. First, the author has used "there" where it should be "their," and next "I" where it should be "me."

Pressed for time, your glee in discovering a good "what-if" scenario dissipates, and you toss the query letter and proposal into the bin marked "Return to Sender." This writers' graveyard is the dead end for aspiring authors or poets since they have not been judged on the merit of the book idea, but disqualified because of grammatical errors.

To ensure query letters and book proposals will be considered on their merits, make certain the text is error-free. To aid your effort, listed below are fifty quick tips designed to provide a working knowledge of proper grammar usage. Presented in a question-and-answer format, they are designed to aid your efforts in submitting a mistake-free book idea to interested agents and publishers. You have thus optimized your opportunity to become published – the ultimate goal of any aspiring writer.

1. Stephen King said, "The adverb is not your friend." What did he mean?

King and many other writing experts believe that if you have to use an adverb to assist the meaning of the verb, use another verb. Before submitting text, whether it is a query letter, a book proposal, or any manuscript, consider adverb surgery. Eliminate as many as possible. This impresses readers since it says to them that you understand good word usage and don't need a crutch to lean on.

Examples:

- The cat raced quickly to avoid the oncoming dump truck. (no)
- The cat raced to avoid the oncoming dump truck. (yes)
- Alex thoroughly searched for the missing paper clips. (no)
- Alex searched two hours for the missing paper clips. (yes)
- Polly was really excited to receive the award. (no)

Notes:

2. Does Stephen King hate adjectives as well? Don't adjectives add flavor?

Once in a while, yes; every other word, no. Nouns are precious commodities. They are the foundation for sentences and should be explosive. As pillars of text, they must stand alone without the need for a fancy friend whose purpose is to tell you how great the noun is. Instead, search for nouns that leap off the page into readers' brains. Inspect your writing to discover if you present the best ones possible. Don't forget that when a query letter, a book proposal, a manuscript, or a collection of poetry is being read, it is tantamount to your having a conversation with the reader, but you are not there. To ensure your writing is visual, uncover the best noun available and you will clip unnecessary adjectives from the text.

Examples:

- The flashy, self-absorbed, spent-looking woman entered the seedy brothel. (no)
- The loquacious madam sauntered into the brothel. (yes)
- Wilbur attended the race with his perky, fun-loving, cheerful

- sister. (no)
- Wilbur attended the race with his gregarious sister. (yes)

Notes:

3. What is wrong with using clichés?

Those who live by the cliché die by the cliché. This "hybrid cliché" suggests that those writers who rely on overused phrases signal their inability to create fresh words to provide description. Whether it is a query letter or book proposal outlining non-fiction, fiction or verses of poetry, a collection of short stories, an essay, or a novel or non-fiction manuscript, don't fall into the "cliché trap." Show (don't tell) readers you possess a vivid imagination and are a professional who takes the time to find the best words to trigger emotion, information, or inspiration.

Examples:
- Charles rolled with the punches when Stan berated his
- behavior. (no)
- He was the cat's meow when he hit the dance floor. (no)
- Sally was concerned about Dan when he talked of his pie-in-
- the-sky dreams. (no)
- Dan likened Alice's eyes to the color of sycamore leaves. (yes)
- Carl decided Rex was meaner than a dog whose tail had been stepped on. (yes)

Notes:

4. I love using metaphors and similes. What's wrong with them?

Metaphor, like simile, can be the author's or poet's friend, as long as it is not too close a friend. Use of multiple metaphors to compare two seemingly different concepts overwhelms readers, leaving them to wonder why the author or poet leans on this lazy crutch when fresh words are available. To impress literary agents and publishers, writers must be unique and present a creative style and use of the language that sets them apart from the multitude of writers submitting material for publishing consideration.

Examples:

Sally ran like the wind to win the race. (no)

Sally sprinted to the lead and never looked back. (yes)

John kept his mouth shut knowing silence is the most powerful message. (yes)

Notes:

Similes can describe two potentially abstract ideas as well. They can be located by watching for words such as "like" and "as." Be careful not to overuse them.

Examples:

- The man in the hat decided he would run like there was no tomorrow. (no)
- Peter grabbed the pole like it was his best friend. (yes)
- She was as eager as a coon dog on a chase. (yes)
- Trip swam like a porpoise in heat. (yes)

Notes:

5. Is there a general rule for the use of "a" and "an"?

Use "a" before consonant sounds and "an" before vowel sounds. To test your use, say the sentence out loud. Many times you can "feel" what is proper from the tone of the words being spoken.

Examples:

- Donna ate a apple a day. (no)
- Polly was an only child. (yes)
- An orange a day will keep doctor bills to a minimum. (yes)
- Prince is an exciting artist and a lover of many varieties of music. (yes)

Notes:

6. I like to use the word "that" as a descriptive word in my text. Am I being unprofessional?

Writers should conduct "that" searches to locate text locations where the word is not required. It is amazing how many can be eliminated without losing any sense of meaning. Be careful, though: non-use of the word where it is required can be as bad as using it too often.

Examples:
- Robert thought that the orchestra was playing a bit flat. (no)
- Robert thought the orchestra was playing a bit flat. (yes)
- Rex chose to stay, a decision that provided him an opportunity to study art. (no)
- Rex chose to stay, a decision providing him an opportunity to study art. (yes)

Notes:

7. When I have a character speak, do I need to use "he said," or "she said," all the time?

No, you do not, but be careful to be clear about who is speaking. Also – you do not need to use explanations in your verbiage such as "he said emphatically," or "she told him excitedly." Your words should do the talking. If they don't, draft new words.

Examples:
- "I'm concerned about Ted," Alice said grumblingly. (no)
- "Let's go to the beach!" Wilbur shouted to everyone. (yes)
- "Are you going to meet me in the morning?" Silowan asked. (yes)

Notes:

8. When do I use "important," vs. "importantly"?

There appears to be no consensus of opinion regarding the correct usage. Using "important" may be preferable, but use of "importantly" won't earn you a trip to the grammar doghouse.

Examples:

- More importantly, he was an above average student at Duke. (yes)
- More important, he was an above average student at Duke. (yes)

Notes:

9. Whether to use "all right" or "alright" is difficult to know. What is proper?

Actually, purists believe that the proper usage is "all right," but modern times appear to favor the use of "alright." Watch how the word is being used. This can be a deciding factor.

Examples:

- Oprah said it was alright for me to kiss Fred. (yes)
- My answers on the quiz were all right. (meaning answers were all correct)
- My answers on the quiz were alright. (meaning answers were satisfactory)
- Richard donned his jacket and said, "Alright, I'm ready to
- go." (yes)

Notes:

10. Deciding whether to use "sit" or "set" causes me to break out in hives. What is proper?

General rule: Sit is only used in the context of sitting down. Set is used in the context of positioning or placing something. Keep this rule in mind and you will never go wrong even though people will tell you there is a better rule.

Examples:

- "Alex said to Sid, "Set down and talk to me." (no)
- Rover decided he had to sit on my lap and drool. (yes)
- Oscar set the plates and saucers beside the table. (yes)
- Sit down and take a break. (yes)

Notes:

11. Are "lie" and "lay" interchangeable?

Don't spend much time trying to figure out which of these words, or their derivatives, is proper since you will end up in a mental institution. A common way of thinking about them is to say, "I use 'lay' when I am going to put something somewhere." Otherwise you "lie" as in "I am going to lie down."

Examples:
- "Lie the Bible down on the table," Pete said. (no)
- "Lie down Abe," Paul said, "or you will be tired for the rest of the day. (yes)
- Lay the music by the piano and begin your singing lessons. (yes)
- He laid the brick on the doorstep before returning to his car. (yes)
- Sylvia was lying in the shade of an oak tree. (yes)

Notes:

12. Is it proper to write, "Can I cut the grass?"

Use "can" in the context of ability to do something while "may" is used in the context of requesting permission.

Examples:
- "Can I have the roast beef sandwich?" Troy asked. (no)
- George asked, "May I escort Olivia to the prom?" (yes)
- He may go to the store, but we'll wait to see if he can behave himself. (yes)

Notes:

13. I hear people say "among" and "amongst." Which is correct?

Both forms are considered acceptable, but "among" is the better of the two since it is shorter and more informal. The same thing is true regarding "amid" and "amidst."

Examples:

- Don't run amongst the bulls or you will get stomped. (no)
- Jonah and Alice were among friends when they entered the pool hall. (yes)
- The robbers decided to split the money among the four boys. (yes)
- He was stronger amid the rest of the men. (yes)

Notes:

14. I get the use of "who," who's," and "whose" mixed up. What is appropriate?

When deciding whether to use "who's" or "whose," read aloud the sentence you are contemplating. Since "who's" is the contraction for "who is," you will be able to tell if the two words fit with the meaning of the sentence or whether the use of "whose," a pronoun, will be proper.

Examples:

- Who's baseball bat is this and why is it laying here? (no)
- The real question he had was, "Who's on first?" (yes)
- Johnny was a lonely boy whose father had abandoned him. (yes)
- Who's going to the basketball game with Sally and Linda? (yes)

Notes:

15. When do I use "nor" and when is "or" appropriate?

"Neither/nor" is a tag team to watch for. "Nor" may be proper without "neither," but seldom.

Examples:

- Neither Abbott or Costello was in attendance. (no)
- Neither Melvin nor Mark was tall. (yes)
- Fred cannot speak nor can he hear. (yes)
- The young boy was neither bright nor industrious. (yes)
- She was not on time, nor was she willing to hurry. (yes)

Notes:

16. Use of "shall" and "will" confuses me. What is proper?

"Shall" is normally used with first-person writing and "will" with second- and third-person text.

Examples:

- Sheila shall run across the yard. (no)
- I shall overcome my tendencies to become angry. (yes)
- Sylvia will leave the church and become a missionary. (yes)
- The umpire will be leaving the game but I shall never forget his ineptness. (yes)

Notes:

17. The words assure, insure, and ensure drive me batty. What is correct?

If you want to "make sure," use ensure. Assure means you are attempting to tell someone everything will be okay. Stick with insure when you are dealing with insurance matters.

Examples:

- He ensured his car for twenty-five thousand dollars. (no)
- Colin assured the nation he would not run for president. (yes)
- To ensure a stable future, Eric attended Harvard business school. (yes)
- I told him to insure the house for $100,000. (yes)

Notes:

18. "Convince" and "persuade" appear to be interchangeable. Are they?

No. If you are attempting to convince someone, it normally deals with the thought process. On the other hand, persuade involves action; attempting to cause someone to do something.

Examples:

- Alexander tried to persuade Solomon he was a saint. (no)
- Alexander attempted to convince Solomon he was a saint. (yes)
- To persuade him to try out for the debate team, she read him the rules. (yes)
- Persuade her to stay and I will bake a raspberry pie. (yes)

Notes:

19. How can I tell when it is proper to use "among" or "between"?

A good general rule is to use "among" when discussing more than two things or persons unless they are being considered individually.

Examples:

- Between the brothers, he was the fastest. (no)
- The shortstop position would be decided among four
- players. (yes)
- Why can't you stop bickering among yourselves? (yes)
- The debate was between Claude, Helga, and their professor. (yes)

Notes:

20. I've been criticized for my use of the word "they" when I'm describing action by a character. What is the problem?

Disagreement between nouns and pronouns – mixing singular and plural – is looked upon with disfavor. Be careful not to describe the work of an organization or other entity as "they" when "it" is proper.

Examples:

- The Police Athletic League is a terrific organization and they help
- officers. (no)
- Each clown puts on their own makeup. (no)
- Each clown puts on his or her own makeup. (yes)
- A good writer watches his or her punctuation usage. (yes)

Authors and poets are talented and they deserve applause for their efforts. (yes)

Notes:

21. I often have trouble deciding whether to use "which" or "that." What is proper?

"Which" is used when adding information about an object already identified. Use of "that" narrows a category or identifies a subject being discussed. "Which" is often preceded by a comma, parentheses or a dash.

Examples:

- The shoes which are in the closet are quite comfortable. (yes)
- The shoes, which are in the closet, need polishing. (yes)
- I heard a song that reminded me of my high school prom. (yes)

Notes:

22. Should I write in first person, second person, third person, or may I combine them?

Writing in first person means the narrator is participating in the action. Writing in second person is normally restricted to instructional books when the author speaks directly to readers. Writing in third person permits the narrator to observe the action. Any of these written communications is proper, but do not mix them without careful thought.

Examples:

- (1st person) From behind the haystack, I watched the enemy soldiers.
- (2nd person) When you decide to write, make sure you use proper grammar.
- (3rd person) Frederick avoided the stare of the lovely woman and walked away.

Notes:

23. I'm confused about tenses. How do I decide what would be most interesting to the reader?

Text may be written in present, past or future tense. Present tense involves action taking place currently. Past tense deals with action that has already occurred. Future tense is action that will happen. The key is not to confuse readers by mixing them.

Examples:

- Lenore called her on the telephone and she picks it up on the third ring. (no)
- Lenore called her on the telephone and she picked it up on the third ring. (yes)
- Frankie was an addict and his drug of choice is speed. (no)
- Frankie was an addict and his choice of drug was speed. (yes)
- I will call my mom because I was going to tell her a secret. (no)
- I will call my mom and tell her a secret. (yes)

Notes:

24. Is it permissible to use "But" or "And" at the start of a sentence?

There is a difference of opinion regarding its use, but it is proper. Be careful not to overuse this word choice or to present a fragmented sentence.

Examples:
- Pam ran to the store. But before the rain fell. (no – fragment)
- Pam ran to the store, but before the rain fell. (yes)
- Art practiced diving in the lap pool. But he left before the competition. (yes)
- The truth was apparent to Tom. But recent developments left him puzzled. (yes)
- Johnny saw the cat. And then turned around when he heard a hiss. (yes)

Notes:

25. When is it proper to use the word "etc." to indicate more is intended?

"Etc." means there are more examples or there is something more the subject said, but you are not going to provide that information. Avoid if possible, and instead use "including," or "such as."

Examples:
- Paul was left with many choices, etc. etc. etc. (no)
- The rain was accompanied by lightning, thunder, hail, etc. (no)
- Jim wondered if Arnie was angry, anxious, or just grouchy. (yes)
- Pat packed many items such as raincoats, socks, boots, and
- hats. (yes)

Notes:

26. Deciding when to use "further" and "farther" causes me severe headaches. What is the distinction?

When designating distance, use "farther." "Further" is best used to denote quantities or abstract concepts or notions.

Examples:
- James was further from the goal than Pistol Pete. (no)
- Suspicious, Owen decided to look into the matter further. (yes)

- Jupiter is farther from the earth than the moon. (yes)
- The farther the golf ball traveled, the less it stayed in
- bounds. (yes)

Notes:

27. Is it wrong to use "however" in my writing?

Words such as "however," "nevertheless," and "fortunately" are overused. I call these words "interrupt words" because writers often use them as filler.

Examples:
- Johnnie ran to the cleaners, however, he was late. (no)
- Johnnie ran to the cleaners. He was late. (yes)
- Fortunately, Rex loved Debbie for her looks not her money. (no)
- Rex loved Debbie for her looks and not her money. (yes)

Notes:

28. Is there such a word as "irregardless?"

No. The proper word is "regardless."

Examples:
- Irregardless of the weather, he paddled in the surf. (no)
- Regardless of the outcome, the championship fight was a
- success. (yes)
- The teacher liked John regardless of his tendency to be late for class. (yes)

Notes:

29."Is it proper to use "as per" in a sentence?

It is only proper if you don't ever want to write anything professionally in your life. Always use "per."

Examples:
- As per your instructions, I will be leaving the fort at five
- o'clock. (no)
- Per your instructions, I will be leaving the fort at five o'clock. (yes)
- John decided to attend the soccer game per the note in his locker. (yes)

Notes:

30. I'm a lover of the words "very" and "really." Is it okay to use them for emphasis?

"Very" and "really" are unnecessary most of the time. Use strong, visual words and they can stand alone.

Examples:
- Sal was very interested in becoming a professor at the
- university. (no)
- Sal was committed to becoming a professor at the university. (yes)
- Steve was so interested in becoming tenured he made a pact with the devil. (yes)

Notes:

31. How do I know whether to use "him" or "he?"

eading the text out loud assists your choice. To test usage, try replacing "him" with "me," and see if the sentence flows. For example, in the following sentence, "Paula danced with him and his brother," replacing "him" with "me" fits. But "Paula danced with I and his brother sounds incorrect, so "he" is not the right choice. If the action is performed *by* the subject, use subjective pronouns I, he, she, or they. If the action is done *to* the subject, use objective pronouns, me, him/her, or them.

Examples:

- Charlie left with he and Margaret for the movies. (no)
- I wanted to know him better before we dated. (yes)
- After all, it was he who called to see if I was feeling better. (yes)
- If the choice is clear, Alex will be with him and not Rex. (yes)

Notes:

32. What about use of "her" or "she?"

Use the same rules as above. Speak the words and see what fits. Test your usage by leaving out one subject. The pronoun should stand alone. In the final example, if you left out "Marlene," it would only sound correct to say "Tony asked her," not "Tony asked she."

Examples:

- Bob took Sheila and she to the movies. (no)
- Bob took Sheila and her to the movies. (yes)
- I left she at the gate, and traveled the distance on foot. (no)
- I left her at the gate, and traveled the distance on foot. (yes)
- Tony asked her and Marlene for the truth. (yes)

Notes:

33. When to use "who" and "whom" is a tough decision. What are my options?

A good general rule to remember: Use "whom" when denoting the recipient and not the subject of the action. To test usage, replace "whom" with "him" and "he." If "he" sounds better, use "who." If "him" sounds better, use "whom."

Examples:

- To who am I am speaking? (no)
- To whom am I speaking? (yes)
- Fred, whom is calling me? (no)
- Fred, who is calling me? (yes)
- Lucy, who is the head cook, brought me a piece of cake. (yes)
-

Notes:

34. Use of "I" or "me" in a sentence is confusing. Is there a set standard?

Usually "I" denotes the one in action while "me" is the object of an action. If there are two subjects or objects of the action, test usage by leaving out one subject to see what sounds right on its own.

Examples:

- Claudia loves Sharon and I. (no) [Claudia loves me.]
- Alfred and me attended the opera opening. (no) [I attended the opera...]
- Abe called out to Sid and me. (yes)
- ["Abe called out to I" sounds wrong. "Me" in the above sentence is correct.]

Notes:

35. Whether to use "one another" or "each other" drives me crazy. How can I decide what is correct?

Your sanity is saved. The term "each other" refers to two people while "one another" is used to denote three or more people. Enough said.

Examples:

- The five boys and I said to each other, "should we go
- fishing?" (no)
- The three girls hung around one another like they were
- sisters. (yes)
- "We love each other," John said to Arlene. (yes)
- Why don't you and Fred and the twins see one another in September. (yes)

Notes:

36. Is bestseller one word or two? How about the same question for such words as work week, schoolyear, and website?

Internet spell-checks can be helpful, but the dictionary is a remarkable resource. If you can't find a word in the dictionary, ask an editor or proofreader.

Examples:

- The book was a bestseller on the *New York Times* list. (preferred)
- He endured a sixty-hour workweek. (yes)
- The school year lasted two hundred sixty days. (yes)
- Dorothy worked online to prepare her thesis. (preferred)

Notes:

37. I like to use abbreviations in my text. Is this alright?

Our fast-food society has adopted coined terms to describe nearly every aspect of life. We thus say paper instead of newspaper, photo instead of photograph, and worse than worse, phone instead of telephone. While this is acceptable if you are using a colloquial voice, professional authors and poets using the formal voice do not accede to this lazy way of writing. Instead they use the proper word in their text. This is impressive to literary agents and publishers who value the written word.

Examples:

Improper	Proper
TV	Television
Ad	Advertisement

Notes:

38. Does the above information apply to use of names like doctor, lieutenant, mister, and reverend?

Abbreviations are proper for certain designations like those stated above unless they are used before a name in direct quotations.

Examples:
- Flashbulbs blinded Doctor Lind as he walked up the courthouse steps. (no)
- Flashbulbs blinded Dr. Lind as he walked up the courthouse
- steps. (yes)
- Lt. Johnson carried himself well. (yes)
- The lieutenant walked with a limp. (yes)
- He loved the play, "Doctor Doolittle." (yes)

Notes:

39. When do I use "who" or "that" when describing the actions of a character?

Use "who" when you are dealing with humans and "that" otherwise. This rule should pull you through.

Examples:
- There was a story by a newspaper reporter that loved the
- written word. (no)
- There was a story by a newspaper reporter who loved the written word. (yes)
- The corporation executives who stole the money should be in prison. (yes)

Notes:

40. I write sentence fragments. Is there an easy way to fix them?

I'm pleased you asked. To effectively turn dastardly fragments into complete sentences, writers should understand that there are two types of clauses combined to create different types of sentences. First, there is the independent clause, the subject and predicate structure that forms the backbone of sentences. They include a noun and a verb. The clause is "independent" since it can stand on its own. A dependent clause that does not contain the noun/verb pairing cannot stand alone.

Examples:

- Because Claude had no money. (no).
- Because he had no money, Claude left the store. (yes)
- Peter brought them tissues, they were sneezing. (no)
- Peter brought them tissues because they were sneezing. (yes)

Notes:

41. All of the sentences I write look the same. How can I vary the structure?

To vary the sentence structure, try using simple sentences, compound sentences, complex sentences, and compound-complex sentences. Each sentence utilizes different combinations of independent and dependent clauses.

Examples:

- Simple: Antonio Banderas walked to the movie set.
- Compound: Antonio Banderas drove to the movie and ran into a mailbox.
- Complex: Antonio Banderas walked the dog before it rained.
- Compound-Complex: Before it rained, Antonio Banderas walked to the movie set and was joined by his wife and pet chicken.

Notes:

42. When there are mistakes in a quote I am using, should I correct them?

Regardless of the text, a quote should be repeated accurately. If you are quoting someone from an interview you have conducted and wish to alter the wording for grammatical purposes so the person will not be embarrassed, you must receive the interviewee's permission. If you decide to use part of the quoted material, and feel that doing so might be objectionable, consult with him or her.

Examples:
- Hugh told me, "Golf is a young man's sport and they love it." (no)
- Hugh told me, "Golf is a young man's sport and he loves it." (yes)
- Frederick said, "I never seen anyone prettier than her." (yes – direct quote)

Notes:

43. I'm dumbfounded regarding when to capitalize "Dad," "Father," "Mom" and "Mother," and when to not do so.

Relax your worried mind. Remember – capitalize when used as proper noun or title. Always use lower case when using "my," "him," or "her."

Examples:
- I love my Mother more than anyone. (no)
- After the film, Mom and I wept. (yes)
- I love my mother more than anything. (yes)
- My dad and I decided to shop in the mall. (yes)
- He saw Fred's mother walking to the market. (yes)
- Dad, watch out! (yes)

Notes:

44. Are "ask" and "asked" interchangeable?

No, they are not and if you mix them up, membership in the Grammar Society of America is forsaken. "Ask" is a present tense word while "asked' deals with past tense. Watch usage since this is a telltale sign of unprofessional conduct for a writer who does not do his homework.

Examples:
- I asked you, "Does he understand what I am saying?" (no)
- I ask you, "Does he understand what I am saying?" (yes)
- The preacher has ask that you parishioners quiet down during prayer. (no)

- The preacher has asked that you parishioners quiet down during prayer. (yes)

Notes:

45. Is it proper to say Mr. and Mrs. Sally Anne Barker?

No, you have created Mr. Sally Barker. He will object to this.

Examples:
- The president intends to invite Mr. and Mrs. John Barker. (yes)
- Mrs. Sally Ann Baker is married to John. (yes)
- Where is the invitation for the Canganys, John and Alice? (yes)

Notes:

46. Is it alright to use the words "the fact that"?

Curse the day you do so. Edit them out since there are other words that will accomplish your intended mission.

Examples:
- The fact is that he was an awful man and I'm pleased he
- failed. (no)
- He was an awful man and I'm pleased he failed. (yes)
- In spite of the fact that Aubrey drank whiskey every day, he was okay. (no)
- Aubrey drank whiskey every day, but he was okay. (yes)

Notes:

47. I like to use contractions since they are more conversational. What is proper?

Scattered use is acceptable, but don't overuse contractions. Read your words out loud to see if a contraction is really required.

Examples:

- They'd be better off dead. (Better – They would be better
- off dead.)
- I have never seen a woman like Rosy. (yes)
- Who would have ever believed he'd be a famous ballplayer? (yes)

Notes:

48. I confuse use of "because" and "since." Is there an easy way to tell when to use them?

Grammatically, there is no real difference between "because" and "since," but "since" is used to relay a sense of time while "because" is used with a cause/effect relationship.

Examples:

- Because she was born, Sally has loved to play in the yard with the dog. (no)
- Since she lost her hearing, Sally has loved to play in the yard with the dog. (yes)
- Because I left the opera early, I missed the finale. (yes)
- Since the last time I saw Clem, I fell in love with Rex. (yes)

Notes:

49. Is there a handy-dandy rule to follow regarding subject and pronoun agreement?

Don't use "their" when the subject is singular. Pronouns such as everybody, everyone, either, neither, somebody and anyone may sound plural, but they are usually treated as singular, and require singular corresponding pronouns and verbs.

Examples:

- Each writer wanted their books back. (no)
- He and she wanted their books back. (yes)
- Each writer wanted his or her book back. (yes: each is singular)
- Everyone wants to be noticed for their academic

- achievements. no)
- Everyone wants to be noticed for his or her academic achievements. (yes)
- It's great to have a dog like Black Sox who entertains
- themselves. (no)
- It's great to have a dog like Black Sox who entertains himself. (yes)

Notes:

50. I know misspellings are careless and confusing one word for another is a no-no, but are there tips you can give me to spot common mistakes in this area?

Please you asked! Computer spell-check is good for catching some misspellings, but not for finding incorrect words used. Here are lists of commonly misspelled words as well as those that appear to be misused on a regular basis:

List of Commonly Misspelled Words

Correct Spelling	Frequently Misspelled
accidentally	accidently
acknowledgment	acknowledgement
a lot	alot
desperate	desparate
development	developement
embarrass	embarass
harassment	harrassment
independent	independant
indispensable	indispensible
irresistible	irresistable
irritable	irritible
memento	momento
millennium	millenium
privilege	privilege
repetition	repitition
sacrilegious	sacreligious
seize	sieze
separate	seperate
yield	yeild

Notes

Homonyms, Homophones, and Other Confusing Words

Note: These words sound alike or look similar, but they can have vastly differing meanings. If you aren't certain which the correct one is, become familiar with their meanings and spellings. Even the best spellers can slip up and use the wrong word because it "sounds" right. But using the wrong word causes readers to stumble, making the writer look careless or lazy – or unintelligent.

accept, except
ad, add
affect, effect
aid, aide, ade
air, heir, err
altar, alter
any way, anyway
backyard, back yard
bare, bear
born, borne
break, brake
burned, burnt
buy, by, bye
carat, carrot, caret, karat
cent, scent, sent
cite, site, sight
compliment, complement
core, corps
counsel, council
course, coarse
dammed, damned
depend, deepened, deep end
die, dye
discrete, discreet
elicit, illicit
everyday, every day

fair, fare
faze, phase
feat, feet
flare, flair
flour, flower
for, fore, four
forth, fourth
forward, foreword
gorilla, guerilla
hale, hail
hangar, hanger
hay, hey
hear, here
heroin, heroine
incite, insight
inquire, enquire
its, it's
lead, led
lessen, lesson
lightning, lightening
loan, lone
loose, lose
manner, manor
marry, merry
meat, meet, mete
medal, meddle
metal, mettle
moose, mousse
naval, navel
one, won
pair, pare, pear
palate, pallet, palette
passed, past
peace, piece
prays, preys, praise
principal, principle

profit, prophet
rain, rein, reign
raise, raze, rays
real, reel
recreate, re-create
regimen, regiment
right, rite, write
road, rode, rowed
root, route
rye, wry
savor, saver
seam, seem
shear, sheer
slight, sleight
so, sew, sow
sole, soul
sore, soar
spade, spayed
stake, steak
stationary, stationery
steal, steel
sweet, suite
tail, tale
taut, taught
team, teem
teas, tease, tees
then, than
they're, there, their
threw, through
tic, tick
to, too, two
toad, towed, toed
tracked, tract
vain, vein
vary, very
verses, versus
vice, vise

ware, where, wear
waste, waist
weather, whether
whale, wail
whined, wined, wind
whole, hole
whose, who's
won't, wont
yoke, yolk

Punctuation Points

The sentence, "'I see beautiful stars in the sky", Alice commented'". is a killer for any aspiring author or poet. By inserting the comma and the period after the quotation marks and by not knowing how to properly use quotation marks, the writer has shouted to the literary world, "I am a novice whose work is not worthy of serious consideration."

Correct punctuation is an essential tool for the writer, a thumbprint regarding his or her professionalism. Punctuation mistakes are red flags that stop the reading process.

As stated in the Author's Note, any serious writer aspiring to publish should hire a professional line editor or copyeditor to scan his or her material prior to submission, but before doing so, work hard to eliminate punctuation errors. This will permit the editor to better evaluate the content. It will also reduce the amount of proofreading expense incurred by the writer.

Below are twenty-six essential tips to aid the effort.

1. I have trouble deciding whether punctuation marks are located inside or outside quotation marks. What is the general rule?

The general rule is that commas and periods are located inside quotation marks. Semi-colons and colons are normally positioned outside the quotation marks. When the entire sentence is a question or exclamation, the question mark or exclamation point is located outside the quotation mark. If the entire sentence is a question, the question mark is located outside the quotation mark. When only the quoted material is a question or exclamation, the question mark or exclamation point is inside the quotation mark.

Examples:

- "Was Rex correct when he answered, "Brazil?" (no)
- "Was Rex correct when he answered, "Brazil"? (yes)
- "*Annie Hall* is my favorite film", Woody Allen said. (no)
- "*Annie Hall* is my favorite film," Woody Allen said. (yes)
- Olivia screamed, "I love you Brad!" (yes)

- Axel hated the phrase, "Be all you can be"; why, we didn't know. (yes)

Notes:

2. When is the use of single quotation marks acceptable?

Single quotes are used to signify a quotation within a quotation. They can also be used around unusual or foreign words. Be sure to include the final single quote mark inside the double quotation marks.

Examples:
- Paul said to Felix, "I used the words I'm back from the *Terminator*." (no)
- Paul said to Felix, "I used the words 'I'm back' from the *Terminator*." (yes)
- Osgood began his speech with the words, "My favorite saying is, 'Ain't life grand?'" (yes)
- "There is a line in a poem," John said, "that reads 'all love is hate in disguise.'" (yes)
- Pete told me to avoid the 'varmit' who fixes trucks with used parts. (yes)

Notes:

3. When to italicize, when to underline, and when to use quotation marks is a perplexing problem. How can I decide?

Writers should italicize the names of films, books, screenplays, operas, plays, television series, and magazines. Quotation marks are used for book chapters, poems, articles, songs, and short stories. By current publishing standards, underlining for any reason is incorrect. Some writing experts believe that the title of a book not yet published should be in all capital letters. This is optional.

Examples:
- Pete and Martin left the movie, <u>A Few Good Men</u>, with haste. (no)
- I read MOBY DICK from cover to cover. (no)
- Claude and Elizabeth enjoyed *A Beautiful Mind*. (yes)

- His poem, "The Artful American," won the festival award. (yes)
- My favorite song is Roy Orbison's, "Runnin' Scared." (yes)

Notes:

4. When I include numbers in my writing, how can I tell whether to use numerical symbols or write the words out?

This varies from publisher to publisher, and there are exceptions, but the general rule is for numbers from zero to ninety-nine, use words; for 100 and above, use the numerical symbol. One more rule: Never begin a sentence using the numerical symbol.

Examples:
- 10 girls kissed the boy's rosy cheek. (no)
- Ten girls kissed the boy's rosy cheek. (yes)
- Oliver left me twenty stories to edit. (yes)
- Frederick won 2 million dollars. (yes)
- Alfred won 4 percent of the vote. (yes)
- Jerry raced 59 miles to meet her. (yes)
- Judy changed the 100-watt light bulb for the second time. (yes)

Notes:

5. How about when numbers are used to denote age?

There are conflicting opinions regarding whether to spell out numbers or use the numeral symbol. Consistency is more important than which rule is followed.

Examples:
- Ralphie turned twenty-five years old last Saturday. (no)
- The zoo featured a fifteen-year-old Panda. (no)
- The zoo featured a 15-year-old Panda. (yes)

Notes

6. When should I use brackets in my sentences?

Tough call at times, but brackets are used sparingly to note an explanation or clarification and not simply more information. Use brackets to further offset information within parentheses or to indicate a missing word.

Examples:

- Theodore was the image of his father [now deceased], but better
- looking. (yes)
- (To elaborate on the discussion [of December 3], see the professor.) (yes)
- Johnson stated his opinion [of] the amendment in the newspaper. (yes)

Notes:

7. When should I use parentheses in my writings?

Parentheses provide clarification or additional information about words being used. Do not use them too often, especially in the same sentence, or where commas would suffice.

Examples:

- Tickets will be available (at a discounted rate) after dinner. (yes)
- The alley cat (a mixed-breed) loved tuna. (yes)
- When Freddie danced with Ruth (she was a foot shorter), he hunched over. (yes)

Notes:

8. What words are capitalized?

A good general rule is that only sentence beginnings and proper nouns are capitalized. Watch capitalizing terms following a colon unless what follows is a proper noun or a complete sentence.

Examples:
- The coach set the following goals: win twenty games and the conference. (yes)
- The Summers family posted the menu: Turkey and dressing will be served. (yes)
- He listed the suspects in order: Polly, Dave, Sue, and
- Leonard. (yes)
- The lineup for today's ballgame includes: shortstop, Mike, and pitcher, Ted. (yes)

Notes:

9. Whether to use commas, and how many to use, drives me crazy. What is the scoop?

The serial comma (the final comma in a list, usually before the words "and" or "or") is being phased out of use. However, include the serial comma in case of ambiguity or for clearer meaning, such as if the last element is two like items separated by "and."

Examples:
- We gathered sticks, rocks, twigs, and bark. (no)
- We gathered sticks, rocks, twigs and bark. (yes)
- She asked whether we were interested in going to the movie, going dancing, spending time at the lake that evening or resting until tomorrow's trip to the amusement park. (yes)
- Books, uniforms, notepads, and pens and pencils were all
- supplied. (yes)
- She wanted to know if I preferred washing, drying, or putting away the dishes. (yes)

Notes:

10. I've never understood the use of hyphens and dashes. Why is this so confusing?

It isn't. Hyphens are versatile tools since they can be used for many different functions. Single hyphens can join two or more words that serve as a compound adjective *before* the noun they are modifying. If they appear after the noun, no hyphen is required. Double hyphens, or dashes, are used to emphasize certain parts of a sentence or to permit a break in the sentence. They also separate complete thoughts.

Examples:

- Jonathan was born into a society considered low class. (yes)
- Jonathan was born into a low-class society. (yes)
- John Dillinger is a well known criminal. (no)
- A well-known criminal is John Dillinger. (yes)
- Sylvia leased a house in Italy—somewhere in Tuscany—for the summer. (yes)
- There were twenty-nine cats entered in the competition. (yes)

Notes:

11. Semi-colons should be banished from the English language. Is there a need for them?

The function of a semi-colon is similar to that of the dash, but the semi-colon can also be used with conjunctive adverbs (however, therefore, nevertheless) to introduce a new thought. Short sentences do not necessarily need semi-colons. Instead, commas may be appropriate. Use semi-colons in lists, especially of phrases.

Examples:

- Ollie loved Sylvia; but she did not know it. (no)
- We tried to drive to Oregon; however, steep mountains blocked
- our path. (yes)
- Ethel and Ricky watched the sky; the stars were glimmering in the
- night. (yes)
- Wanda ordered tuna on rye a pickle spear; potato wedges with cheese, four apple turnovers, and a large coffee, all to go. (yes)

Notes:

12. Is a comma required before the beginning of a quote in a sentence?

A full-sentence quote should be introduced by a comma, but partial quotes and entertainment titles (books, television, plays, film) don't require a comma to introduce them.

Examples:

- Pat recognized the play, *Of Mice and Men*, as a classic. (no)
- Humphrey Bogart said, "Here's looking at you kid." (yes)
- The author titled his play "To Love or Not to Love." (yes)
- Oscar wrote the book "Ugly Men Love Olivia." (yes)

Notes:

13. Deciding whether I need a comma to separate clauses in a sentence is difficult. Is there a general rule to follow?

If there are subjects in both clauses, separate the clauses with a comma. If there are not, do not use the comma.

Examples:

- Paulie glanced in the girls' locker room, but didn't see any naked girls. (no)
- Scott glanced in the girl's locker room and didn't see any naked girls. (yes)
- Sheila watched the stars, but Pete watched her. (yes)
- Claude rounded the bend and headed for home plate. (yes)
- Mary washed dishes in the cramped kitchen, and Bob cleared the table. (yes)

Notes:

14. How can I tell if I have written a "run-on" sentence?

This occurs when the writer uses a comma where a period would be appropriate. Avoid writing long sentences when breaking them up would provide more clarity.

Examples:
- John went to the bathroom and then walked into the living room and then left for the movie before he went to see Claudia about their exam grades. (no)
- There was a smell in the air of burnt toast and he loved that smell. (no)
- Pete loved Alicia. He also loved Cathy and Julie. (yes)
- Art was a fan of Sammy Sosa; he watched Cubs games all the time. (yes)

Notes:

15. When is the use of a long dash (called an em dash) appropriate?

Use of a long dash indicates there is a break in the sentence. In *Elements of Style*, the dash is defined as "a mark of separation stronger than a comma, less formal than a colon, and more relaxed than parentheses."

Examples:
- Paulie was a cool guy—and lived in Las Vegas in the winter. (no)
- Paulie was a cool guy. He lived in Las Vegas in the winter. (yes)
- Sally wanted to teach him a lesson—that he better not mess with her. (yes)
- The principal stood out—in the minds of many—because he always wore white socks. (yes)

Notes:

Note: *Em dashes (roughly the width of an 'm', and different from an en dash or hyphen in its look and usage), are symbols that aren't on a standard keyboard but are available in word processing software either as a key command or symbol to be inserted. If you're not sure how to insert them, use two hyphens with no spaces between words or hyphens.*

Examples:

- She waited—and waited—for the bus.
- She waited—and waited—for the bus.

Notes:

16. Is the first word of a quote capitalized?

Doing so is dependent on how the quote is introduced. Complete phrases require capitalization, but partial quotes may not.

Examples:

- The jury foreman stated, "That they live up the street." (no)
- The jury foreman stated, "We find the defendant guilty as charged." (yes)
- Eleanor explained Ruth's behavior by saying "she's just not herself." (yes)

Notes:

17. I am mixed up about apostrophes and single quotation marks and sometimes my computer is too. What's the story?

There is a difference between an apostrophe and a single quotation mark. Your computer will often automatically insert the wrong one. An apostrophe is in the shape of a '9' and an open quote mark is in the shape of a '6'. You might have to manually insert the correct symbol and override your word processing software. Remember, an apostrophe is used to show possession (Sheila's dog, the school's gym, all four tires' tread), and in contractions or where letters or numbers are missing (don't read, where's my car, I'm here, '44 was a good year).

Examples:

- She screamed, "There is a 'Cadillac-size' cockroach in the cabinet." (yes)
- I don't want any 'cause they're stale. (no)
- I don't want any 'cause they're stale. (yes)
- She grew up in the '70s. (no)
- She grew up in the '70s. (yes)

Notes:

18. Apostrophe rules are confusing. What is acceptable?

Apostrophes are used to form possessives of proper and common nouns, but not pronouns. When a contraction is used, the apostrophe will designate what has been eliminated. Apostrophes are occasionally used to designate plurals of letters such as "abc's" or "the three r's" for clarity." Never add apostrophes to make a noun plural.

Examples:
- Sammy ran after the lost dog's. (no)
- Don't leave me home with Sally. (yes)
- Peter was a 1960s kind of guy. (yes)
- Peter was a '60s kind of guy. (yes)
- Bob Clark's vacation home is splendid. (yes)
- The Clarks' vacation home is splendid. (yes)

Notes:

19. Use of "it's" or "its" bugs me. Does it make a difference?

"It's" is the contraction for "it is." To test usage, read out loud the sentence you are forming. If you stumble using "it is," then "its" is correct.

Examples:
- Ray told his children, "Its time to leave for the park." (no)
- Ray told his children, "It's time to leave for the park." (yes)
- The school was proud of it's principal. (no)
- The school was proud of its principal. (yes)

Notes:

20. I'm confused about how to indicate the possessive of words ending in "s". Help please.

Typically, if a word ends in "s," and the word is singular, add an apostrophe and an "s" to the end. This may look awkward, but it is correct. If the word is plural and ends in "s", simply add the apostrophe.

Examples:

- Jack Nicklaus' wife shouted "hooray" when he sank the winning putt. (no)
- Jack Nicklaus's wife shouted "hooray" when he sank the winning putt. (yes)
- James Johnsons' girls decided to try out for the play. (no)
- James Johnson's girls decided to try out for the play. (yes)

Notes:

21. When should I use ellipses and how should they be spaced?

Ellipsis points serve a dual purpose: to indicate missing words in a sentence or to permit a sentence to trail off without an ending. Proper usage requires leaving a space after the word before the use of the ellipses and before the next word once the ellipses have been used. If one is used after a complete sentence, a fourth dot is used to represent the period.

Examples:

- This is a fine mess. . . . Get the hell out of here. (no)
- President Roosevelt said, "We have nothing to fear . . . but fear itself." (yes)
- "Romeo," she called, "let me explain . . . " (yes)

Notes:

22. Do I leave one space or two after a complete sentence and the beginning of the next one?

It is now correct to use one space after a period when using word processing programs. For those of you who love the typewriter, two spaces are permissible.

Notes:

23. What is the correct punctuation to be used with parentheses?

Punctuation is positioned after the use of the closing parenthesis. If the material inside the parenthesis requires its own punctuation, position it accordingly.

Examples:
- Alex ran toward Felix, (a half-breed) who scampered away. (no)
- Alex ran toward Felix (a half-breed), who scampered away. (yes)
- The best of times (why should it be questioned?), bring out the best in man. (yes)

Notes:

24. Should I indent each paragraph, and if so, how many spaces? Also – should there be spaces between my paragraphs?

Publishers' requirements vary, but the current trend is to add a line space between paragraphs and use no indentation.

Examples:
- See writing samples in Appendix.

Notes:

25. What in the world are split infinitives? Do I need them?

Stay away from them or you will be shot. Infinitives are verbs that have a "to" in front of them like "to catch," or "to think." The trouble arises when words such as "so," "really," and other "ly" words separate the "to" from the verb. This causes a split infinitive and is unacceptable.

Examples:
- Jimmy loves apples, but loves to also eat bananas (no).
- Jimmy loves apples, but he also loves to eat bananas (yes).
- Ben and Jerry wanted to really watch the television program. (no).

- Ben and Jerry really wanted to watch the television program. (yes)

Notes:

26. I think exclamation points are nifty. Is it okay to use them?

Less rather than more is the standard rule. Too many exclamation points provide a hint that you are not a professional writer. Never use !!!!!! – it is totally unprofessional. One exclamation point is all you need, if that, since your writing should show enough emotion through strong word choice.

Examples:
- I love to ice skate!!!!!! (no)
- Freddie won first prize! (yes)
- Black Sox slept with a grin on his face! (yes)
- Sally exclaimed, "What an exciting game!" (yes)

Notes:

Miscellaneous Tips

- Never use "%" in text, but rather spell out "percent." It is alright to use the symbol in illustrations or charts.

- Never us "&" in text unless it is part of a logo or business name. Always spell out the word "and".

- Avoid using overused or trite phrases such as "the fact that," "is a person who," "as to whether," or "in regard to." They sound like filler and add only unnecessary verbiage.

- Be careful not to use "of" where "have" is required. "Phil should have gone to the market," is proper while "Phil should of gone to the market" is not.

Helpful Reminders

- Good writing requires hard work even for the best wordsmiths. Many bestselling authors and poets have spent years writing one book.

- There are few absolutes regarding grammar and punctuation rules in the publishing industry, but rather accepted standards and conventions. This book has presented universally accepted guidelines, but be certain to check the style guide used by the publishing company you are submitting your material to.

- Remember – typos and other errors tend to cluster. If you find one mistake, read each sentence around it and you'll likely discover more.

- Reading your text out loud is a good way to discover errors. Another is to wait a few days after you have composed material and then look at it with a fresh perspective.

- Better yet, have a professional proofreader scan the text before any submission. This will enhance your chances for a mistake-free manuscript.

Bibliography

Balzac and the Little Chinese Seamstress, Dai Sijie, Random House, New York, 2001

Book, The Magazine For The Reading Life, July/August, 2001

Down and Out In London and Paris, George Orwell, Harcourt, New York, 1933

Every Saint Has A Past, Every Sinner Has A Future, Terry Cole-Whitaker, Putnam, New York City, 2001

How To Write a Book Proposal, Michael Larsen, Writer's Digest Books, Cincinnati, Ohio, 1997

Jack Kerouac, Selected Letters, Edited by Ann Charters, Penguin, New York, 1996

Novel Ideas, Barbara Shoup and Margaret Love Denman, Alpha Books, Indianapolis, Indiana, 2001

On Writing, Stephen King, Scribner's, New York City, 2001

On Writing Well, William Zinser, HarperCollins, New York, 2001

Presumed Innocent, Scott Turow, Warner Books, New York, 1987

Seabiscuit, Laura Hillenbrand, Ballantine, New York, 2001

1,818 Ways To Write Better and Get Published, Scott Edelstein, Writer's Digest Books, Cincinnati, 1991

The Complete Guide To Book Publicity, Jodee Blanco, Allworth Press, New York, 2000

The First Five Pages: A Writer's Guide to Staying Out of the Rejection Pile, Noah Lukeman, Simon and Schuster, 2003

The Writer's Chapbook, George Plimpton et al, The Modern Library, New York, 1999

Twentieth Century Dictionary of Quotations, Edited by The Princeton Language Institute, The Philip Lief Group, Bantam Doubleday Dell Publishing Group, New York City, 1993

Various Issues – Writer's Digest Magazine

Writer's Guide To Book Editors, Publishers, and Literary Agents, Jeff Herman, Prima Publishing, 2002

Writing Down The Bones, Natalie Goldberg, Shambhala, Boston and London, 1986

Your Novel Proposal, From Creation to Contract, Blythe Camenson and Marshall J. Cook, Writer's Digest Books, Cincinnati, Ohio, 1999

Resources

Alderson, Daniel, *Talking Back To Poems: A Working Guide for the Aspiring Poet*

James Scott Bell, *Plot and Structure*

Briggs, John, *Fire in the Crucible: The Self-creation of Creativity and Genius*

Brande, Dorothea, *Becoming A Writer*

Burroway, Janet, *Writing Fiction: A Guide to Narrative Craft*

Buzan, Tony, *Use Both Sides of the Brain*

Epel, Naomi, *Writers Dreaming*

Forster, E. M., *Aspects of a Novel*

Hartwell Fiske, Robert, *The Dictionary of Concise Writing: 10,000 Alternatives to Wordy Phrases*

Hemingway, Ernest, *A Moveable Feast*

Hirsch, Edward, *How to Read a Poem and Fall in Love with Poetry*

Keyes, Ralph, *The Courage To Write; How Writers Transcend Fear*

Maisell, Eric, *Staying Sane In The Arts*

May, Rollo, *The Courage to Create*

Nachmanovitch, Steven, *Free Style Improvisation in Life and Art*

Perry, Aaren Yeatts, *Poetry Across the Curriculum*

Rico, Gabrielle Lusser, *Writing the Natural Way*

Uleland, Brenda, *If You Want To Write*

Welty, Eudora, *One Writer's Beginnings*

Notes

Notes

To Order Copies of

How to Become a Published Author: Idea to Publication

Visit www.markshawbooks.com,
or email at mshawin@yahoo.com.

Seminars,
Speaking Engagements

Mark Shaw is available to conduct seminars focusing on writing tips, publishing strategies, and storytelling ideas at high schools, colleges, universities, libraries, writer's centers, writer's groups, youth groups, senior centers, corporations, and legal organizations. For more information, visit www.markshawbooks.com or call 415.747.7598.

Mentoring

Mark Shaw is available to mentor writers on a daily basis at no charge. For more details visit www.markshawbooks.com.

Mark Shaw

Mark Shaw is a former criminal defense lawyer turned author/journalist with thirty-plus published books. At the ripe young age of sixty-two, he earned a Masters Degree in Theological Studies from San Francisco Theological Seminary.

For more than ten years, Mark has mentored writers around the world with aspirations to become published. Many have become published through the guidelines in this book and his seminars, How to Become a Published Author: "Idea to Publication." He has taught writing and publishing at numerous libraries, colleges, and universities in the United States as well as at seminars presented in Paris and Taiwan.

Published books include The Reporter Who Knew too Much, The Poison Patriarch, Denial of Justice, Collateral Damage, Fighting for Justice, Stations Along the Way, Road to the Miracle, Beneath the Mask of Holiness: Thomas Merton and the Forbidden Love Affair that Set Him Free, and Melvin Belli, King of the Courtroom.

Previous works are *Miscarriage of Justice*, *The Jonathan Pollard Story*, *Forever Flying, the* autobiography of famed aviator R. A. "Bob" Hoover, and Larry Legend, a biography of NBA superstar Larry Bird. He has also written *Down for the Count*, an investigative book about the Mike Tyson rape trial, *Bury Me in a Pot Bunker*, the autobiography of controversial golf course designer Pete Dye, *The Perfect Yankee,* a chronicle of New York Yankee pitcher Don Larsen's perfect game in the 1956 World Series, and *Clydesdales, The World's Most Magical Horse.* Mark has also written five books about writing and becoming published.

More than 30 editions of Mark's books are in print. *Forever Flying, The Perfect Yankee, Larry Legend, Jack Nicklaus, Golf's Greatest Champion,* and *Bury Me in a Pot Bunker* have been published in paperback. Bury Me in a Pot Bunker has been translated in Japanese.

Mr. Shaw's background includes six years as a noted criminal defense attorney in the Midwest. He practiced entertainment law in Los Angeles and Indianapolis. Mark remains a member of the bar in California and Indiana.

Mark co-founded the *Aspen Daily News,* a daily newspaper in Colorado. He has hosted radio talks shows in Bloomington and Indianapolis, Indiana.

Mr. Shaw began his career in the entertainment industry as an on-air television personality for ABCs Good Morning America, CBS's People, the syndicated World of People, and the Disney Channel's The Scheme of Things. He has hosted various talk shows including A.M. Los Angeles and Mid-Morning L.A., and was a legal correspondent for the nationally syndicated program, On Trial.

Mark was the legal analyst who correctly predicted the outcome of the Mike Tyson and O. J. Simpson trials for, among others, CNN, ABC, and ESPN. He wrote several columns analyzing the case for USA Today. In 2004, he analyzed the Kobe Bryant case for ESPN and USAToday.com.

Mark created and produced the Television Special, A Beverly Hills Christmas with James Stewart, for Fox Broadcasting. He was co-executive producer for two motion pictures, Freeze Frame and Diving In. After co-writing the screenplay for the film Hazel for Universal Studios, Mr. Shaw became a member of the Writers Guild of America. He has written articles and columns for, among others, Examiner.com, Huffington Post, USA Today, The Aspen Daily News, The National Pastime, The Bloomington Voice, Indianapolis Monthly, and Indiana Lawyer.

An avid collector of Ernest Hemingway books and a longtime suffering fan of the Chicago Cubs, Mark is married to Wen-ying Lu, Head of Cataloging at the Santa Clara University Libraries. They live in the San Francisco area.

Testimonials Regarding

"The Mark Shaw Method"

"Whenever I am asked how best to pitch a book to publishers, I direct aspiring authors to Mark Shaw's book, *How to Become A Published Author*. Mark's educated and no-nonsense approach demystifies the field, and was instrumental in helping me land my first book deal."

–Christine Montross, *New York Times* best selling author of *Body of Work* and *Falling Into the Fire.*

"How may I ever thank you? You really made it possible for me to learn how to complete my book and create a successful book proposal. Your patience and encouragement are most appreciated."

–Lisa Mantoba, Fort Charles, Louisiana

"Thank you, thank you. Your words of advice regarding my writing skills have really paid off."

–Peter Lynch, Paris, France

"Mark, thanks for caring about writers so much. Your advice is so practical in nature and I feel blessed to have had you in my corner."

–Rex Billings, San Francisco, California

"Your command of the subject is beyond my wildest dreams. Thank you for this book and your help."

–Avon Privette, Zebulon, North Carolina

"This book and your mentoring permitted me to become a published author. Thank you."

–John Daisy, Perth, Australia